Smart Cities and Urban Development in India

SMART CITIES and Urban Development in India

By

N. Mani
Professor and Head,
Post-graduate and Research Department of Economics,
Erode Arts and Science College, Erode, Tamil Nadu

New Century Publications
New Delhi, India

NEW CENTURY PUBLICATIONS
4852 / 24, 1st Floor,
Ansari Road, Daryaganj,
New Delhi – 110 002 (India)

Tel.: 011-4101 7798; 4358 7398; 98112 66355
E-mail: info@newcenturypublications.com

www.newcenturypublications.com

Editorial office:
4800 / 24, Bharat Ram Road,
Ansari Road, Daryaganj,
New Delhi – 110 002

Edition: 2026

ISBN: **978-81-7708-432-0**

First Published: July 2016

Published by New Century Publications and printed at Milan Enterprises, New Delhi.

Designs: Patch Creative Unit, New Delhi.

PRINTED IN INDIA

About the Book

The share of urban population in India's total population was 25.7 percent in 1991 which increased to 27.8 percent in 2001. About 377 million Indians comprising of about 31 percent of the country's population, live in urban areas according to Census 2011. Projections are that by 2031, 40 percent of India's population will be residing in urban areas.

In recent years, the urban sector in India has undergone a major change following the country's transition towards a market-based economy and the spirit of decentralization embodied in the Constitution (Seventy-fourth) Amendment Act, 1992 (relating to municipalities) which came into force on June 1, 1993. Municipalities are now constitutional bodies forming third tier to the federal polity of India.

Taking into account the existing and future scenario, Government of India has launched, in recent years, a number of schemes/programmes to augment and modernize urban infrastructure. Development of smart cities is a step in that direction.

The Smart Cities Mission, launched by the Prime Minister in June 2015, will cover 100 cities and its duration will be 5 years (2015-16 to 2019-20). The first list of 20 urban areas that will be developed as smart cities was announced by the Government on January 28, 2016. 13 more cities were added to the list on May 24, 2016, making a total of 33 cities.

This book provides a detailed account of problems arising from growing urbanization in India. It particularly focuses on policies and programmes of the Government to deal with the challenges posed by rising urbanization which is attributable in large measure, to migration of rural people to urban areas in search of employment and a better standard of living.

About the Author

Dr. N. Mani is presently Head, Post-graduate and Research Department of Economics, Erode Arts and Science College, Erode, Tamil Nadu. He holds M.A., M.Phil. and Ph.D. degrees from Bharathiar University, Coimbatore. Specializing in development economics, he has 26 years of teaching experience to post-graduate and undergraduate classes. He successfully completed a major research project sponsored by University Grants Commission (UGC), New Delhi. He is currently engaged in a research project sponsored by Indian Council of Social Science Research (ICSSR), New Delhi.

Dr. Mani has published 8 books and several papers on varied subjects in reputed journals. He is also the President of Tamil Nadu Science Forum and was organizing secretary of the National Children Science Congress, 2006. He has successfully guided and supervised the works of 6 Ph.D. and 14 M.Phil. scholars. He is a member of various academic bodies including Indian Society of Labour Economics and Indian Society of Agricultural Economics.

Contents

Preface

The share of urban population in India's total population was 25.7 percent in 1991 which increased to 27.8 percent in 2001. About 377 million Indians comprising of about 31 percent of the country's population, live in urban areas according to Census 2011. This is a smaller proportion compared to other large developing countries, for example, 45 percent in China, 54 percent in Indonesia, 78 percent in Mexico and 87 percent in Brazil. With the rapid growth of the Indian economy in recent years, which is expected to continue, the rate of urbanisation will increase and projections are that by 2031, 40 percent of India's population will be residing in urban areas.

Urbanization in India has become an important and irreversible process, and an important determinant of national economic growth and poverty reduction. The process of urbanization is characterized by a dramatic increase in the number of large cities, although India may be said to be in the midst of transition from a predominantly rural to a quasi urban society. It is acknowledged that this transition to a quasi-urban society, however, has not been accompanied by a commensurate increase in the supply of basic urban services like water supply, sewerage and drainage network, garbage disposal facilities, city-wide roads, public transport, and public safety systems like street lighting and pedestrian pathways. The supply of land and housing has not kept pace with the increase in urban population.

In recent years, the urban sector in India has undergone a major change following the country's transition towards a market-based economy and the spirit of decentralization embodied in the Constitution (Seventy-fourth) Amendment Act, 1992 (relating to municipalities) which came into force on June 1, 1993. Municipalities are now constitutional bodies forming third tier to the federal polity of India.

Excessive concentration of population in cities and unprecedented increase in the demand for civic facilities and amenities has led to problems of land shortage, housing shortfall, inadequate transportation etc. Management of essential infrastructure like water supply, sewerage, drainage, solid waste disposal has become more challenging. The concentration of economic activities and population in some of the mega cities (like Mumbai, Kolkata, Delhi, Chennai, Hyderabad, Bengaluru and Ahmedabad) has put tremendous strain on the delivery of services. At the same time there has been growing realization that there is a need for decentralization of activities so as to reduce the burden on these cities.

Taking into account the existing scenario and the urgency to augment urban infrastructure backed by strengthening of urban governance of the cities/towns, Government of India has launched, in recent years, a number of schemes/programmes with the participation of State Governments and other relevant agencies. Development of smart cities is a step in that direction.

The Government of India under Prime Minister Narendra Modi has a vision of developing 100 smart cities for modern and resurgent India. Launched by the Prime Minister in June 2015, Smart Cities Mission is a bold new initiative. It is meant to set examples that can be replicated both within and outside the smart city, catalysing the creation of similar smart cities in various regions and parts of the country. The Government has defined eligibility criteria for cities to qualify for inclusion under this programme.

The Smart Cities Mission will cover 100 cities and its duration will be 5 years (2015-16 to 2019-20). The Mission may be continued thereafter in the light of an evaluation to be done by the Ministry of Urban Development, incorporating the learnings from the Mission.

The first list of 20 urban areas that will be developed as smart cities was announced by the Government on January 28, 2016. 13 more cities were added to the list on May 24, 2016, making a total of 33 cities.

As the proportion of the urban population continues to grow, investments in urban infrastructure for the provision of services such as roads, water supply and sewerage, transportation and the like will need to be much higher than they have been in the past.

Attention needs to be focussed not only on the growing challenges of urbanisation but on the relationship between urban and rural development. The rapid transformation in the country's urban scenario must be taken into account and provided for, in order that urban growth becomes compatible with healthy socio-economic development of the nation. It will be necessary to take note of the prevailing dichotomy in rural and urban development and evolve a mechanism for bringing about rural-urban cohesion in the management of growth. This can be achieved through the process of spatial planning, which is an integrating concept that makes it possible to achieve the composite development of human settlements while stimulating economic growth.

A large part of civic amenities, particularly water supply, sanitation and sewerage, are managed with assets that have outlived their operational efficiency. The required massive upgradation and renovation of these assets, is constrained by high population density and concentrated commercial activities at the locations where these service assets are installed. The lack of comprehensive urban planning in the past to promote regular upgradation and renewal has resulted in a large backlog of development activities.

Attitudes to urban growth within the country tend to swing between two extremes. Cities are seen either as an unavoidable evil or in a more positive way as *engines of growth*. The former view is held by those who focus on the growth of slums and squatter colonies, the congestion on the roads and environmental degradation. The others, in contrast, focus on the bustling formal and informal sectors in urban areas and their contribution to the economy, the diversification of occupations away from traditional land-based ones to newer forms of production and services, and the lower levels of poverty as compared to rural areas. From this point of view, the moderate pace of urbanisation in the country has been a cause of disappointment. There is, however, no rural versus urban conflict either in terms of national growth, or in development priorities.

The present book aims to provide a detailed account of problems arising from growing urbanization in India. It particularly focuses on policies and programmes of the Government to deal with the challenges posed by rising urbanization which is attributable, to a large measure, to migration of rural people to urban areas in search of employment and a better standard of living.

Erode **N. Mani**

Abbreviations/Acronyms

ADB	Asian Development Bank
AHUs	Air Handling Units
AICTE	All India Council for Technical Education
AUWSP	Accelerated Urban Water Supply Programme
BAU	Business-As-Usual
BCIL	Biodiversity Conservation India Limited
BCM	Billion Cubic Metres
BEE	Bureau of Energy Efficiency
BEL	Bharat Electronics Limited
BIS	Bureau of Indian Standards
BOT	Build-Operate-Transfer
BOV	Battery Operated Vehicles
BRTS	Bus Rapid Transit System
CDM	Clean Development Programme
CER	Carbon Emission Reduction
CESE	Centre for Environmental Sciences and Engineering
CFL	Compact Fluorescent Lamp
CMP	Comprehensive Mobility Plan
CNG	Compressed Natural Gas
CPCB	Central Pollution Control Board
CPHEEO	Central Public Health and Environmental Engineering Organization
CPWD	Central Public Works Department
CRZ	Coastal Regulation Zone
CSE	Centre for Science and Environment
DCR	Development Control Rules
DDWS	Department of Drinking Water Supply
DIMMTS	Delhi Integrated Multi-Modal Transit System
DLCC	District Climate Change Committee
DSM	Demand Side Management
DTC	Delhi Transport Corporation
DUAC	Delhi Urban Arts Commission
EACs	Employees Assistance Centres

ECBC	Energy Conservation Building Code
ESR	Elevated Service Reservoir
GHGs	Green House Gases
GoI	Government of India
GPS	Global Positioning System
GRIHA	Green Rating for Integrated Habitat Assessment
HBA	House Building Advance
HTL	High Tide Line
HUDCO	Housing and Urban Development Corporation
HUPA	Housing and Urban Poverty Alleviation
HVs	Hybrid Vehicles
HVAC	Heating Ventilation Air Conditioning
ICLEI	International Council for Local Environmental Initiatives
ICT	Information and Communication Technology
IDSMT	Integrated Development of Small and Medium Towns
IEA	International Energy Agency
IEP	Integrated Energy Policy
IGBC	Indian Green Building Council
IGNOU	Indira Gandhi National Open University
IMG	Inter Ministerial Group
IPCC	Intergovernmental Panel on Climate Change
JCM	Joint Consultative Machinery
JNNURM	Jawaharlal Nehru National Urban Renewal Mission
L&DO	Land and Development Office
LCS	Low Cost Sanitation
LPD	Litres Per Day
LRHD	Low-Rise High Density
MBR	Master Balancing Reservoir
MDGs	Millennium Development Goals
MNRE	Ministry of New and Renewable Energy
MoEF	Ministry of Environment and Forests
MoRD	Ministry of Rural Development

MoUD	Ministry of Urban Development
MoWR	Ministry of Water Resources
MSW	Municipal Solid Waste
NBC	National Building Code
NBCC	National Buildings Construction Corporation
NCRPB	National Capital Region Planning Board
NCU	National Commission on Urbanisation
NEERI	National Environmental Engineering Research Institute
NERUDP	North-Eastern Region Urban Development Programme
NGOs	Non-governmental Organizations
NIT	National Institute of Technology
NIUA	National Institute of Urban Affairs
NURM	National Urban Renewal Mission
NUTP	National Urban Transport Policy
PCRA	Petroleum Conservation Research Association
PHE	Public Health Engineering
PHED	Public Health Engineering Department
PPP	Public-Private-Partnership
PWD	Public Works Department
QIP	Quality Improvement Programme
RDF	Refuse Derived Fuel
RECs	Regional Engineering Colleges
RTO	Road Transport Office
RWAs	Resident Welfare Associations
SBM	Swachh Bharat Mission
SLR	Sea Level Rise
SPA	School of Planning and Architecture
SPV	Solar Photo Voltaic
STPs	Sewerage Treatment Plants
SWM	Solid Waste Management
TCPO	Town and Country Planning Organisation
TERI	The Energy and Resources Institute
ToR	Terms of Reference
UD	Urban Development

UIDSSMT	Urban Infrastructure Development Scheme for Small and Medium Towns
UIDSST	Urban Infrastructure Scheme for Satellite Towns
UIG	Urban Infrastructure and Governance
ULBs	Urban Local Bodies
UNFCCC	United Nations Framework Convention on Climate Change
WWF	World Wide Fund

1

Approach to Urban Development

Urbanization is a key indicator of economic development and should be seen as a positive factor for overall development. As an economy grows, its towns and cities expand in size and volume. Urbanization is a natural consequence of economic changes that take place as a country develops. At the same time, urbanization helps to contribute to the growth process at large. This is manifest in the increasing contribution of urban sector to national income.

1.1 Urbanization and its Effects

The process of urbanization has gathered considerable momentum in recent times and this has put urban infrastructure and services under severe strain. For example, several cities in India have only two to four hours of water supply during the entire day. Smaller cities, because of inadequate financial resources, have found it particularly difficult to cope with the increasing demands on services.

The positive role of urbanization is often over-shadowed by the evident deterioration in the physical environment and quality of life in the urban areas caused by widening gap between demand and supply of essential services and infrastructure. This results from increasing population, pressure on urban centres, most of which are financially and organisationally ill-equipped to respond to infrastructural needs. Public investment in urban infrastructure has also been less than adequate. The challenge of reorienting the urbanization process, thus, lies in overcoming the infrastructural deficiencies and taking the best advantage of economic momentum inherent in urbanization.

1.1.1 Positive Effects of Urbanization: Like many other

demographic changes, urbanization has both positive and negative effects. Cities and towns have become the engines of social change and rapid economic development. Urbanization is associated with improved access to education, employment, and healthcare, resulting in increase in the age at marriage, reduction in family size and improvement in health indices. As people have moved towards and into cities, information has flowed outward. Better communication and transportation now link urban and rural areas both economically and socially creating an urban-rural continuum of communities with improvement in some aspects of lifestyle of both. The ever increasing reach of mass media communicates new ideas, points of reference, and available options are becoming more widely recognized, appreciated and sought. This phenomenon has affected health care, including reproductive health, in many ways. For instance, radio and television programmes that discuss gender equity, family size preference and family planning options are now reaching formerly isolated rural populations. This can create demand for services for mothers and children, higher contraceptive use, and fewer unwanted pregnancies, smaller healthier families and lead to more rapid population stabilisation.

1.1.2 Negative Effects of Urbanization: However, the rapid growth of urban population also poses some serious challenges. Urban population growth has outpaced the development of basic minimum services. Housing, water supply, sewerage and solid waste disposal are far from adequate. Increasing waste generation at home, offices and industries, coupled with poor waste disposal facilities result in rapid environmental deterioration. Increasing automobiles add to air pollution. All these have adverse effect on ecology and health. Poverty persists in urban and peri-urban areas. Awareness about the glaring inequities in close urban setting may lead to social unrest. As a consequence cities are facing the problem of expanding urban slums.

1.2 Rising Urbanization in India

Urbanization is directly associated with economic development. In fact, a shift of population from rural to urban areas is an indicator of economic development. The shift of population to urban areas was slow during British rule because the process of economic development itself was slow during that period. Urban population which formed 10 percent of total population in 1911, moderately increased to 14 percent in 1941. This was in sharp contrast to the urbanization trend taking place in Europe.

India ranks poorly among the countries of the world in respect of degree of urbanization. The share of urban population in total population was 25.7 percent in 1991 which increased to 27.8 percent in 2001, as per Census 2001.

About 377 million Indians comprising of about 31 percent of the country's population, live in urban areas according to Census 2011. This is a smaller proportion compared to other large developing countries, for example, 45 percent in China, 54 percent in Indonesia, 78 percent in Mexico and 87 percent in Brazil. With the more rapid growth of the Indian economy in recent years, which is expected to continue, the rate of urbanization will increase. Projections are that by 2031, about 600 million Indians will reside in urban areas.

1.2.1 Concentration of Urban Population: There is a concentration of the urban population in large cities and existing urban agglomerations. As per Census 2011, there are 53 million plus cities accounting for about 43 percent of India's urban population. Class-I cities with population over 3 lakh accounted for about 56 percent of the urban population and with a population ranging from 1 lakh to 3 lakh accounted for another 14 percent. This pattern of population concentration in large cities reflects spatial polarisation of the employment opportunities. While it is expected that gains from an agglomeration economy would lead to some polarisation of economic activities, there is a need for developing an optimal portfolio of cities by drawing regional development plans and promoting growth centres that are employment intensive and consistent with the economic potential including the natural endowment of cities and regions. The availability of water to provide for the needs of a large urban population must be a critical factor in plans for urban development.

Though the proportion of urban population concentrated in larger cities continues to remain high, there is some evidence that other urban growth nodes are emerging underscoring the need for adequate policy attention to smaller cities and peri-urban areas as against the narrow focus of concentrating on large cities. Census 2011 notes that the number of towns in India increased from 5,161 in 2001 to as many as 7,935 in 2011.

An accelerated pace of urbanization would imply significant spill over of existing cities into peri-urban areas. As borne out by a recent study by the World Bank—*India Urbanization Review: Urbanization beyond Municipalities* (2012) already there are evidences that peri-urban areas in the vicinity of large cities are centres of intense economic activities. A large number of new towns are 'born' in the vicinity of existing cities with million plus population. If these trends are any indication of how the future will unfold, much of India's urbanization challenge will be to transform land-use and expand infrastructure in its largest cities and neighbouring suburbs.

Jobs and people are flowing from metropolitan cores to nearby settlements—regardless of whether they are classified as urban or rural often giving rise to haphazard urbanization in the peri-urban areas. The challenge is to ensure that new cities and existing metropolises are connected and land-use change is coordinated with infrastructure development to accommodate urban redevelopment and urban spatial expansion.

1.2.2 Inter-State Variations in Urbanization: There is wide variation among states in urbanization. At one end of the spectrum is the National Capital Territory of Delhi, with 93 percent of its population living in urban areas. At the other end, Himachal Pradesh is the least urbanised state with only 9.8 percent of its population in urban areas. Tamil Nadu is the most urbanised among the larger states with 43.9 percent urban population, followed by Maharashtra with 42.4 percent and Gujarat with 37.4 percent. Among the larger states, Bihar has the lowest proportion of urban population (10.5 percent), below Assam (12.7 percent) and Odisha (14.9 percent). Pattern of population concentration in large cities reflects spatial polarization of employment opportunities.

1.2.3 Twelfth Five Year Plan (2012-17) on Urbanization: Pointing out the challenges of rising urbanization, the Twelfth Plan remarked, "In 2001, India's urban population, living in approximately 5,200 urban agglomerations, was about 285 million. It has increased to almost 380 million in 2011. Projections are that by 2030, out of a total population of 1.4 billion, over 600 million people may be living in urban areas. The process of urbanization is a natural process associated with growth. It is well known that agglomeration and densification of economic activities (and habitations) in urban conglomerations stimulates economic efficiencies and provides more opportunities for earning livelihoods. Possibilities for entrepreneurship and employment increase when urban concentration takes place, in contrast to the dispersed and less diverse economic possibilities in rural areas. This enables faster inclusion of more people in the growth process and is therefore more inclusive. There is no doubt that the condition of the poor in rural India must continue to get major attention but the urban sector development should not be viewed as negating such attention or weakening it in any way. On the contrary, we must acknowledge that there is a synergistic relationship between rural prosperity and the continuum of urban development from small towns through larger cities to metros. A holistic approach to spatial development is needed if the country wishes to achieve more inclusive growth.

An interesting aspect of the urbanization trend revealed by the Census is that the number of towns in India increased from 5,161 in 2001 to as many as 7,935 in 2011. It points out that almost all of this increase reflects the growth of 'census' towns (which increased by 2,532) rather than 'statutory' towns (which increased by only 242). 'Statutory' towns are towns with municipalities or corporations whereas 'census' towns are agglomerations that grow in rural and peri-urban areas, with densification of populations, that do not have an urban governance structure or requisite urban infrastructure of sanitation, roads, etc. As more Indians will inevitably live within urbanized conglomerations, with densification of villages, sprouting of peri-urban centres around large towns, and also migration of people into towns, the quality of their lives and livelihoods will be affected by the infrastructure of India's urban conglomerations. The infrastructure of India's present towns is very poor. Sewage, water, sanitation, roads and housing are woefully inadequate for their inhabitants. The worst affected are the poor in the towns. As more urban conglomerations form and grow without adequate infrastructure, the problems will only become worse. Therefore, India's urban agenda must get much more attention". [1]

1.2.4 Consequences of Rising Urbanization: Rising urbanization in India has led to tremendous pressure on civic infrastructure systems, water supply, sewerage and drainage, uncollected solid waste, parks and open spaces, transport etc. It has also led to deterioration in the quality of city environments. In several cities, the problems of traffic congestion, pollution, poverty, inadequate housing, crime, and social unrest are assuming alarming proportions. Further, growing urbanization is characterized by incomplete devolution of functions to the elected bodies, lack of financial resources, unwillingness to progress towards municipal autonomy, adherence to outdated methods in property taxation, hesitation in levy of user charges, unsatisfactory role of parastatals in the provision of water supply and sanitation services etc.

As the proportion of the urban population continues to

grow, investments in urban infrastructure for the provision of services such as roads, water supply and sewerage, transportation and the like will need to be much higher than they have been in the past.

The likely increase in urban productivity and population due to the new economic policies of the Government of India will place a heavy demand on all kinds of urban infrastructure and services. The infrastructure bottlenecks in urban centres are likely to pose serious impediments in enhancing the productivity.

Rising urbanization has increased the functional responsibilities of municipalities. To meet the scale and challenge of urbanization, municipal governments are always looking for additional funds from various sources.

Since a significant part of national income originates in urban areas, efforts must be made to maintain and enhance urban productivity which, in turn, depends on the level and quality of urban infrastructure. The demand for urban infrastructure services has increased, and is likely to accelerate further, due to rising personal incomes, rapid growth of population, and general increase in economic activities. Inability of municipal governments to meet the rising demand would adversely affect growth prospects of the economy.

Urbanization will be central to India's strategy of achieving faster and more inclusive growth because agglomeration and densification of economic activities (and habitations) in urban conglomerations stimulates economic efficiencies and provides more opportunities for earning livelihoods. Thus, urbanization increases avenues for entrepreneurship and employment compared to what is possible in dispersed rural areas. It, thereby, enables faster inclusion of more people in the process of economic growth.

1.3 Features of Urban Infrastructure Services

Urban infrastructure services have the following features:

1. Most urban infrastructure services are natural monopolies and their marginal cost declines over a very large range of

output. As such, it is feared that the private sector might exploit the monopolistic situation. Such services include water, waste water management, telephone, electricity, bridge, and road networks.

2. Many services like sanitation and solid waste disposal (SWD) have significant external economies. As a consequence, market-based systems may fail to provide the service in adequate quantity and quality.
3. It is difficult to exclude anyone from using certain public services like roads or street lighting. The consumer may refuse to pay for the service since he may be able to use it free of charge legally or otherwise.
4. Certain infrastructure services being necessities (like water) have almost inelastic demand. Private provision of these could result in exploitative pricing unless prices are regulated.
5. Requirement of heavy investment in capital equipment discourages private sector entry into certain infrastructure segments.

The above mentioned characteristics have for long been used as valid arguments for blocking entry of the private sector into infrastructure. The arguments, however, are slowly losing their validity due to many technological and organizational innovations. Unbundling of services has been a major mechanism through which the misconception about the economies of scale argument has been overcome. Technological innovations in the areas of sanitation and sewerage have permitted low-cost supply options. Increasing range and quality of service has reduced the cost of providing the service, making the operation commercially viable and also opening up areas for private sector operations. The recognition of the demand aspect has made remunerative pricing possible in some segments.

By and large, governments have not been very effective suppliers of many services. The cost of government failures has been much higher than the possible cost of market failure.

Commercialisation of infrastructure projects basically means efficient provision of service to the consumers' satisfaction on cost-recovery basis. Since the public sector in most cases is an inefficient provider due to its inherent characteristics, promotion of privatisation itself becomes an instrument for commercialisation.

1.4 Functions of Local Bodies

Functional responsibilities of local bodies vary from country to country and within a country. Still some common patterns are discernible. Broadly speaking, the functions of a local body (e.g., a municipality) can be divided into the following three categories.

1.4.1 Essential Civic Functions: The main function of a municipality is to provide and maintain core (or essential) civic services. These include: refuse collection, street lighting, water supply, sewage disposal, fire protection, abattoirs, and primary health services. These are services for which decision-making rests with the municipalities.

1.4.2 Regulatory Functions: These functions pertain to regulation of industry, trade and construction activities. Municipalities issue licences, permits and levy fees of various kinds, and also impose fines for violation of rules and regulations. Charges for regulatory functions should be so fixed as to cover at least the cost of administration and surveillance. If these services are subsidised it would put strain on resources.

1.4.3 Agency Functions: These are functions (e.g., protection of environment) which are funded out of State revenues by specific transfers.

1.5 Financing of Local Bodies

In the public finance literature, the following general rules are mentioned as regards the financing of local bodies.

1. Where the benefits of a local public service are measurable and accrue to readily identifiable individuals/households

within a jurisdiction, user charges are the most appropriate method of financing the service.
2. Local public services which are services to general public in the sense that identification of beneficiaries and measurement of benefits to individuals/households is difficult, should be financed by taxes on local residents. Such services include traffic control, street lighting, security, and general administration.
3. Services the benefits of which spill over to neighbouring jurisdictions should be financed by intergovernmental transfers. These services include health, education, anti-pollution measures, and other social welfare activities.
4. Long-term borrowings are the appropriate source to finance capital projects with long-term gains.

Higher level governments generally assign certain taxes to local bodies to augment their resources. Tax literature suggests the following principles regarding assignment of taxes to local bodies.

1. Municipal governments should be assigned those taxes that are leviable on bases which are *immobile* or *location-specific* and those whose burden cannot be exported outside the municipal jurisdiction. Property tax is a case in point.
2. Local tax base should be easily identifiable and its incidence transparent.
3. Tax yield should be stable, predictable, and buoyant.
4. Rate schedule of the tax should possess a reasonable degree of progressivity.
5. The tax should be easy to administer.

Based on the foregoing considerations, the following taxes are generally assigned to local bodies: (a) property tax, (b) entertainment tax, (c) tax on professions, (d) tax on advertisements and (e) octroi/tolls.

In India, urban infrastructure services are provided by local level agencies. Funds have generally been in the form of loans/grants from the Central and State Governments. Own resources of urban local bodies (ULBs) have been insufficient even to meet the O&M requirements of these services. Since most urban infrastructure services have been treated as public services and the concept of cost recovery has never been considered relevant, a commercial approach to these services has not developed. Even if the facilities were funded by loans, the repayment of loans generally took adjustments or paid out of grants made by State Governments. Even when user charges are levied, the price per unit is too low to cover even the variable cost of providing the service.

The fact that infrastructure services do not pay for themselves, and the government does not have the financial capacity to continue to subsidise the beneficiaries, has resulted in low availability of funds. With increasing requirements, this has meant deficiency in volumes as well as quality of service. Consequently, a parallel unorganised sector for provision of many of these services has developed, resulting in high prices and qualitatively deficient services. From a societal point of view, these are expensive solutions. It is high time that a commercial approach is adopted.

In order to augment resources in the urban infrastructure, 100 percent foreign direct investment (FDI) has been permitted in the development of integrated township since 2001. However, investments have not materialised because of very rigid existing conditions relating to land procurement especially in urban areas. Moreover, there are problems relating to lack of clear titles, old protective tenancy and rent control. The system of maintenance of land records need to be improved through computerisation. This, together with rationalisation of stamp duty, would make things easier for those interested in entering into partnership for development of townships.

In terms of financing patterns, the foundation of urban infrastructure has to be user charges. It is possible for urban institutions to access funds from the capital markets to finance a large portion of capital expenditure on urban infrastructure, which can be serviced by user charges in the future. While municipal bond issues have indeed taken place, the magnitude of resources raised is as yet insignificant. The user-charge financed approach can facilitate a massive increase in capital expenditure on urban infrastructure without worsening the fiscal problem. In addition, the tariff restructuring or subsidy design allows for more efficient and targeted impact on the poor.

1.5.1 Cost Effectiveness: The major demands of the strategy to minimise cost should be technological appropriateness, proper attention to maintenance, curbing misuse of services and efficient institutional arrangements for providing services. To promote cost effectiveness, different infrastructure projects may be packaged together like water supply and drainage projects. Coordination between different departments providing different services will also reduce overall cost of production.

The supply orientation in infrastructure policy has not succeeded to respond adequately to the evolution of demand. A commercial approach requires that demand-orientation service should be supplied in response to demand rather than in anticipation of demand. This will also improve cost recovery and financial viability of such projects.

1.5.2 Innovations for Better Urbanization: Managing India's ongoing urbanization will place huge requirements on financial as well as human resources in the country. Given the scarcity of resources in the medium term, innovation will have a significant role to play. It is critical to promote innovation and research in several ways.

Given the huge requirement of funds, it is critical to incentivise cost reducing innovations in the fields of materials and processes. The support can be in the form of incubation assistance and low cost funds. Incentives could be in the form of recognition and rewards.

Creating innovative solutions is not enough. These solutions need to be spread across the country to maximise impact.

1.5.3 Pooled Finance Development Fund (PFDF): Direct access to capital markets for funding urban infrastructure projects, often leveraging government grants, is an established option in global markets. However, capital market investors require well structured projects with a clear understanding of inherent risks, appropriate pricing of such risks, and an established system for ensuring timely payment of dues.

In this context, the Government of India launched the Pooled Finance Development Fund (PFDF) scheme. The PFDF scheme is meant to provide credit enhancement grants to a pool of (primarily) medium and smaller municipalities to enable them to access the capital market through pooled finance municipal bonds for investment in urban infrastructure projects. The PFDF scheme is meant for creation of essential municipal infrastructure, with priority on water and sanitation projects. In case access to the PFDF scheme is being sought for projects in other areas, it must be first demonstrated that adequate service quality exists in the water and sanitation sectors in areas under the jurisdiction of the respective municipalities. The main objectives of the PFDF scheme are fourfold:

1. Facilitate ULBs to access the capital and financial market for investment in essential municipal infrastructure.
2. Facilitate development of bankable urban infrastructure projects.
3. Reduce the cost of borrowings to local bodies with appropriate credit enhancement measures and through restructuring of existing costly debts.
4. Facilitate development of municipal bond market.

1.5.4 Tax Free Municipal Bonds: In 2000-01, the Government inserted a new clause (vii) in Section 10(15) of the Income Tax Act, 1961, exempting interest income from bonds issued by local authorities. Funds raised from Tax Free Municipal Bonds are to be used only for capital investments in urban infrastructure for providing one or more of the following:

1. Potable water supply.

2. Sewerage or sanitation.
3. Drainage.
4. Solid waste management.
5. Roads, bridges and flyovers.
6. Urban transport (if this is a municipal function under respective state legislation).

Ministry of Urban Development, Government of India has been designated as the nodal agency for processing applications for issue of tax free bonds.

Guidelines were issued by the Ministry of Urban Development on February 8, 2001 for regulating issue of tax free municipal bonds. Under the guidelines, such bonds will be issued for raising resources for capital investment in creation of new infrastructure as well as augmentation of existing systems.

Guidelines for issue of municipal tax free bonds were revised in consultation with the Ministry of Finance and circulated to all the State Governments and UT Governments on March 7, 2006.

Municipal bonds were successfully issued by several municipal corporations like, Bangalore, Ahmedabad, Ludhiana, Nagpur, Nasik, and Madurai for raising resources for urban infrastructure.

1.6 Municipal Commercial Borrowings

In India, Plan allocations of Central and State Governments are the chief source of financing capital projects of municipal governments. Other sources of finance include: (a) internal resources of municipalities, (b) institutional resources (HUDCO etc.), and (c) multilateral agencies.

The scope for additional funds from Central and State Governments is limited in view of the pressing need to reduce fiscal deficit. Similarly, institutional finances at low cost are unlikely to be available in the wake of financial sector reforms. Under such circumstances, municipal authorities should be permitted access to the capital market to mobilise additional resources. Recent expansion and modernisation of capital market in India suggests that inflow of capital into equity and debt market is quite high if attractive rate of return is offered.

1.6.1 Rationale for Municipal Commercial Borrowings: It is both fair and efficient that projects with long-term benefits are financed through long-term borrowings. If long-term capital projects are financed out of current revenues and/or short-term borrowings, the future generations would enjoy free-riding. Since the benefits of a capital project are reaped over a long period of time, i.e. by more than one generation of tax payers, the financing of such projects should place the repayment burden on the present as well as future generations.

1.6.2 Factors Determining Success of Municipal Bonds: To attract a share of capital market for municipalities, the following conditions need to be satisfied.

1. Urban infrastructure projects should be commercially viable.
2. Municipal bonds are rated by some recognised credit rating institution. This will help build confidence of investors in the bond issue as well as help in its subsequent trading on the secondary market.
3. Such bonds should carry tax concessions.
4. Revenues accruing to the municipal entity are sufficiently elastic.
5. Security behind the debt taken by the municipal entity is sound.
6. Municipal entity makes provision for the creation of debt-servicing funds and the legal procedures for seeking recourse in the event of default.
7. Municipal entity is competent to pledge revenues for debt-servicing and extend collateral in terms of commercial property, plant and machinery and other assets.

1.6.3 Limitations: Municipal access to capital market, though desirable, is hindered by a variety of factors which may be classified into two categories: (a) restrictions imposed by the higher level government, and (b) other constraints.

The Constitution of India imposes various types of restrictions on the borrowing powers of the State Governments which, in turn, impose restrictions on the borrowing powers of the municipalities under them. Since borrowings by the lower level government are guaranteed, in most cases, by the higher level government, the latter has a right to impose such restrictions. These restrictions apply to: (a) type of debt, (b) amount of debt, (c) term of the debt, and (d) use of debt funds. Approval of the higher level government, which is often cumbersome, is needed before the debt is floated.

Thus, no municipal authority can borrow without an explicit sanction of its State Government. When the loan amount exceeds ₹ 25 lakh or the repayment period is over 30 years, local borrowings need Central approval under the provisions of the Local Authorities Loan Act, 1914 (a Central Legislation).

Among the 'other constraints', the more important are the following: Low credit worthiness of municipalities, their poor tract record as borrowers, and lack of trustworthy financial intermediaries.

Despite the foregoing hurdles, some municipalities in India have successfully tapped the bond market.

1.7 Privatisation of Municipal Services

The scope for privatisation of some municipal services in order to reduce costs is a moot question.

Municipalities alone cannot handle huge infrastructural projects like water supply, sewage disposal, and urban transport. Involvement of central, state, and private sector is required to meet the scale of investment needed in these areas. Similarly, greater participation of private sector is desirable in the provision of civic services, particularly those the consumption of which can be attributed to individuals and households. There are many types of arrangement in respect of public-private partnership depending on situation. However, care should be taken not to dilute current social commitments while embarking on public-private partnership.

The historical and ideological resistance to private sector participation persists in most places. Consequently, few local bodies have tried out private sector participation in civic services on any significant scale. Wherever it has happened, the experiment has remained limited to disposal of solid wastes, and maintenance of parks.

The disenchantment with utility enterprises of municipalities is not conceptual but borne out of their inefficient and sometimes corrupt management. The merits of privatisation are seen in terms of improvement in efficiency and reduction in the budgetary burden of state-owned enterprises.

Though the need for private sector participation is widely felt, it is not openly expressed. Very rarely political parties have spoken publicly against the public sector. Contrarily, there is a stiff opposition by political parties to any move to undermine the importance of public sector. The strong unions of public sector enterprises come in handy for politicians to prevent the erosion of state and municipal activities.

1.8 Urban Governance

Despite the 74th Constitutional Amendment, which required States to transfer eighteen functions to the ULBs, there is significant variation in devolution of functions, functionaries and funds across the States. City mayors lack the powers and tenure to be truly accountable for delivery of urban services. At the metropolitan level, Metropolitan Planning Committees (MPCs) are yet to evolve and District Planning Committees must function not only in letter but in the intended spirit too. In most States either State agencies or parastatals are in-charge of urban service delivery rather than ULBs. This maze like structure of management and accountability hampers good urban management.

Urban governance today is characterised by fragmentation of responsibility, incomplete devolution of functions and funds to the elected bodies and urban local bodies (ULBs), unwillingness to progress towards municipal autonomy, adherence to outmoded methods of property tax and reluctance to levy user charges. State Governments continue to take decisions on such matters as rates of user charges, property tax, octroi, role of parastatals in water supply and sanitation services etc., with little reference to the ULBs that are affected by these decisions.

Far from strengthening the constitutional role of the elected ULBs, such developments only reinforce the perception that ULBs are subordinate entities under the day-to-day control of the State Governments, beholden to them not only for the development of the cities but often for their very survival. There appears to be a lack of confidence that many of the ULBs are capable of meeting their obligations as institutions of local self-governance. In the present set up, initiatives for local developmental activities rarely come from the ULBs. Experience shows that functional autonomy becomes a reality only when it is accompanied by financial independence. State governments, therefore, need to strengthen the autonomous functioning of the ULBs through positive measures, and in particular, ensure their financial self-reliance.

The key urban concern is the growing gap between demand and supply of basic services. While there has been a steady growth in the housing stock, infrastructure and services, the gaps between demand and supply have been rising, even in terms of conservative norms.

Since overall government resources are limited and must be applied to other priority sectors such as health and education, it is necessary that cities, especially the larger ones, and progressively even the smaller ones, are encouraged and enabled to draw resources from the market and the private sector. For this, they must improve their governance and ability to implement projects. They will also have to manage their land resources more strategically, both to ensure better land use and to secure what will be a principal resource for their future financial needs. They must become able to recover adequate service charges, and equitably, from their inhabitants, which will require them to demonstrate an ability to deliver better and more reliable services.

In short, urban governance is very weak, with poor co-ordination amongst the many agencies that must work together to create and maintain good functioning habitats. Personnel and institutional capabilities for urban management have to be developed on a massive scale across the country. Capabilities for planning locally are woefully inadequate, which is leading to projects not aligned with local priorities and poor coordination amongst separate initiatives.

Information technology (IT) can play an important role in improving governance. With municipal administration becoming increasingly complex, the benefits of IT adoption are becoming more visible across several municipalities. E-governance must be a mandatory reform under the renewed Jawaharlal Nehru National Urban Renewal Mission (JNNURM) and its implementation should be required in all cities receiving assistance under the capacity building component of the Mission. A major constraint in full fledged transition to e-governance is lack of a suitable national level architecture. This has led to States and ULBs independently developing e-governance platforms which are often mutually incompatible. This has also prevented States from replicating successful architecture developed in other States leading to avoidable expenditure. To address this problem, the Ministry of Urban Development should finalise a suitable national level architecture with sufficient flexibility for customization at the State and ULB level.

1.8.1 Building Capacity for Managing Urbanization: Lack of sufficient capacity across all levels of Government is a root cause of India's urban development challenges. Many States have lagged in programme utilisation due to inadequate capabilities of governance and management. Traditionally, capacity building, though critical, has been given low priority, which is evident in the absence of dedicated municipal cadres and robust urban management structures. Substantial skill gaps exist across almost all areas of urban management. This is driven as much by the lack of credible and specialized supply side institutions as it is by poor demand from those responsible for urban management in cities. Addressing the capacity deficit must be a key endeavour.

E-governance initiatives including online project management information system should be implemented across all ULBs. There should be a State level nodal agency for implementation and monitoring of all e-governance initiatives within the State. It should also identify the training needs and coordinate with relevant agencies to conduct trainings.

1.9 Urban Planning

A key weakness of India's urbanization efforts is that the agenda is being implemented through disjointed projects/activities with inadequate or no planning for the urban area as a whole. The Master Plan approach generally focuses on only the core area of the city, has little linkages to any financial and operating strategy and, in many cases has been used as a regulatory tool instead of being a blue print for development of dynamic and smart cities. A master plan typically freezes the land use pattern and building bye-laws and so on determines the permissible limits of floor space index (FSI) and minimum setback areas. Often these provisions do not take into account the potential of the city to grow, especially where trunk infrastructure has been laid. This results in sub-optimal use of land as well as the infrastructure.

Absence of any long-term plan prevents development of 'good cities' in which all the parts of the system—urban services, transportation, housing, commercial activities—fit together harmoniously. Planning must be holistic before it is detailed, for example, urban housing and urban poverty issues cannot be separated from other aspects of urban planning. Holistic planning, even if not detailed, is required at the local urban level, at the metropolitan level and at State and national levels too.

Urban planning is a key determinant of demand for mobility: whether it is a compact city where the various functions—residential and commercial, services, education and recreation—are located and how they interconnect; whether public transport is available for newly developed areas etc. City governments should be made accountable for greenhouse gas emissions caused by poorly planned suburban sprawl.

Low rise and higher density is a way to improve the overall energy efficiency of urban areas. General urban consolidation and more intensive mixed use of local activity centres close to public transport nodes provide opportunities to lower carbon emissions.

The planning of housing areas can significantly affect living comfort during heat waves. Innovative cooling systems contribute to limitation of emissions.

Planting trees around buildings to shade urban surfaces and green roofs to reduce their temperature lead to substantial reductions in energy consumption for air conditioning and sequester carbon while growing. Trees to shade roads and parking lots reduce evaporative emissions from gasoline, which contribute to increased levels of urban ozone. Biomass from trees and shrubs can be used as wood energy to replace fossil fuels, thus contributing to climate adaptation.

Planners should take into account specific effects of climate change while planning for a district/region. Some issues which need to be tackled at the regional level include flexible management of resources, including allocation of water, preservation of threatened areas.

Sound urban practices lead to long-term sustainability. The National Commission on Urbanization (NCU) India (1988) recommended low-rise high density (LRHD) built form for Indian cities. It stated that such a form is less expensive to maintain and has other advantages like equity. According to NCU, income profile and affordability suggest that a range of small and medium-sized plots, between 50 square metres and 100 square metres (with some plots perhaps up to 200 square metres) can satisfy the needs of over 95 percent of the urban population. NCU felt that this typology is more economical than apartments because less space is required for public circulation and lifts, besides it also provides much better living conditions. According to NCU, a 50 square metres plot per family with 5 members would generate a net density of 1,000 persons per hectare (i.e. a gross residential density of 500 persons per hectare). Similarly, a 100 square metres plot would generate a gross residential density of 250 persons per hectare. It also stated that high gross densities in the inner city can be tackled by interventions in the city structure and by adjusting land use allocation within the city itself to create spaces for social overheads. Its recommendations for built form specified that residential sites should be provided so that:

1. 50 percent of the land is in plots between 25 and 100 square metres.
2. 25 percent of the land is in the plots between 100 and 200 square metres.
3. 25 percent of the land is either in this size of plots or any other sizes.

NCU further stated that as long as Indian cities remain within stipulated density thresholds (i.e. neighbourhood densities of 250 to 1,000 persons per hectare) there are efficient and cost-effective solutions within available resources. The densification can be increased at selected nodal points depending on the holding capacity of the area. Densification should be related to the mass public transport network.

High population density aggravates negative externalities like air pollution, noise and loss of green space. However, it may improve accessibility of services, reduce per capita domestic energy consumption and also promote infrastructure efficiency and use of public transport.

In general, advantages of densification can be summarized as follows: (a) protection of the countryside, green space and biodiversity, (b) reduction of travel distance, emission of green house gases and thus global warming, (c) reduction in use of material for construction of infrastructure, (d) economies of scale in providing social and institutional services like hospitals, banks etc. and (e) better interactive community life.

The disadvantages are as follows: (a) overcrowding, (b) traffic congestion, (c) ill health, (d) crime and (e) high energy demand in compact high rise buildings.

Arriving at an optimum form would require a balance between densification and expansion.

1.10 Urban-Rural Co-ordination

Attention needs to be focussed not only on the growing challenges of urbanization but on the relationship between urban and rural development. The rapid transformation in the country's urban scenario must be taken into account and provided for, in order that urban growth becomes compatible with healthy socio-economic development of the nation. It will be necessary to take note of the prevailing dichotomy in rural and urban development and evolve a mechanism for bringing about rural-urban cohesion in the management of growth. This can be achieved through the process of spatial planning, which is an integrating concept that makes it possible to achieve the composite development of human settlements while stimulating economic growth.

The rural hinterland has played a critical role in sustaining urbanization. This is reflected in the indicators of sources of primary inputs, competitively priced labour for urban economic activities, primary funds as reflected in comparative urban and rural credit-deposit ratios and market for urban products. However, the unending migration of the rural poor to urban areas may have a destabilising effect on urbanization and its sustainability. Income and employment opportunities will have to rise in the rural areas, through both the farm and non-farm sectors and habitats and basic services have to be improved so that with rural development and congenial habitats, rural areas emerge as sustainable centres of economic activities and human settlements.

In a country still largely rural and agricultural in character, it is natural that programmes for agricultural and rural development should receive the greatest emphasis, in particular those for rural employment creation and assistance to the rural poor. Urban development should, however, be seen as complementary to rural development and policies affecting the process of urbanization should be such as to strengthen the links between towns and cities and their hinterland. Urban areas of all sizes operate as market centres for agricultural output and provide a variety of service functions in addition to operating as centres of manufacturing activity. These functions should be strengthened such that towns and cities serve the rural areas more effectively.

The process of urbanization should then be seen as aiding employment and income generation in rural areas rather than as a competitive process. Larger towns serve as distribution centres for seed, fertilisers and credit for farmers as well as serving as organised markets for their produce. The bigger cities provide services and facilities to both the smaller towns as well as rural areas in their hinterland. Thus, national policy on urban development should view the whole range of urban settlements as having a role to play in the national development process.

It is also important to view the provision of services in rural areas in an integrated manner. Availability of shelter, safe water supply and facilities for hygienic sanitation are as necessary in the rural areas as in the urban. Owing to different residential densities, however, different technologies can be used in different sizes of settlements in providing these services.

It is only through purposive public programmes providing essential services like water and sewerage along with low cost shelter programmes like sites and services that the urban landscape of the country can be improved to enable the urban population to function more efficiently. Particular attention must be paid to the functioning of the small, medium and intermediate cities in order to aid them in their role as market centres and as suppliers of goods and services for agriculture. The environmental and infrastructural conditions in some of these towns and cities have been neglected so long that their efficient functioning is beginning to be hampered.

Although the theme of a *rural-urban divide* still colours some policy discourse in India, there is a growing recognition that urbanization is necessary to realise India's growth potential, and that rural-urban linkages must be strengthened. Indeed this will accelerate growth of the rural sector also.

The fortunes of the agricultural sector are crucially linked to the manner in which growth in the industry and services sectors unfolds. People living in rural areas typically tap the opportunities that cities provide for employment, entrepreneurial avenues, and education. As urbanization grows, demand for food items other than foodgrains, i.e. vegetables, lentils, milk, eggs and so on, also grows. This leads to investments in infrastructure, logistics, processing and packaging in rural and peri-urban areas. Such investments and other economic inter-linkages connect and build synergy between rural and urban centres. Thus, the rural sector also benefits from good management of neighbouring urban conglomerations.

1.11 Major Issues in Urbanization

The concentration of urban population in a few large cities has led to tremendous pressure on civic infrastructure systems like water supply, sewerage and drainage, solid waste management, parks and open spaces, transport etc. It has also led to deterioration in the quality of city environment. In several cities, the problems of traffic congestion, pollution, poverty, slums, crime and social unrest are assuming alarming proportions. Climate change is likely to exacerbate the existing stresses that these settlements already face. It may also impact measures that are being undertaken for sustainable development of these areas.

Attitudes to urban growth within the country tend to swing between two extremes. Cities are seen either as an unavoidable evil or in a more positive way as *engines of growth*. The former view is held by those who focus on the growth of slums and squatter colonies, the congestion on the roads and environmental degradation. The others, in contrast, focus on the bustling formal and informal sectors in urban areas and their contribution to the economy, the diversification of occupations away from traditional land-based ones to newer forms of production and services, and the lower levels of poverty as compared to rural areas. From this point of view, the moderate pace of urbanization in the country has been a cause of disappointment. There is, however, no rural versus urban conflict either in terms of national growth, or in development priorities.

Good urban governance calls for adequate policy and legal frameworks, the existence of regulatory and planning authorities, human skills, a sound revenue base, accounting and accountability. Substantial work has already been done to upgrade the urban infrastructure and several parastatals and urban development authorities have acquired considerable skills in planning and executing projects. In particular, parastatal agencies and bodies such as development authorities need to play a supportive role to the elected bodies rather than taking over functions which properly belong to the ULBs. The objective of devolution and decentralisation should be carried forward by making parastatals and authorities partners and agencies of the democratically elected ULBs, thus making a gradual transition to local management while continuing to use the expertise of the organisations set up and supervised by the State Governments.

A large part of civic amenities, particularly water supply, sanitation and sewerage, are managed with assets that have outlived their operational efficiency. The required massive upgradation and renovation of these assets, is constrained by high population density and concentrated commercial activities at the locations where these service assets are installed. The lack of comprehensive urban planning in the past to promote regular upgradation and renewal has resulted in a large backlog of development activities.

Another crucial aspect requiring immediate attention is that physical infrastructure assets created in urban areas have generally been languishing due to inadequate attention and/or improper O&M. The fiscal flows to the sector have laid emphasis only on the creation of physical assets. Not much effort has been made either to manage these assets efficiently or to achieve self-sustainability. It is, therefore, necessary that a link be established between asset creation and management, as both are important components for ensuring sustained service delivery.

To sum up, India is a part of the global trend towards increasing urbanization. Cities hold tremendous potential as engines of economic and social development, creating jobs and generating wealth through economies of scale. They need to be sustained and augmented through the high urban productivity for country's economic growth. National economic growth and poverty reduction efforts will be increasingly determined by the productivity of these cities and towns. For Indian cities to become growth oriented and productive, it is essential to achieve a world class urban system. This in turn depends on attaining efficiency and equity in the delivery and financing of urban infrastructure.

Cities and towns are emerging as centres of domestic and international investments where most of the commercial activities take place. The higher productivity of any urban area depends on the availability and quality of infrastructure services. Urban economic activities are dependent upon urban infrastructure like roads, water supply, power, telecommunication, mass transportation and other civic infrastructure like sanitation and solid waste management. Massive urban growth has led to complex problems of inadequacy of basic urban services.

Rapid economic growth will inevitably lead to an increase in urbanization as cities provide large economies of agglomeration for individual activity. Unfortunately, the state of urban infrastructure has deteriorated to an extent that the country is not able to fully benefit from these economies. Poor urban infrastructure inflicts a severe hardship on people. Congested roads, poor public transport, inadequate availability of water, improper treatment of sewage, uncollected solid waste and above all grossly inadequate housing, all these severely decrease the quality of life and lower the well-being of urban population.

The rural-urban continuum should be strengthened so that gaps between rural and urban lifestyles are reduced. Effective urban strategies and programmes cannot be developed in isolation of those in the rural areas.

Endnote

1. Government of India, Planning Commission, *An Approach to the Twelfth Five Year Plan*, October 2011, p. 108.

2

Constitutional Provisions and Institutional Framework for Urban Development

Towns and cities contribute substantially to the economic development of the country. These urban centres also play an important support role in the development of rural hinterland. To keep this economic transformation in line with needs and realities at the grassroots level, it is necessary that the people and their representatives are fully involved in the planning and implementation of the programmes at local level. If democracy in Parliament and State Legislatures is to remain strong and stable, its roots must reach towns and villages and the cities where the people live.

Rapid urbanization has increased the functional responsibilities of municipalities in India. To meet the scale and challenge of urbanization, municipal governments are always looking for additional funds from various sources. Since a significant part of national income originates in urban areas, efforts must be made to maintain and enhance urban productivity which, in turn, depends on the level and quality of urban infrastructure. The demand for urban infrastructure services has increased, and is likely to accelerate further, due to rising personal incomes, rapid growth of population, and general increase in economic activities. Inability of municipal governments to meet the rising demand would adversely affect growth prospects of the economy.

2.1 Constitutional Provisions Regarding Local Bodies

The Constitution of India has made detailed provisions for ensuring protection of democracy in Parliament and in State Legislatures. Hence, democracy in these institutions has survived and flourished. However, the Constitution did not make local self-government in urban areas a clear-cut Constitutional obligation. While Article 40 of the Constitution requires the strengthening of the units of local self-government in the States, particularly panchayati raj institutions (PRIs), there is no specific reference to municipalities except implicitly in Entry 5 of List II (State List) in the Seventh Schedule of the Constitution, which places the subject of local self-government as a responsibility of the State. Entry 5 reads as under:

"Local Government, that is to say, the constitution and powers of municipal corporations, improvement trusts, district boards, mining settlement authorities and other local authorities for the purpose of local self-government or village administration".

As a consequence of inadequate Constitutional provision for local self-government, democracy in municipal governance was not stable. Though the respective municipal acts of the States provided for regular elections to municipal bodies, they were frequently suspended and superseded for indefinite periods of time. Frequent and indefinite suspensions or supersessions eroded the very basis of local self-government and had a negative effect on democracy at the grassroots level. The general position with regard to financial resources of the municipal bodies was also not satisfactory. Over the years, there was a steady encroachment on the assigned functions and revenues of urban local bodies (ULBs) by specialized agencies of the State Governments.

In short, local bodies could not function effectively because of: (a) inadequate devolution of functions and financial powers (b) failure to hold regular elections and prolonged supersession and (c) lack of participation from weaker sections of society. Consequently, local bodies in many States had become weak and ineffective as units of self-government in the democratic set up of India.

The weakened status of ULBs crystallized public opinion

in favour of a Constitutional guarantee to safeguard the interests of urban local bodies in order to provide for the following:

1. Regular and fair conduct of elections to these bodies.
2. Holding of elections within a specified time limit in case of supersession.
3. Adequate representation of SC/ST and women in the elected bodies.
4. Placing on firm footing the relationship between the State Governments and the urban local bodies with respect to: (a) functions and taxation powers of the urban local bodies and (b) arrangement for revenue sharing between the State Government and the urban local bodies.
5. Involvement of elected representatives at grassroots level in planning at the district and metropolitan levels.

2.2 Decentralisation Initiative, 1992

The Seventy-third and Seventy-fourth Amendment Bills relating to panchayats and municipalities respectively were introduced in the Parliament in September 1991 to provide constitutional remedy for the inadequacies plaguing these bodies which were unable to perform effectively as vibrant democratic units of self-government. The Bills were referred to two joint bodies of Parliament and after necessary revision were reintroduced in July 1992, and passed by the Parliament in December 1992. Both the Bills were ratified by the required number of States [Article 368(ii)] and the President gave his assent in April 1993. The Seventy-third Amendment Act relating to *panchayats* came into force from April 24, 1993. The Seventy-fourth Amendment Act relating to municipalities came into force from June 1, 1993. The changes made by the Seventy-third and Seventy-fourth Amendment Acts to the Constitution were of historical importance and are summarised in Table 2.1.

In short, panchayats and municipalities are now constitutional bodies forming third tier to the federal polity of India. India's decentralisation initiative in the form of Seventy-third and Seventy-fourth Amendments poses challenges and offers opportunities.

Table 2.1: Seventy-third and Seventy-fourth Constitutional Amendment Acts

Act	Date on which came into force	Amendments made
Constitution (Seventy-third Amendment) Act, 1992	24. 4. 1993	A new Part IX relating to panchayats was inserted. In clause (3) of Article 280, sub-clause (bb) was inserted which provides for measures to supplement the resources of the panchayats. Eleventh Schedule added to the Constitution which provides an illustrative list for the devolution of functions to panchayats.
Constitution (Seventy-fourth Amendment) Act, 1992	1. 6. 1993	A new Part IXA relating to municipalities was inserted. In clause (3) of Article 280, sub-clause (c) was re-lettered as sub-clause (d) and before sub-clause (d) as so re-lettered, sub-clause (c) was inserted which provides for measures to supplement the resources of the municipalities. Twelfth Schedule added to the Constitution which provides an illustrative list for the devolution of functions to municipalities.

Source: Government of India, Ministry of Law, Justice and Company Affairs, *The Constitution of India*, (Supplement to the Third Edition), 1994.

2.3 Constitution (Seventy-third Amendment) Act, 1992

The passage of the Constitution (Seventy-third Amendment) Act, 1992 marked a watershed in the history of modern India. With this amendment, a uniform structure of *panchayats* emerged throughout the country.

Article 243G read with Eleventh Schedule of the Constitution explicitly requires the States to devolve powers and authority on *panchayats* which may be necessary to enable them to function as institutions of self-government. The Eleventh Schedule of the Constitution is reproduced in Table 2.2.

Table 2.2: Eleventh Schedule of the Constitution (Article 243G)

1.	Agriculture, including agricultural extension.
2.	Land improvement, implementation of land reforms, land consolidation and soil conservation.
3.	Minor irrigation, water management and watershed development.
4.	Animal husbandry, dairying and poultry.
5.	Fisheries.
6.	Social forestry and farm forestry.
7.	Minor forest produce.
8.	Small-scale industries, including food processing industries.
9.	Khadi, village and cottage industries.
10.	Rural housing.
11.	Drinking water
12.	Fuel and fodder.
13.	Roads, culverts, bridges, ferries, waterways and other means of communication.
14.	Rural electrification, including distribution of electricity.
15.	Non-conventional energy sources.
16.	Poverty alleviation programmes.
17.	Education, including primary and secondary schools.
18.	Technical training and vocational education.
19.	Adult and non-formal education.
20.	Libraries.
21.	Cultural activities.

Contd...

22.	Markets and fairs.
23.	Health and sanitation, including hospitals, primary health centres and dispensaries.
24.	Family welfare.
25.	Women and child development.
26.	Social welfare, including welfare of the handicapped and mentally retarded.
27.	Welfare of the weaker sections, and in particular, of the scheduled castes and the scheduled tribes.
28.	Public distribution system.
29.	Maintenance of community assets.

2.4 Constitution (Seventy-fourth Amendment) Act, 1992

The passage of the Constitution (Seventy-fourth Amendment) Act, 1992 was a landmark in the history of municipal administration in India. Article 243W read with Twelfth Schedule of the Constitution provides the illustrative list for the devolution of functions to the municipalities. The Twelfth Schedule of the Constitution is reproduced in Table 2.3. Many States have amended their municipal laws to ensure conformity with the new constitutional provisions.

Through this amendment a new Part IX-A relating to municipalities was incorporated in the Constitution to provide for, *inter alia,* the constitution of three types of municipalities, viz. *nagar panchayat* for a transitional area, i.e. an area in transition from a rural to urban area [1]; municipal council for smaller urban area, and municipal corporation for larger urban area (Article 243Q).

The Constitution (Seventy-fourth Amendment) Act, 1992 conferred constitutional status to the structure and mandate of municipalities so as to enable them to function as vibrant democratic and self-governing institutions at the grassroots level. [2]

The objectives of the Seventy-fourth Amendment included decentralisation of power and popular participation in the planning, management, and delivery of civic services.

Table 2.3: Twelfth Schedule of the Constitution (Article 243W)

1.	Urban planning including town planning.
2.	Regulation of land-use and construction of buildings.
3.	Planning for economic and social development.
4.	Roads and bridges.
5.	Water supply for domestic, industrial and commercial purposes.
6.	Public health, sanitation conservancy and solid waste management.
7.	Fire services.
8.	Urban forestry, protection of the environment and promotion of ecological aspects.
9.	Safeguarding the interests of weaker sections of society, including the handicapped and mentally retarded.
10.	Slum improvement and upgradation.
11.	Urban poverty alleviation.
12.	Provision of urban amenities and facilities such as parks, gardens, playgrounds.
13.	Promotion of cultural, educational and aesthetic aspects.
14.	Burials and burial grounds; cremations, cremation grounds and electric crematoriums.
15.	Cattle ponds; prevention of cruelty to animals.
16.	Vital statistics including registration of births and deaths.
17.	Public amenities including street lighting, parking lots, bus stops and public conveniences.
18.	Regulation of slaughter houses and tanneries.

The main provisions introduced by the Seventy-fourth Amendment are as under:

2.4.1 Constitution of Municipalities: It provides for constitution of 3 types of municipalities depending upon the size and area namely: (a) *nagar panchayat* for an area in transition from rural to urban area, (b) municipal council for smaller urban area and (c) municipal corporation for larger urban area. Demographic and other conditions—which are determining factors for constituting a particular type of municipality—differ a great deal from one State to another. It has, therefore, been left to the State Legislatures to decide which specific type of municipality will be constituted for particular urban area.

2.4.2 Composition of Municipalities: The seats shall be filled by direct elections. Besides the seats filled by direct elections, some seats may be filled by nomination of persons having special knowledge and experience in municipal administration. Persons so nominated shall not have the right to vote in the meetings of the municipality. The Legislature of a State may, by law, also provide for the representation in a municipality of members of the House of the People and the members of the Legislative Assembly of the State representing constituencies which comprise wholly or partly the municipal area and also the Members of the Council of States and the members of the Legislative Council of the State registered as electors within the municipal area. The manner of election of chairpersons of municipalities has been left to be specified by the State Legislature.

2.4.3 Constitution of Wards Committees: This provides for constitution of ward committees in all municipalities with a population of 3 lakh or more.

2.4.4 Reservation of Seats: In order to provide for adequate representation of SC/ST and of women in the municipal bodies, provisions have been made for reservation of seats. The proportion of seats to be reserved for SC/ST to the total number of seats shall be same as the proportion of the population of SC/ST in the municipal area. The reservation would be made in respect of seats to be filled by direct elections only. Not less than one-third of the total number of seats reserved for SC/ST shall be reserved for women belonging to SC/ST. This is a mandatory provision.

In respect of women, the seats shall be reserved to the extent of not less than one-third of the total number of seats. This includes seats reserved for women belonging to SC/ST. These reservations will apply for direct elections only. This is also a mandatory provision. There will be no bar on State

Legislatures from making provisions for reservation of seats in any municipality or office of Chairperson in the municipalities in favour of backward class of citizens. This is an optional provision.

2.4.5 Duration of Municipalities: The municipality has a fixed term of 5 years from the date appointed for its first meeting. Elections to constitute a municipality are required to be completed before the expiration of the duration of the municipality. If the municipality is dissolved before the expiry of 5 years, the elections for constituting a new municipality are required to be completed within a period of 6 months from the date of its dissolution.

2.4.6 Powers and Functions of the Municipalities: All municipalities would be empowered with such powers and responsibilities as may be necessary to enable them to function as effective institutions of self-government. The State Legislature may, by law, specify what powers and responsibilities would be given to the municipalities in respect of preparation of plans for economic development and social justice and for implementation of schemes as may be entrusted to them. An illustrative list of functions that may be entrusted to the municipalities has been incorporated as the Twelfth Schedule of the Constitution.

2.4.7 Finances of Municipalities: It has been left to the Legislature of a State to specify by law matters relating to imposition of taxes. Such law may specify the following:

1. Taxes, duties, fees, etc. which could be levied and collected by the municipalities, as per the procedure to be laid down in the State law.
2. Taxes, duties, fees, etc. which would be levied and collected by the State Government and a share passed on to the municipalities.
3. Grants-in-aid that would be given to the municipalities from the State.
4. Constitution of funds for crediting and withdrawal of moneys by the municipalities.

2.4.8 Finance Commission: The Finance Commission constituted under Article 243-I to review the financial positions of Panchayati Raj Institutions shall also review the financial position of the municipalities and will make recommendations to the Governor.

The recommendations of the Finance Commission will cover the following:

1. Distribution between the State Government and Municipalities of the net proceeds of the taxes, duties, tolls and fees leviable by the State.
2. Allocation of share of such proceeds between the municipalities at all levels in the State.
3. Determination of taxes, duties, tolls and fees to be assigned or appropriated by the municipalities.
4. Grants-in-aid to municipalities from the Consolidated Fund of the State.
5. Measures needed to improve the financial position of the municipalities.

2.4.9 Elections to Municipalities: The superintendence, direction and control of the preparation of the electoral rolls for, and the conduct of, all elections to the panchayats and municipalities shall be vested in the State Election Commissions.

2.4.10 Audit and Accounts: The maintenance of the accounts of the municipalities and other audit shall be done in accordance with the provisions in the State law. The State Legislatures will be free to make appropriate provisions in this regard depending upon the local needs and institutional framework available for this purpose.

2.4.11 Committee for District Planning: Planning and allocation of resources at the district level for the panchayati raj institutions are normally to be done by the zilla parishad. With regard to urban areas, municipal bodies discharge these functions within their respective jurisdictions. However, some important questions may arise, which would concern the urban-rural interface, and it may be necessary to take an overall view with regard to development of the district as a whole and decide on allocation of investments between the rural and urban institutions. Provision has, therefore, been made for the constitution of a Planning Committee at the district level with a view to consolidating the plans prepared by the panchayats and the municipalities and preparing a development plan for the district as a whole. The District Planning Committee in preparing the Draft Development Plan shall have regard to the following:

1. Matter of common interest between the panchayats and the municipalities including spatial planning.
2. Sharing of water and other physical and natural resources.
3. Integrated development of infrastructure and environment conservation.
4. Extent and type of available resources, whether financial or otherwise.

The Draft District Development Plan so prepared and recommended by the District Planning Committee shall be forwarded by the chairperson of the Committee to the State Government.

2.4.12 Metropolitan Planning Committees: It is provided in the Act that in every metropolitan area (with a population of 10 lakh or more), a Metropolitan Planning Committee shall be constituted for preparing a draft development plan for the metropolitan area as a whole.

The Metropolitan Planning Committee shall take into account the following for preparation of the Draft Development Plan:

1. Plan prepared by the municipalities and the panchayats in the metropolitan area.
2. Matter of common interest between the municipalities and panchayats including coordinated spatial plans of the area.
3. Sharing of water and other physical and natural resources.
4. Integrated development of infrastructure and environmental conservation.
5. Overall objectives and priorities set by the Government of

India and the State Government.

6. Extent and nature of investments likely to be made in the metropolitan area by agencies of the Government.
7. Other available resources, financial and otherwise.

In short, the salient features of the Seventy-fourth Amendment are the following:

1. It provides a framework for the assignment of appropriate governmental functions to municipalities through the Twelfth Schedule of the Constitution read with Article 243W. The Twelfth Schedule defines the functional domain of municipalities. Many of the functions included in this Schedule have distributional and developmental attributes. The Twelfth Schedule generally contains traditional functions of municipalities. However, some non-traditional functions are also discernible from the list. These are: (a) protection of the environment and promotion of ecological aspects, (b) safeguarding the interests of weaker sections of society including the handicapped and mentally retarded, (c) urban poverty alleviation, and (d) promotion of cultural and aesthetic aspects.
2. States are statutorily required to constitute a finance commission (Article 243-I and 243-Y), once in every 5 years, to recommend to their legislatures measures to improve municipal finances including: (i) assignment of taxes, duties, tolls, and fees, (ii) sharing of state taxes, and (iii) provision of grants-in-aid.
3. Finance Commission constituted by the Government of India is obligated to recommend measures to augment the Consolidated Fund of State Governments to supplement the resources of the municipalities on the basis of the recommendations made by the State Finance Commissions [Article 280(3)(c)].
4. It is mandatory to constitute in every State at the district level a District Planning Committee to consolidate and prepare development plan for the district as a whole (Article 243ZD). Similarly, it is mandatory to constitute in

every metropolitan area a Metropolitan Planning Committee to prepare a development plan for the metropolitan area as a whole (Article 243ZE).

5. It mandates that a municipality if dissolved by a State Government, must be reconstituted within six months [Article 243U(3)]. This is meant to ensure the continuity of civic affairs by elected representatives of the people.
6. It ensures reservation of seats for women and other disadvantaged categories (Article 243T).

In terms of Article 243ZC of the Constitution, nothing in Part IXA shall apply to Scheduled areas and Tribal areas as referred to in Article 244 of the Constitution. However, Parliament may by law, extend the provisions of Part IXA to these areas subject to such exceptions and modifications as may be specified in that law.

In order to provide time to allow changes to be made in the then existing laws which were inconsistent with the provisions of the Constitution (Seventy-fourth Amendment) Act, a transition period of 1 year was provided for.

The amended State municipal laws provide for detailed provisions for constitution and composition of municipalities, reservation of seats for SC/ST and women, fixed term of 5 years and re-election of municipalities within a period of 6 months in case of dissolution, functions and financial powers of municipalities, setting up of State Finance Commission etc.

2.5 New Status of Municipalities: An Assessment

The Seventy-fourth Amendment was made with the intention to make municipalities self-governing units. The situation existing before and after the Seventy-fourth amendment is summarised in Table 2.4.

In the federal polity of India, local bodies are institutions created by the State Governments (Entry 5 of List II of the Seventh Schedule). They enjoy only those powers and responsibilities which are assigned to them. Twelfth Schedule of the Constitution lists the functions and responsibilities that may be transferred to municipalities.

Table 2.4: Status of Municipalities in India

Before the 74th Amendment	After the 74th Amendment
No all-India framework for devolution of functions.	12th Schedule read with Article 243W of the Constitution provides guide points for assignment of functions to municipalities.
High degree of arbitrariness in the system of fiscal transfers from the State Governments to municipalities. No periodic assessment of financial needs of municipalities.	State Finance Commission (SFC) to be constituted statutorily in every State every Fifth year (Article 243-I and 243-Y) to review the financial position of municipalities and suggest measures to improve the same.
No role for the National Finance Commission as regards the finances of urban local bodies.	National Finance Commission is required to augment the Consolidated Fund of State Governments to supplement the resources of the municipalities on the basis of the recommendations made by the SFCs [Article 280(3)(c)].
Absence of constitutional bodies to prepare development plans for local areas.	Mandatory constitution of District Planning Committees (Article 243ZD) and Metropolitan Planning Committees (Article 243ZE) for consolidation and preparation of development plans.
Failure to hold regular elections and prolonged supersessions.	A municipality if dissolved by a State Government must be reconstituted within six months [Article 243U(3)].
Lack of participation from weaker sections of society.	Reservation of seats for women and other disadvantaged categories (Article 243T).

The permissive nature of Seventy-fourth Amendment is clear and the State Governments enjoy full discretion as regards the transfer of functions to municipalities.

No doubt, municipalities have acquired constitutional status after the said Amendment, they are completely dependent on respective State Governments in terms of self-governance.

2.5.1 Desirability and Feasibility of Uniformity in Municipal Functions: A careful reading of the Twelfth Schedule shows that many of the functions listed in it found place in the Municipal Acts of various States even before the enactment of the conformity legislations by them. Hence, the Twelfth Schedule has been generally accepted as a guiding list of municipal functions.

Should there be all-India uniformity in delegating functions and financial powers to local bodies? There is a weak case for all-India uniformity as regards functional domain of local bodies. State Governments and their local bodies have diverse economic and social conditions. It is by no means rational to expect uniformity in the functions and powers of the Greater Bombay Municipal Corporation and the municipality of a small township of a backward State. Similarly, it is debatable if local bodies should have uniform taxation powers.

Though it will be useful to prepare a reference list regarding functions (Eleventh and Twelfth Schedules), assigned taxes, shareable taxes, user charges, fees etc., all-India uniformity in these matters would be too much to expect.

Even at the level of a State, uniformity is not desirable in view of diverse city conditions and intra-State disparities. This fact has been recognised by the Constitution while providing for the constitution of 3 types of municipal bodies: nagar panchayats, municipal councils, and municipal corporations (Article 243Q). However, it does not distinguish between the functional domains of the 3 types of municipal bodies. The determination of the functions of municipalities of different sizes is left to the wisdom of the State Governments.

However, there exists a case for uniformity of functions among similar municipalities in a State. If a State chooses to allocate dissimilar functions and powers to similar municipalities (say municipal councils), there can be genuine resentment among the municipalities discriminated against. It is here that objective criteria based on population size, geographical area, or constitutional categorisation (Article 243Q) are needed to prevent misuse of political authority.

The Constitution should provide, at least, a list of minimum functions to be transferred to municipalities of various types by the State Governments.

2.5.2 Role of State Finance Commissions: The State Finance Commission is set up under Article 243-I read with Article 243-Y of the Constitution. It is required to review the financial position of the municipalities and make recommendations as to:

(a) the principles which should govern–

i. the distribution between the State and the municipalities of the net proceeds of taxes, duties, tolls and fees leviable by the State, which may be divided between them, and the allocations between the municipalities of their respective shares of such proceeds.

ii. the determination of the taxes, duties, tolls and fees which may be assigned to, or appropriated by, the Municipalities.

iii. the grants-in-aid to municipalities from the Consolidated Fund of the State.

(b) the measures needed to improve the financial position of the municipalities.

(c) any other matter referred to the Finance Commission in the interest of sound finance of the municipalities.

As required under the Constitution, all State Governments set up Finance Commissions. These State Finance Commissions (SFCs) are expected to strengthen local bodies so that they may function as democratic units for the socio-economic development of urban and rural areas of our country.

The task of the First Finance Commission of a State was difficult and arduous in the absence of precedence and it was expected to make suo moto all such studies in areas which never existed before. Nevertheless, the work of the First Finance Commission was crucial because it paved the way for subsequent commissions. The following observations may be made in this regard.

1. New Constitutional arrangement (Seventy-fourth Amendment) implies that the whole range of a State's tax revenue is open to sharing with municipalities. SFCs are expected to evolve principles of tax assignment, tax sharing, and grants to municipalities with a view to mitigate their weak financial position. They are also required to evolve criteria with regard to adequacy and objectivity of grants.
2. Sharing of State tax revenue with municipalities depends wholly on the discretion of State Government.
3. In determining devolution of funds, the SFCs would do well to keep in mind, *inter alia*, the following factors.

(a) Resource position of the State.

(b) Normative deficits of municipalities. Any system which underestimates the gap between revenue and expenditure should be discouraged.

(c) Degree of dependence of municipalities for funds on the State Government.

(d) Capacity of a municipality to utilise devolved resources.

(e) A State Finance Commission may consider introduction of a system of incentives and disincentives into the entire governmental grants on objective lines. Municipalities which are able to raise resources through levy of user charges and benefit taxes should be considered for incentive grants from the State Government.

A. Determination and Filling of Budgetary Gaps: A State Finance Commission has to determine the budgetary gaps of municipalities for the period of its award. Thereafter, it has to devise formulae for filling the gaps so determined.

(a) Determination of the Budgetary Gaps: Two approaches may be followed for this purpose: (a) trend growth rate and (b) normative approach.

Under the first approach, average annual growth rate in a variable during a reference period (say 1994-95 through 2006-07) is worked out and the same is projected for a future period (say 2007-08 through 2011-12). It is assumed that past behaviour of the variable will be repeated in future. Thus, *actuals* or *accounts* of revenue and expenditure of a government may be used to compute the average annual growth rate of the two aggregates over a stated period. Applying the computed average to a future period, one can work out estimated revenue, expenditure and budgetary gap for any future year.

Under the second method, revenue of a government is assessed normatively and certain norms are applied to assess expenditure. In other words, *needs* and *capacities* of different governments are assessed normatively and such normative assessments are used to meet budgetary gaps of the governments. More specifically, fiscal performance of a government is judged on the basis of *what ought to be* rather than *what it actually is*.

In the context of the work of a State Finance Commission, normative approach should apply to both the State Government and municipalities and that the assessment of revenue and expenditure should be done in a manner so as to maintain incentives for greater revenue efforts and economy in spending.

(b) Filling the Gap: Once budgetary gaps of municipalities are determined, the next task of a State Finance Commission is to devise formulae for filling these gaps. For this purpose, it has to work out a judicious mix of tax devolution and grants.

It is noteworthy that the term *gap-filling* in the context of State-municipal fiscal relations has a different connotation than at the national level.

At the national level, even after the transfer to the States of a share of divisible taxes, the resources of some of the States may remain inadequate to meet their needs. Thus, a Finance Commission determines the grants equal to deficit of each State so that the non-Plan revenue accounts of the States are balanced or left with a surplus every year. In other words, deficits of non-Plan revenue account which remain after tax devolution are covered through grants. This is called the gap-filling approach (or more appropriately net gap-filling approach).

It is possible that even before tax devolution from the Centre, some high-income States have surplus in their non-Plan revenue account. Thus, while a State cannot be denied a part of a shared Central tax even if it has no demonstrated financial need, grants are given upon genuine financial needs of the States.

However, the working of a State Finance Commission is different. Like the National Finance Commission, it is not bound by any constitutional restrictions regarding the type of taxes to be shared with municipalities. In fact, the whole field of State taxation is open to it for determining tax devolution. In other words, tax devolution and grants are to be used simultaneously to cover the budgetary gaps of municipalities. In this case, gap-filling means how to cover the projected budgetary gaps of municipalities through a judicious mix of tax devolution and grants with due regard to the underlying principles of the two methods to effect transfers from a higher to a lower level government.

2.6 Ministry of Urban Development (MoUD)

Ministry of Urban Development and Poverty Alleviation was bifurcated into two Ministries, viz. the Ministry of Urban Development and Ministry of Urban Employment and Poverty Alleviation in 2004. The Ministry of Urban Employment and Poverty Alleviation was subsequently named as Ministry of Housing and Urban Poverty Alleviation (M/o HUPA) in 2006. However, Ministry of Urban Development is the Cadre

Controlling Ministry in respect of M/o HUPA also.

The Ministry of Urban Development is responsible for formulating policies, supporting and monitoring programmes and coordinating the activities of various Central Ministries, State Governments and other nodal authorities in so far as they relate to issues in urban development.

Urban development is a State subject but the Government of India plays a co-ordinating and monitoring role and also supports urban development through Central and Centrally-sponsored schemes. MoUD addresses various issues of urban sector through policy guidelines, legislative guidance and sectoral programmes.

MoUD is the nodal ministry for planning and co-ordination of urban transport matters at the central level. It had prescribed a National Urban Transport Policy in 2006 with the objective to ensure easily accessible, safe, affordable, quick, comfortable, reliable and sustainable mobility for all. To bring uniform legislative cover for all metro rail projects in the country Metro Railways Amendment Act came into force in September 2009.

The other set of responsibilities of MoUD pertain to construction and maintenance of Central Government buildings, including residential accommodation, with the exception of those under the Ministry of Defence, Atomic Energy, Railways and Communications. It is also responsible for management of Central Government lands and properties, most of which are confined to Delhi and some of the metropolitan cities. These functions are discharged through the Central Public Works Department (CPWD) and Land and Development Office (L&DO).

Under its administrative control, MoUD has four attached and three subordinate offices, one public sector undertaking and five statutory/autonomous bodies, including one non-statutory registered society.

2.6.1 Attached Offices: These are as under.

A. Central Public Works Department (CPWD): It the largest of organizations under MoUD. It is a multifaceted comprehensive construction management agency provides services from project concept to completion and maintenance management in the post-construction stage. It is a total service provider, capable of giving single window service for all facets of built environment with complete accountability and responsibility.

CPWD is an organization with a large bank of engineering, architectural and horticulture human resources, which renders most comprehensive services in the field of planning, designing, construction and maintenance management for all building and infrastructure projects with total quality assurance.

It operates through a wide network zones, circles, divisions, subdivisions and sections. Divisions are the main executing units of the CPWD. Thrust has been given to execute important and time bound projects in a project mode to address the specific requirements of the clients and to pay exclusive attention to the project in hand and accordingly project units have been created for execution of major projects in time bound manner.

It handles wide range of projects pertaining to housing, office space, hospitals, educational institutions, roads, national highways, bridges, flyovers, airports, tourism and culture, environmental and other utility services. It also executes border fencing, flood lighting and road projects in difficult terrain under hostile conditions.

B. Directorate of Printing: With presses in various parts of the country, it caters to the printing requirements of the Central Government Ministries and Departments. It is the Government Printer for executing printing works for all Ministries and Departments of Government of India including forms for civil and defence departments. It is also responsible for the stocking and distribution of various forms for Ministries/Departments, as per their requirements. It also renders advice, from time to time, to various State Governments and Central Government Ministries/Departments on technical matters relating to printing and allied subject in printing technology as well.

C. Directorate of Estates: It is mainly responsible for administration and management of the office buildings and residential accommodation of Government of India employees. There are at present 8 Regional Stations at Mumbai, Kolkata, Chennai, Shimla, Chandigarh, Faridabad, Ghaziabad and Nagpur under its administrative control.

D. Land and Development Office (L&DO): It administers nazul and rehabilitation leases in Delhi, in addition to managing the Central Government lands in Delhi. In addition, the following items of work are also being handled by L&DO:

1. Allotment of land to various Government/Semi-government Departments and various political, social, charitable, educational and religious institutions under the directions of the Government of India.
2. Administration and management of various leases granted by L&DO, Notified Area Committee, Central Public Works Department and Regional Settlement Commissioner, New Delhi etc. in accordance with the terms of lease deeds and orders/instructions issued by the Government of India from time to time.
3. Substitution, mutation etc. of lease hold residential and commercial properties and conversion into free hold by execution of conveyance deeds.

2.6.2 Subordinate Offices: These are as under.

A. Government of India Stationery Office: It looks after the stationery requirements of all the Central Government Ministries/Departments.

B. Department of Publications: It stocks and sells Government publications.

C. Town and Country Planning Organisation (TCPO): It is the technical arm of MoUD in matters of town planning, regional planning and urban development. It assists and advices the State Governments, urban local bodies and development authorities on matters pertaining to urbanization, town planning, urban transport, metropolitan planning, human settlements, urban and regional information system and training.

2.6.3 Public Sector Undertaking: National Buildings Construction Corporation (NBCC) is a public sector civil construction agency under administrative control of MoUD and its activities are spread all over the country and abroad. NBCC was conferred with the status of *Navratna* by the Government of India on June 23, 2014. NBCC provides civil engineering construction services in a wide gamut of projects of varied nature and complexities in different geographical locations, both within India and abroad. In view of its vast experience and quality of services, a number of Central Government Ministries and various State Governments are utilizing the services of NBCC as their extended engineering arm.

2.6.4 Statutory and Autonomous Bodies: These are as under.

A. Delhi Development Authority (DDA): It was created in 1957 under the provisions of the Delhi Development Act to promote and secure the development of Delhi. It has statutory jurisdiction for overall development and land use in the National Capital Territory of Delhi. DDA has played a vital role in the orderly development of Delhi.

B. Delhi Urban Arts Commission (DUAC): It has statutory mandate to preserve and develop aesthetic quality and environment in Delhi. DUAC was set up by an Act of Parliament in 1973 to advise the Government of India in the matter of preserving, developing and maintaining the aesthetic quality of urban and environmental design within Delhi and to provide advice and guidance to any local body in respect of any project of building operations or engineering operations or any development proposal which affects or is like to affect the skyline or the aesthetic quality of the surroundings or any public amenity provided therein.

The area of urban Delhi has expanded and it has become more densely built in the years since the DUAC was constituted. This gives even greater relevance to the injunctions in the original mandate. Ecology and heritage are more pressing concerns now, the difficulties of seeing the city as a whole in a situation where there are many decision-making bodies is more evident than before, and there is urgent need to have a vision for the future of the city's constituent elements.

Presently, following are the main concerns of DUAC: (a) threats to the remaining oases of open spaces, riverine and forest, (b) need to improve the quality of life in historic precincts, (c) need to ensure that dilapidated areas are redeveloped elegantly and (d) find ways in which traffic networks can work efficiently but with a humane quality.

C. National Capital Region (NCR) Planning Board: National Capital Region (NCR) is a unique example of inter-state regional development planning for a region, having a total area of over 33,500 square kilometres spanning over 15 districts in the states of U.P, Haryana, Rajasthan and National Capital Territory of Delhi.

Constituted in March 1985 under the NCR Planning Board Act, 1985, it has the important goal of evolving harmonized policies for control of land uses and development of infrastructure in the NCR so as to avoid any haphazard development of the Region. The key rationale was to promote balanced and harmonized development of the Region, *and to* contain haphazard and unplanned urban growth by channelising the flow and direction of economic growth (on which the urban phenomenon feeds) along more balanced and spatially-oriented paths.

National Capital Region Transport Corporation (NCRTC) was incorporated on August 21, 2013 for designing, developing, implementing, financing, operating and maintaining Regional Rapid Transit System (RTS) in the NCR.

D. National Institute of Urban Affairs (NIUA): Set up in 1976, it is an autonomous non-statutory body, registered under the Societies Registration Act, 1860, for carrying out urban research in the country. It is also involved in collection, processing, storing and dissemination of information relating to urban local bodies, their functioning, management, finances, development programmes and training.

NIUA is a premier institute for research, training and information dissemination in urban development and management. It enjoys the support and commitment of MoUD, Government of India, State Governments, urban and regional development authorities and other agencies concerned with urban issues. Policies and directions of NIUA are determined by the Governing Council consisting of a president (who is appointed by the Government of India), 2 vice-presidents, 3 members of the Government of India in their ex-officio capacity, 12 other members, and the director (the chief executive) as the member-secretary.

NIUA Memorandum of Association lays down, *inter alia*, the following as its main functions:

1. To act as an autonomous, scientific and research organisation to undertake, promote and coordinate studies on urbanization.
2. To act as a centre for advanced study of urban problems and to provide and promote the necessary training and research facilities.
3. To evaluate the social, administrative, financial and other aspects of the implementation of urban development plans and programmes.
4. To mobilise available expertise in the field of urban affairs and to offer and co-ordinate technical and consultancy services.
5. To constitute or cause to be constituted or give affiliation to regional, state or local centres to promote the purpose of NIUA.
6. To organise and sponsor training courses, workshops and seminars in various fields.
7. To act as a clearing house of information, and to operate a documentation centre and disseminate information on urban affairs.
8. To undertake and facilitate publication and distribution of

books, research papers, monographs, a journal and other communication material pertaining to urban affairs.

The core activities of NIUA are carried out by an experienced and multidisciplinary team of urban planners, economists, geographers, statisticians, sociologists, systems analysts and management experts. Specialised staff equipped with the latest computer hardware and advanced software packages provide the necessary support services to research, training, publication and other activities of NIUA.

E. Rajghat Samadhi Committee: It was created by an Act of Parliament, namely Rajghat Samadhi Act, 1951. It is an autonomous body entrusted with the following responsibilities:

1. To administer the affairs of the Samadhi of Mahatma Gandhi and to keep it in proper order and in a state of good repair.
2. To organize and regulate periodical functions at the Samadhi.
3. To do such other things as may be required.

2.7 Programmes and Schemes for Urban Development

2.7.1 National Urban Information System (NUIS): Ministry of Urban Development launched NUIS scheme in March 2006 to develop GIS databases for 137 towns/cities in the country in two scales, i.e. 1:10,000 and 1:2000. The total number of towns in NUIS Scheme is 152. The inclusion/addition/deletion of towns is done as requested by State Government and approved by TAC. In addition, utility mapping in 1:1000 scale will also be undertaken for 24 towns. Apart from spatial data, NUIS has another component, i.e. National Urban Data Bank and Indicators (NUDBI). The spatial and attribute databases thus generated will be useful for preparation of master/development plans, detailed town planning schemes and serve as decision support for e-governance. The work of spatial data will be undertaken by the Survey of India, Dehradun, the National Mapping Agency. Memorandum of Understanding was signed between Ministry of Urban Development and the National Mapping Agency on March 13, 2006 for Urban Spatial data generation.

A. NUIS Scheme Guidelines: Town and Country Planning Organisation, Ministry of Urban Development has prepared Guidelines for implementation of NUIS scheme.

B. NUIS Scheme and Design Standards: For effective implementation of NUIS scheme, Ministry of Urban Development constituted NUIS Standards Committee (NSC) on June 12, 2002. The Authoring Group of NUIS Design and Standards prepared a report which outlines the content at 1:10,000/1:2,000/1:1,000 scales, design standards framework, USIS, NUDB&I and NUO data elements to be adopted as National NUIS Standards. The standards address different levels of planning and management and a comprehensive document has been finalized, which has been approved by the Technical Coordination Committee (TCC) of NNRMS-Standing Committee-Urban on May 3, 2006.

C. Road Map of NUIS Scheme: Town and Country Planning Organisation, Ministry of Urban Development has prepared for proper implementation of the scheme. The road map contains components of NUIS Scheme stepwise major activities, stakeholders, fund management schedules and milestones for implementation of NUIS Scheme.

D. Capacity Building: The capacity building is one of the major objectives of NUIS Scheme. About 30 training programmes, 20 participants per each programme at various levels, over a period of 2 years, have to be organised to train the urban managers and field staff in the areas of remote sensing and geographical information system (GIS). In order to achieve the same, as per the NUIS guidelines, the capacity building has been decentralised and major Training Institutes like IIRS Dehradun, NRSA Hyderabad, STI (SOI) Hyderabad, SAC, Ahmedabad, IRS-AU, Chennai and RRSSCs—who are imparting training in the areas of remote sensing and GIS application in urban planning and management—have been identified. The State Nodal Agencies have to identify and nominate the personnel for capacity building programmes Organised by TCPO/MoUD in the prescribed nomination form.

E. Monitoring and Implementation Group: TAC has constituted the Monitoring and Implementation group to resolve all technical and operational issues, to finalise timelines for activities, to resolve the issues related to Area of mapping, data acquisition, generation of GIS database, integration of 1:10,000, 1:2000 and 1:1000 scale spatial database, issues related to NUDB&I, to monitor the mapping of utilities, to assure the quality of data through required quality check, to suggest the methodology for application development, to develop real time sample data base and provide training to State agencies.

2.7.2 Promotion of Barrier-free Built Environment for the Disabled and Elderly Persons: Ministry of Urban Development is the nodal Ministry for implementation of barrier-free built environment for the disabled and elderly persons as envisaged in Section 46 of The Persons with Disabilities (Equal Opportunities, Protection of Rights and Full Participation) Act, 1995.

The Ministry has prepared model building by-laws which contain provisions for improving access to various public buildings by disabled and elderly persons. These building bye-laws have been sent to the State Governments/Union Territories.

2.7.3 Regional Centres for Urban and Environmental Studies (RCUES): RCUES were established with the purpose of meeting the training and research needs in the urban sectors in various States. These centres assist the State Governments in disseminating information about the various policies and programmes of MoUD in the field of urban governance and also undertake research activities and organise training courses, seminars, workshops and conferences on topics relating to local self-government, urban development, urban management, water supply and sanitation, property tax, municipal audit and accounting, public housing and low cost sanitation and urban poverty alleviation programmes etc. Following are the 4 regional centres for urban and environmental studies:

1. **RCUES Mumbai:** All Indian Institute of Local Self Government, Mumbai.
2. **RCUES Lucknow:** University of Lucknow, Lucknow.
3. **RCUES Hyderabad:** Osmania University, Hyderabad.
4. **RCUES New Delhi:** Centre for Urban Studies, Indian Institute of Public Administration, New Delhi.

2.7.4 National Heritage City Development and Augmentation Yojana (HRIDAY): HRIDAY was launched on January 21, 2015. The scheme is aimed at preserving and revitalizing the soul and unique character of the heritage cities in India. Initially, the following 12 cities have been identified for development under the scheme: Ajmer, Amritsar, Amaravati, Badami, Dwarka, Gaya, Kanchipuram, Mathura, Puri, Varanasi, Velankanni, and Warangal.

HRIDAY scheme offers a paradigm shift in India's approach to city development, bringing together urban planning/economic growth and heritage conservation in an integrated manner with specific focus on sanitation, security, tourism, heritage revitalization and livelihoods retaining the city's cultural identity. The scheme aims at restoring, reviving and strengthening the soul and heritage of the cities.

2.7.5 Atal Mission for Rejuvenation and Urban Transformation (AMRUT): Providing basic services (e.g., water supply, sewerage, urban transport) to households and build amenities in cities which will improve the quality of life for all, especially the poor and the disadvantaged, is a national priority. This means that the focus should be on infrastructure creation that has a direct link to provision of better services to people and this was explicitly stated by the President of India in his speeches to the Joint Sessions of the Parliament on June 9, 2014 and February 23, 2015.

Therefore, the purpose of AMRUT is to: (a) ensure that every household has access to a tap with assured supply of water and a sewerage connection, (b) increase the amenity value of cities by developing greenery and well-maintained open spaces (e.g. parks) and (c) reduce pollution by switching to public transport or constructing facilities for non-motorized transport (e.g. walking and cycling).

AMRUT makes States equal partners in planning and implementation of projects, thus actualizing the spirit of cooperative federalism.

2.7.6 E-municipalities/E-nagar palika for Urban Local Bodies: Urban local bodies (ULBs) of India are the constitutionally provided administrative units that provide basic infrastructure and services in cities and towns. The ULBs are responsible for providing all the civic services and amenities to the citizens.

Government of India has launched a National e-Governance Plan (NeGP). NeGP intends to institute and enable mechanisms to improve the system of governance and thus provide better services to the citizens by effective use of ICT. E-governance in municipalities is one of the Mission Mode Projects under the NeGP, which is expected to result in improved service delivery by local governments for the citizens.

The broad aim for implementing E-governance in municipality/nagar palika is to:

1. Focus on clearly identified citizen services that would be covered with clearly laid down service levels and outcomes to be achieved.
2. Improve efficiency and effectiveness in interaction between local government and citizens and other stake holders.
3. Improve quality of internal local government operations and management information systems to support and stimulate good governance.
4. Bring about transparency and accountability in urban local body operations.
5. Help improve reach of the delivery of services to citizens.

2.8 Women in Local Governance Structures

Legislative enactments have dramatically increased

women's access to decision-making structures in recent years. The Seventy-third and Seventy-fourth Constitutional Amendments passed in 1993 provide for reservation of 33 percent of elected seats for women at different levels of local governance in both rural and urban local bodies. Also there would be one-third reservation for women to posts of chairperson of these bodies. One-third of the seats are further reserved for women belonging to the SC/ST community. The Panchayats (Extension to Schedule Areas) Act, 1996 (PESA) made this amendment applicable to Schedule V areas. This has dramatically increased women's participation in local bodies. For every 5 year tenure of local governments, about 1 million women get elected to panchayats and local bodies. In some states, the number of elected women exceeds the reserved one-third quota.

The Constitution provides for rotation of seats reserved for women but does not prescribe the number of terms for which seats may be served for rotation. Seats are reserved for one term, two terms or more depending upon the provisions made by the State Legislature in the State law. The option to reserve seats for more than one terms is open, but it is for the State Legislature to decide the number of terms for which seats will remain reserved. Tamil Nadu has taken a positive step by freezing the reserved seats for women for two terms.

Local government institutions have not been given full financial and political powers to function independently but 29 subjects ranging from agriculture to poverty eradication have been devolved to these institutions. In theory, the presidents of the gram panchayats, block panchayats and district panchayats are responsible for prioritising the developmental needs of the villagers and allocating the grants accordingly. In practice, the level of responsiveness and manner of functioning of the panchayats varies considerably across states. As far as women's participation is concerned, the legislative enactments have ensured that they are represented in all states.

Many of the elected women entering the public arena for

the first time lack confidence, feel isolated, and have no previous political experience. They need to develop their innate leadership skills. Studies conducted in different parts of the country show that 95 percent of the elected women representatives (EWRs) are first-timers in politics and join politics because that is what their male family/village members want. As first timers without previous exposure to politics, many of the elected women lack the capacity to function properly in the panchayats and municipalities, and consequently are not taken seriously by their colleagues. Sustained training and networking efforts are being undertaken both by government and non-government agencies to ensure that women's capacity to participate improves. With just a few years of experience, women have emerged as articulate, motivated leaders all over the country.

Gender budgeting involving grassroots elected women representatives is being used for advocacy in several places. Increased networking and formation of confederations of elected women representatives has helped to strengthen women's leadership. This approach has been especially successful in southern and western India. The formation of these networks promotes solidarity among the elected women representatives, otherwise divided by caste, religion and geographical boundaries. Thus, formation of these networks is the first step in the direction of empowering women. Their position as panchayat members adds to their ability to intervene and negotiate with the community. The presence of EWRs in the dispute resolution process lends support and confidence to other women. The networks have also been able to promote capacity building.

2.8.1 Proxy Politics: Constitutional provisions apart, there are complaints from various parts of the country regarding effective participation of women in local governance structures. Proxy politics, power brokering and gender discrimination continue, and many women sarpanches have to face violence for challenging existing societal power centres.

In other cases, women are in PRI only in name. In reality, it is the male family members who hold the power. In spite of the affirmative action in panchayati raj in favour of marginalized communities, exclusion of caste, poverty, tribal status, gender and caste sharply demarcate those who have political power from those who do not. Central and State Governments should not delay any further the devolution and decentralization of powers from higher bodies (Government of India or State Governments) to the panchayati raj structures. This devolution right now is lagging in almost all the States. The three Fs—funds, functions and functionaries—in most States are still in the same position prior to 1993. In the absence of this basic requirement, the Constitutional provisions are not only being violated, but there is lack of clarity at the field level which leads to dysfunctional situations.

India has primarily relied upon the method of reservation to ensure women's presence in decision-making bodies. This has increased *de jure*, but not necessarily *de facto*, participation. There is need to encourage women's participation in other kinds of groups and associations which contribute to an atmosphere of leadership by women, as well as supporting training and networking for elected women.

2.8.2 Amendment to Article 243T of the Constitution to Provide for 50 Percent Reservation for Women in Urban Local Bodies: The Constitution (112th Amendment) Bill, 2009, to provide for 50 percent reservation of women in Urban Local Bodies was introduced in Lok Sabha on November 24, 2009. Through this Bill the Government of India seeks to increase the representation of women in urban local bodies (ULBs) from the present level of one-third to 50 percent which would also include enhancement of reservation for women up to 50 percent in seats reserved for scheduled castes, scheduled tribes, and 50 percent reservations for women in the posts of chairpersons. This would result in increased representation of women in ULBs and is likely to yield significant benefits in terms of higher priority to women's issues in critical areas of urban Governance and service delivery such as water supply, sanitation, solid waste management, education and health, etc. Presently the bill is under the consideration of the Parliamentary Standing Committee on Urban Development.

To sum up, urban local bodies (ULBs) should be made responsible for providing all urban infrastructures in the city area and entrusted with the functions of planning, co-ordination and policy for supply of services. The multiple agencies in-charge of providing various services should be merged under the ULB. The ULB should be responsible for deciding on the operations to be contracted out carrying out preliminary preparation of contract documents and monitoring of private operation. The ULB may coordinate with the metropolitan or regional/state level agencies and with other ULBs whenever required.

In many states, the devolution of administrative powers related to planning, financing and managing municipal services has not yet become effective. The expected improvement in services, as an outcome of decentralization, is based on the notion that as expenditure responsibilities are devolved, local elected representatives would have decision-making authority. However, the range of issues on which elected municipal representatives can take a decision is limited.

There is a wide variation in availability of infrastructure and services in different cities. The larger cities have the ability to raise resources from the capital market, while smaller towns lag behind because of lack of resources and expertise. ULBs and state development agencies have an important role to play in the development of urban infrastructure.

In the context of the growing demand for urban services, the rationalisation and the augmentation of revenue system have not made commensurate progress resulting in increasing dependence of urban local bodies (ULB) on the financial assistance from the States and Central Government. Own revenues of the local bodies are not adequate even to meet operation and maintenance expenditure. In the case of smaller local bodies, the weak financial position is also combined with lack of organisational and technical capabilities. The weak financial and organisational base of ULB's has, in turn, led to highly subsidised and inequitable supply of various urban services with critical dependence on State grants.

Endnotes

1. Here, 'a transitional area', 'a smaller urban area', or 'a larger urban area' means such area as the Governor may specify by public notification having regard to the population of the area, the density of the population, the revenue generated for local administration, the percentage of employment in non-agricultural activities and such other factors.
2. Following is the Statement of Objects and Reasons appended to the Constitution Seventy-third Amendment) Bill, 1991 which was enacted as the Constitution (Seventy-fourth Amendment) Act, 1992.

   In many States local bodies have become weak and ineffective on account of a variety of reasons, including the failure to hold regular elections, prolonged supersessions and inadequate devolution of powers and functions. As a result, urban local bodies are not able to perform effectively as vibrant democratic units of self-government.

   Having regard to these inadequacies, it is considered necessary that provisions relating to Urban Local Bodies are incorporated in the Constitution particularly for: (i) putting on a firmer footing the relationship between the State Government and the Urban Local Bodies with respect to: (a) the functions and taxation powers; and (b) arrangements for revenue sharing; (ii) Ensuring regular conduct of elections; (iii) ensuring timely elections in the case of supersession; and (iv) providing adequate representation for the weaker sections like scheduled castes, scheduled tribes and women.

3

Smart City: Conceptual Settings

Since the days of the industrial revolution, cities have been the engines of economic growth. The revolution was effective in developing prosperity for many countries, but the development was not always *smart*, sacrificing health conditions, for instance, for greater productivity.

Now with greater use of technology, a number of cities are accumulating data, delivering innovation, and enhancing lives of citizens.

The people who live in cities are driven economic performers who are seeking to take advantage of technologies to further their personal and collective opportunities. Cities provide them these opportunities and in doing so draw many like-minded parties into their midst. With this drive and an increase in active participants, there are downsides, most notably energy consumption, waste and congestion. In this day and age people are increasingly concerned with climate change and awareness of limited resources all while demanding more efficiencies and technological development.

Citizens are not the only factors to consider in the evolution of cities into smart cities. Governmental and commercial entities are going to play an increasingly important role in development and implementation of technologies that pave the way to the smart city.

3.1 Smart City Defined

There is no universally accepted definition of a smart city. It means different things to different people. It could be smart design, smart utilities, smart housing, smart mobility, smart technology etc. Thus, it is rather difficult to give a definition of a smart city. However, smart cities could be considered as cities which have smart (intelligent) physical, social, institutional and economic infrastructure while ensuring centrality of citizens in a sustainable environment. It is expected that such a smart city will generate options for all residents to pursue their livelihoods and interests meaningfully and with joy.

The conceptualisation of smart city, therefore, varies from city to city and country to country, depending on the level of development, willingness to change and reform, resources and aspirations of the city residents. A smart city would have a different connotation in India than, say, in US. Even in India, there is no one way of defining a smart city. In the imagination of any city dweller in India, the picture of a smart city contains a wish list of infrastructure and services that describes his or her level of aspiration. To provide for the aspirations and needs of the citizens, urban planners ideally aim at developing the entire urban eco-system, which is represented by the four pillars of comprehensive development—institutional, physical, social and economic infrastructure. This can be a long-term goal and cities can work towards developing such comprehensive infrastructure incrementally, adding on layers of *smartness*.

Smart cities provide core infrastructure and give a decent quality of life to its citizens, a clean and sustainable environment and application of *smart solutions*. The focus is on sustainable and inclusive development and the idea is to look at compact areas, create a replicable model which will act like a light house to other aspiring cities.

The core infrastructure elements in a smart city should include the following:

1. Adequate water supply.
2. Assured electricity supply.
3. Sanitation, including solid waste management.
4. Efficient urban mobility and public transport.
5. Affordable housing, especially for the poor.
6. Robust IT connectivity and digitalization.

7. Good governance, especially e-governance and citizen participation.
8. Sustainable environment.
9. Safety and security of citizens, particularly women, children and the elderly.
10. Health and educational facilities.

Accordingly, the purpose of a smart city is to drive economic growth and improve the quality of life of people by enabling local area development and harnessing technology, especially technology that leads to smart outcomes.

3.2 Key Features of a Smart City:

3.2.1 Institutional Infrastructure:

1. Good governance.
2. City development plans based on ICT and spatial mapping.
3. Safety and security.
4. Public participation.

3.2.2 Physical Infrastructure:

1. 24x7 smart utility services (water, power etc).
2. Smart urban mobility.
3. Smart but affordable housing.
4. Zero emission sanitation services.
5. Integrated ICT infrastructure.

3.2.3 Social Infrastructure:

1. Smart and quality education.
2. Smart and quality healthcare.
3. Entertainment and sports facilities.
4. Convention centres and auditoriums.
5. Botanical garden.

3.2.4 Economic Infrastructure:

1. Industrial parks and export processing zones.
2. IT/BT parks.
3. Trade, services, financial and tourism centres.
4. Skill development centres.
5. Logistics hubs etc.

3.3 Smart Solutions for a Smart City

Application of smart solutions involves the use of technology, information and data to make infrastructure and services better. For example, applying smart solutions in the transport sector—intelligent traffic management system, reduction in average commuting time, reduction in cost of commuting—has positive effects on productivity and quality of life of citizens. Another example can be waste water recycling and smart metering which can make a huge contribution to better water management in the city.

As far as smart solutions are concerned, an illustrative list is given below. This is not, however, an exhaustive list, and cities are free to add more applications.

3.3.1 E-governance and Citizen Services:

1. Public information and grievance redressal.
2. Electronic service delivery.
3. Citizen engagement.
4. Citizens as city's eyes and ears.
5. Video crime monitoring.

3.3.2 Waste Management:

1. Waste to energy and fuel.
2. Waste to compost.
3. Waste water to be treated.
4. Recycling and reduction of C&D waste.

3.3.3 Water Management:

1. Smart metres and management.
2. Leakage identification and preventive maintenance.
3. Water quality monitoring.

3.3.4 Energy Management:

1. Smart metres and management.
2. Renewable sources of energy.
3. Energy efficient and green buildings.

3.3.5 Urban Mobility:

1. Smart parking.
2. Intelligent traffic management.
3. Integrated multi-modal transport.

3.3.6 Others:

1. Tele-medicine and tele-education.
2. Incubation/trade facilitation centres.
3. Skill development centres

3.4 Barcelona (Spain): World's Smartest City

Juniper Research named Barcelona the top smart city in 2015, prevailing over New York (US), London (UK), Nice (France) and Singapore.

What were some of the things that that city did that caused it to stand out?

The city was not actually top of the class across any of the metrics: Masdar City in the United Arab Emirates won out where environment and sustainability were assessed for example, while Singapore's smart traffic system is second to none. However, the breadth of Barcelona's involvement in the smart city concept, and consistent above-average performance across all metrics judged lead it to the top step.

It was noted that Barcelona "performed consistently well across all metrics". What were the metrics used to gauge smart cities?

Analysts in the mobile and digital technology sector, considered that the Spanish city performed well across subjects like smart grids and smart traffic management. The company also took into account information dealing with smart street lighting and each city's technological capability and social cohesion, among other items.

Moreover, while Barcelona was recognised for implementing environmentally sustainable projects, the research found that New York and London needed to improve their performance on this issue.

4

Smart Cities Mission in India

4.1 Emerging Urbanization Scenario in India

Urbanization in India has become an important and irreversible process, and an important determinant of national economic growth and poverty reduction. The process of urbanization is characterized by a dramatic increase in the number of large cities, although India may be said to be in the midst of transition from a predominantly rural to a quasi urban society.

It is acknowledged that this transition to a quasi-urban society, however, has not been accompanied by a commensurate increase in the supply of basic urban services like water supply, sewerage and drainage network, garbage disposal facilities, citywide roads, public transport, and public safety systems like street lighting and pedestrian pathways. The supply of land and housing has not kept pace with the increase in urban population.

In recent years, the urban sector in India has undergone a major change following the country's transition towards a market-based economy and the spirit of decentralization embodied in the Constitution (Seventy-fourth) Amendment Act, 1992. The Act came into force on June 1st, 1993. Recent years have also witnessed important changes in the thinking about cities and their role in economic growth and reduction in poverty. There is a wide acceptance of importance of urban governance, and recognition of challenges of accountability and responsiveness of the local self-governments to people.

Excessive concentration of population in cities and unprecedented increase in the demand for infrastructure/facilities and amenities has led to problems of land shortage, housing shortfall, inadequate transportation etc. Management of essential infrastructure like water supply, sewerage, drainage, solid waste disposal has become more challenging. The concentration of economic activities and population in some of the mega cities (like Mumbai, Kolkata, Delhi, Chennai, Hyderabad, Bengaluru and Ahmedabad) has put tremendous strain on the delivery of services. At the same time there has been growing realization that there is a need for decentralization of activities so as to reduce the burden on these cities.

Taking into account the existing scenario and the urgency to augment urban infrastructure backed by strengthening of urban governance of the cities/towns, Government of India has launched, in recent years, a number of schemes/programmes with the participation of State Governments and other relevant agencies.

4.2 Smart Cities Mission: Background

Cities are engines of growth for the economy of every nation, including India. Nearly 31 percent of India's current population lives in urban areas and contributes 63 percent of India's GDP (Census 2011). With increasing urbanization, urban areas are expected to house 40 percent of India's population and contribute 75 percent of India's GDP by 2030. This requires comprehensive development of physical, institutional, social and economic infrastructure. All are important in improving the quality of life and attracting people and investments to the City, setting in motion a virtuous cycle of growth and development. Development of Smart Cities is a step in that direction.

The Government of India under Prime Minister Narendra Modi has a vision of developing 100 smart cities for modern and resurgent India. It proposes to place the citizen at the centre of governance and deploy ICT and digital data to improve efficiencies and sustainability. Smart Cities Mission of the Government of India is based on the idea of developing the entire urban eco-system on the principles of complete and integrated planning. Launched by the Prime Minister in June 2015 Smart Cities Mission is a bold new initiative. It is meant to set examples that can be replicated both within and outside the smart city, catalysing the creation of similar smart cities in various regions and parts of the country. The Government has defined eligibility criteria for cities to qualify for inclusion under this programme.

The Smart Cities Mission will cover 100 cities and its duration will be 5 years (2015-16 to 2019-20). The Mission may be continued thereafter in the light of an evaluation to be done by the Ministry of Urban Development, incorporating the learnings from the Mission.

The Government plans to identify 20 smart cities in 2015, 40 in 2016 and another 40 in 2017.

4.3 Typical Features of a Smart City

Some typical features of comprehensive development in smart cities are as follows:

1. Promoting mixed land use in area-based developments, i.e. planning for *unplanned areas* containing a range of compatible activities and land uses close to one another in order to make land use more efficient. State Governments will enable some flexibility in land use and building by-laws to adapt to change.
2. Housing and inclusiveness, i.e. expansion of housing opportunities for all.
3. Creating walkable localities by reducing congestion, air pollution and resource depletion, boosting local economy, promoting interactions and ensuring security. The road network is created or refurbished not only for vehicles and public transport, but also for pedestrians and cyclists, and necessary administrative services are offered within walking or cycling distance.
4. Preserving and developing open spaces, i.e. parks, playgrounds, and recreational spaces in order to enhance the quality of life of citizens, reduce the urban heat effects in areas and generally promote eco-balance.
5. Promoting a variety of transport options, namely transit-oriented development (TOD), public transport and last mile

para-transport connectivity.

6. Making governance citizen-friendly and cost effective by increasingly relying on online services to bring about accountability and transparency, especially using mobiles to reduce cost of services and providing services without having to go to municipal offices. Forming e-groups to listen to people and obtain feedback and use online monitoring of programmes and activities with the aid of cyber tour of worksites.
7. Giving an identity to the city, based on its main economic activity, such as local cuisine, health, education, arts and craft, culture, sports goods, furniture, hosiery, textile, dairy etc.
8. Applying smart solutions to infrastructure and services in area-based development in order to make them better. For example, making areas less vulnerable to disasters, using fewer resources, and providing cheaper services.

4.4 Strategic Components of a Smart City

Area-based developments in the Smart Cities Mission include the following:

1. City improvement (retrofitting).
2. City renewal (redevelopment).
3. City extension (greenfield development).
4. Pan-city initiative.

4.4.1 Retrofitting: It will introduce planning in an existing built-up area to achieve smart city objectives, along with other objectives, to make the existing area more efficient and liveable. In retrofitting, an area consisting of more than 500 acres will be identified by the city in consultation with citizens. Depending on the existing level of infrastructure services in the identified area and the vision of the residents, the cities will prepare a strategy to become smart. Since existing structures are largely to remain intact in this model, it is expected that more intensive infrastructure service levels and a large number of smart applications will be packed into the retrofitted smart city. This strategy may also be completed in a shorter time frame, leading to its replication in another part of the city.

4.4.2 Redevelopment: It will effect a replacement of the existing built-up environment and enable co-creation of a new layout with enhanced infrastructure, using mixed land use and increased density. Redevelopment envisages an area of more than 50 acres, identified by urban local bodies (ULBs) in consultation with citizens. For instance, a new layout plan of the identified area can be prepared with mixed land use and high ground coverage. Two examples of the redevelopment model are the Saifee Burhani Upliftment Project in Mumbai (also called the Bhendi Bazaar Project) and the redevelopment of East Kidwai Nagar in New Delhi being undertaken by the National Building Construction Corporation.

4.4.3 Greenfield Development: It will introduce most of the smart solutions in a previously vacant area (more than 250 acres) using innovative planning, plan financing and plan implementation tools (e.g. land pooling/land reconstitution) with provision for affordable housing, especially for the poor. Greenfield developments are required around cities in order to address the needs of the expanding population. One well-known example is the GIFT City in Gujarat. Unlike retrofitting and redevelopment, greenfield developments could be located either within the limits of the ULB or within the limits of the local Urban Development Authority (UDA).

4.4.4 Pan-city Development: It envisages application of selected smart solutions to the existing city-wide infrastructure.

The smart city proposal of each short-listed city is expected to encapsulate either a retrofitting or redevelopment or greenfield development model, or a mix thereof and a Pan-city feature with smart solution(s). It is important to note that pan-city is an additional feature to be provided. Since smart city is taking a compact area approach, it is necessary that all the city residents feel there is something in it for them also. Therefore, the additional requirement of some (at least one) city-wide smart solution has been put in the scheme to make it inclusive.

For North-Eastern and Himalayan States, the area proposed to be developed is one-half of what is prescribed for any of the alternative models, i.e. retrofitting, redevelopment or greenfield development.

Area-based development will transform existing areas, including slums, into better planned ones, thereby improving liveability of the whole city. New areas (greenfield) will be developed around cities in order to accommodate the expanding population in urban areas. Application of smart solutions will enable cities to use technology, information and data to improve infrastructure and services. Comprehensive development in this way will improve quality of life, create employment and enhance incomes for all, especially the poor and the disadvantaged, leading to inclusive cities.

4.5 Proposal Preparation

The Government has not prescribing any particular model to be adopted by the smart cities. The approach is not *one-size-fits-all.* Each city has to formulate its own concept, vision, mission and plan (proposal) for a smart city that is appropriate to its local context, resources and levels of ambition. Accordingly, they have to choose their model of smart city and answer the question: What kind of smart city do they want? For this, cities will prepare their Smart City Proposal (SCP) containing the vision, plan for mobilisation of resources and intended outcomes in terms of infrastructure upgradation and smart applications.

4.5.1 Essential Features of SCP: It may be noted that even though a particular model is not being prescribed, it is expected that the SCPs will include a large number of infrastructure services and smart solutions. In particular, the elements that must form part of a SCP are as under:

1. Assured electricity supply with at least 10 percent of the smart city's energy requirement coming from solar energy.
2. Adequate water supply including waste water recycling and storm water reuse.

3. Sanitation including solid waste management.
4. Rain water harvesting.
5. Smart metering.
6. Robust IT connectivity and digitalization.
7. Pedestrian-friendly pathways.
8. Encouragement to non-motorised transport (e.g., walking and cycling).
9. Intelligent traffic management.
10. Non-vehicle streets/zones.
11. Smart parking.
12. Energy efficient street lighting.
13. Innovative use of open spaces.
14. Visible improvement in the area (e.g., replacing overhead electric wiring with underground wiring).
15. Encroachment-free public areas.
16. Ensuring safety of citizens, especially children, women and elderly.

Cities will have to add more *smart* applications to this list in order to improve their SCP. In the case of redevelopment and greenfield models of smart cities, in addition to the essential features mentioned above, at least 80 percent buildings should be energy efficient and green buildings. Additionally, of the total housing provided in greenfield development, there should be at least 15 percent in the affordable housing category. Since cities are competing with each other for selection under the Smart Cities Mission, the SCPs have to be prepared with great care and the proposed smart city made *smart* enough.

Cities will prepare SCPs using the principles of strategic planning process and the proposal will contain area-based development plans and Pan-city initiatives. The SCP is collaborative because the objectives and funds of all government departments, parastatals, private agencies and the citizens are dovetailed during the process of preparing the SCP. It is realized that the task of preparing the SCPs is quite challenging and States/ULBs will require assistance of experts. There are two ways of obtaining technical assistance support—by hiring consulting firms and engaging with handholding agencies.

A. Consulting Firms: The Ministry of Urban Development (MoUD) will technically qualify a panel of consulting firms and the States/UTs are at liberty to draw upon this panel. The States have the option of appointing a consulting firm outside the panel by following transparent and fair procedures as per State financial rules.

B. Handholding Agencies: During the preparation of the Smart Cities Mission, a number of foreign Governments offered to provide technical assistance (TA) support. Additionally, other external organizations, including bilateral and multilateral institutions, as well as domestic organizations have suggested to MoUD that they can give technical assistance support. These include World Bank, Asian Development Bank (ADB), UN Habitat, UNIDO etc. Such organizations, which have experience in the field of smart city development, can also extend support to the States/UTs as hand-holding agencies in preparing the SCPs. MoUD will assist in tying up the arrangements.

4.6 Process of Selection of Smart Cities

Each aspiring city competes for selection as a smart city in what is called a City Challenge. There are two stages in the selection process. After the number has been indicated to the respective chief secretaries, the State/UT will undertake the following steps:

4.6.1 Stage 1 of the Competition: Short Listing of Cities by the States: The State/UT begins with short listing the potential smart cities on the basis of conditions precedent and scoring criteria and in accordance with the total number allocated to it. The first stage of the competition will be intra-state, in which cities in the State will compete on the conditions precedent and the scoring criteria laid out. These conditions precedent have to be met by the potential cities to succeed in the first round of competition and the highest scoring potential smart cities will be short listed and recommended to participate in Stage 2 of the Challenge. The information sent by the ULBs in the prescribed forms has to be evaluated by the State Mission Director and the evaluation placed before the State-level High Powered Steering Committee (HPSC) for approval.

The cities emerging successful in the first round of competition will be sent by the State/UT as the recommended shortlist of Smart Cities to MoUD by the stipulated date. The State Government has to fill the prescribed form and send it with the recommended list. The MoUD will thereafter announce the list of 100 smart cities.

4.6.2 Stage 2 of the Competition: The Challenge Round for Selection: In the second stage of the competition, each of the potential 100 smart cities prepares their proposals for participation in the City Challenge. This is a crucial stage as each city's Smart City Proposal (SCP) is expected to contain the model chosen—whether retrofitting or redevelopment or greenfield development or a mix thereof—and additionally include a pan-city dimension with smart solutions. The SCP will also outline the consultations held with the city residents and other stakeholders, how the aspirations are matched with the vision contained in the SCP and importantly, what is the proposal for financing of the smart city plan including the revenue model to attract private participation. Evaluation criteria for the SCPs have been worked out by MoUD based on professional advice and this should act as guidance to the cities for preparing their proposal.

By a stipulated date, to be indicated by MoUD to the States/UTs, proposals will be submitted to MoUD for all these 100 cities. These will be evaluated by a committee involving a panel of national and international experts, organizations and institutions. The winners of the first round of Challenge will be announced by MoUD. Thereafter, while the winning cities start taking action on making their city smart, those who do not get selected will start work on improving their SCPs for consideration in the second round. Depending on the nature of the SCPs and outcomes of the first round of the Challenge, the MoUD may decide to provide handholding assistance to the potential smart cities to upgrade their proposals before starting the second round.

4.7 Number of Smart Cities in Each State/Union Territory

The total number of 100 smart cities has been distributed among the States and UTs on the basis of equitable criteria. The formula gives equal weightage (50:50) to urban population of the State/UT and the number of statutory towns in the State/UT. Based on this formula, each State/UT will, therefore, have a certain number of potential smart cities, with each State/UT having at least one. This distribution is given in Table 4.1.

Table 4.1: Number and Names of Cities Allocated to States Based on Urban Population and Number of Statutory Towns

State/UT	Number of cities	Names of cities
A&N Islands	1	Port Blair
Andhra Pradesh	3	Vishakhapatnam, Tirupati, Kakinada
Arunachal Pradesh	1	Pasighat
Assam	1	Guwahati
Bihar	3	Muzaffarpur, Bhagalpur, Biharsharif
Chandigarh	1	Chandigarh
Chhattisgarh	2	Raipur, Bilaspur
Daman & Diu	1	Diu
Dadra & Nagar Haveli	1	Silvassa
Delhi	1	Delhi (NDMC)
Goa	1	Panaji
Gujarat	6	Gandhinagar, Ahmedabad, Surat, Vadodara, Dahod, Dholera Sir
Haryana	2	Karnal, Faridabad
Himachal Pradesh	1	Dharamshala
Jammu & Kashmir	1	*

Jharkhand	1	Ranchi
Karnataka	6	Mangaluru, Belagavi, Shivamogga, Hubballi-Dharwad, Tumakuru, Davanegere
Kerala	1	Kochi
Lakshadweep	1	Kavarrati
Madhya Pradesh	7	Bhopal, Indore, Gwalior, Jabalpur, Satna, Ujjain, Sagar
Maharashtra	10	Greater Mumbai, Thane, Kalyan-Dombivili, Navi Mumbai, Nashik, Amravati, Solapur, Nagpur, Pune, Aurangabad
Manipur	1	Imphal
Meghalaya	1	Shillong
Mizoram	1	Aizawl
Nagaland	1	Kohima
Odisha	2	Bhubaneshwar, Rourkela
Puducherry	1	Oulgaret
Punjab	3	Ludhiana, Jalandhar, Amritsar
Rajasthan	4	Jaipur, Udaipur, Kota, Ajmer
Sikkim	1	Namchi
Tamil Nadu	12	Madurai, Tiruchirapalli, Chennai, Tiruppur, Coimbatore, Vellore, Salem, Erode, Thanjavur, Tirunelveli, Dindigul, Thoothukudi
Telangana	2	Greater Hyderabad, Greater Warangal
Tripura	1	Agartala
Uttar Pradesh	13**	Moradabad, Aligarh, Saharanpur, Bareilly, Jhansi, Kanpur, Allahabad, Lucknow, Varanasi, Ghaziabad, Agra, Rampur
Uttarakhand	1	Dehradun
West Bengal	4	New Town Kolkata, Bidhannagar, Durgapur, Haldia
Total	100	

*Jammu & Kashmir has asked for more time to decide on the potential smart city; **12 cities have been short-listed from Uttar Pradesh against 13 cities allocated to the state.

The number of potential smart cities from each State/UT will be capped at the indicated number. (This distribution formula has also been used for allocation of funds under Atal Mission for Rejuvenation and Urban Transformation—AMRUT). The distribution of smart cities will be reviewed after two years of the implementation of the Mission. Based on an assessment of the performance of States/ULBs, some re-allocation of the remaining potential smart cities among States may be required to be done by MoUD.

4.8 First 33 Smart Cities

The Government announced on January 28, 2016 the names of the first 20 urban areas that will be developed as smart cities. 13 more cities were added to the list on May 24, 2016, making a total of 33 cities. The selected cities will be equipped with basic infrastructure, efficient urban mobility and public transport, IT connectivity and e-governance mechanisms.

The list of first 33 smart cities is given in Table 4.2.

4.9 Implementation by Special Purpose Vehicle (SPV)

The implementation of the Mission at the city level will be done by a special purpose vehicle (SPV) created for the purpose. The SPV will plan, appraise, approve, release funds, implement, manage, operate, monitor and evaluate the smart city development projects. Each smart city will have a SPV which will be headed by a full time CEO and have nominees of Central Government, State Government and ULB on its Board. The States/ULBs shall ensure that: (a) a dedicated and substantial revenue stream is made available to the SPV so as to make it self-sustainable and could evolve its own credit worthiness for raising additional resources from the market and (b) Government contribution for smart city is used only to create infrastructure that has public benefit outcomes. The execution of projects may be done through joint ventures, subsidiaries, public-private partnership (PPP), turnkey contracts etc. suitably dovetailed with revenue streams.

Table 4.2: First 33 Smart Cities

S.No.	Name of the City	S. No.	Name of the City
20 Cities Announced on 28.1.2016		18.	Chennai
1.	Bhubaneswar	19.	Ludhiana
2.	Pune	20.	Bhopal
3.	Jaipur	**13 Cities Announced on 24.5.2016**	
4.	Surat	21.	Lucknow
5.	Kochi	22.	New Town Kolkata
6.	Ahmedabad	23.	Bhagalpur
7.	Jabalpur	24.	Dharamshala
8.	Vishakapatnam	25.	Agartala
9.	Sholapur	26.	Imphal
10.	Davangere	27.	Panaji
11.	Indore	28.	Chandigarh
12.	New Delhi	29.	Faridabad
13.	Coimbatore	30.	Raipur
14.	Kakinada	31.	Ranchi
15.	Belagavi	32.	Warangal
16.	Udaipur	33.	Port Blair
17.	Guwahati		

The SPV will be a limited company incorporated under the Companies Act, 2013 at the city-level, in which the State/UT and the ULB will be the promoters having 50:50 equity shareholding. The private sector or financial institutions could be considered for taking equity stake in the SPV, provided the shareholding pattern of 50:50 of the State/UT and the ULB is maintained and the State/UT and the ULB together have majority shareholding and control of the SPV.

Funds provided by the Government of India in the Smart Cities Mission to the SPV will be in the form of tied grant and kept in a separate Grant Fund. These funds will be utilized only for the purposes for which the grants have been given and subject to the conditions laid down by the MoUD.

The State Government and the ULBs will determine the paid-up capital requirements of the SPV commensurate with the size of the project, commercial financing required and the financing modalities. To enable the building up of the equity base of the SPV and to enable ULBs to contribute their share of the equity capital, Government of India grants will be permitted to be utilized as ULBs share of equity capital in the SPV, subject to certain prescribed conditions.

After selection of the cities in Stage II of the Challenge, the process of implementation will start with the setting up of the SPV. As already stated, it is proposed to give complete flexibility to the SPV to implement and manage the smart city project and the State/ULB will undertake measures for this purpose. The SPV may appoint project management consultants (PMCs) for designing, developing, managing and implementing area-based projects. SPVs may take assistance from any of the empanelled consulting firms in the list prepared by MoUD and the handholding agencies. For procurement of goods and services, transparent and fair procedures as prescribed under the State/ULB financial rules may be followed. Model frameworks as developed by MoUD may also be used for smart city projects.

4.10 Financing of Smart Cities

Smart City Mission will be operated as a Centrally-sponsored Scheme (CSS) and the Central Government proposes to give financial support to the Mission to the extent of ₹ 48,000 crore over 5 years, i.e. on an average ₹ 100 crore per city per year. An equal amount, on a matching basis, will have to be contributed by the State/ULB. Thus, nearly ₹ 1 lakh crore of Government/ULB funds will be available for development of smart cities.

The project cost of each smart city proposal will vary depending upon the level of ambition, model and capacity to execute and repay. It is anticipated that substantial funds will be required to implement the smart city proposal and towards this end, Government grants of both the Centre and State will be leveraged to attract funding from internal and external sources. The success of this endeavour will depend upon the robustness of SPV's revenue model and comfort provided to lenders and investors. A number of State Governments have successfully set up financial intermediaries (such as Tamil Nadu, Gujarat, Odisha, Punjab, Maharashtra, Karnataka, Madhya Pradesh and Bihar) which can be tapped for support and other States may consider some similar set up in their respective States. Some form of guarantee by the State or such a financial intermediary could also be considered as instrument of comfort referred to above. It is expected that a number of schemes in the smart city will be taken up on PPP basis and the SPVs have to accomplish this.

Government of India funds and the matching contribution by the States/ULB will meet only a part of the project cost. Balance funds are expected to be mobilized from sources as mentioned below:

1. States/ULBs own resources from collection of user fees, beneficiary charges and impact fees, land monetization, debt, loans etc.
2. Additional resources transferred due to acceptance of the recommendations of the Fourteenth Finance Commission (FFC).
3. Innovative finance mechanisms such as municipal bonds with credit rating of ULBs, pooled finance mechanism, tax increment financing (TIF).
4. Other Central Government schemes like Swachh Bharat Mission, Atal Mission for Rejuvenation and Urban Transformation (AMRUT), National Heritage City Development and Augmentation Yojana (HRIDAY).
5. Leverage borrowings from financial institutions, including bilateral and multilateral institutions, both domestic and external sources.
6. States/UTs may also access the National Investment and Infrastructure Fund (NIIF), which was announced by the Finance Minister in his 2015 Budget Speech.
7. Private sector through PPPs.

The distribution of funds under the Scheme will be as follows:

1. Project funds: 93 percent.
2. Administrative and Office Expenses (A&OE) funds: 7 percent.

4.11 Funds Release

After the Stage 1 of the challenge, each potential smart city will be given an advance of ₹ 2 crore for preparation of SCP which will come from the city's share of the A&OE funds and will be adjusted in the share of the city.

In the first year, Government proposes to give ₹ 200 crore to each selected smart city to create a higher initial corpus. After deducting the ₹ 2 crore advance and A&OE share of the MoUD, each selected smart city will be given ₹ 194 crore out of ₹ 200 crore in the first year followed by ₹ 98 crore out of ₹ 100 crore every year for the next 3 years.

The yearly instalment of funds will be released to SPVs after they meet the following conditions:

1. Timely submission of the City Score Card every quarter to the MoUD.
2. Satisfactory physical and financial progress as shown in the utilization certificate and the annual city score card.
3. Achievement of milestones given in the roadmap contained in SCP.
4. Fully functioning SPV as set out in the guidelines and the articles of association. A board resolution should certify that all these conditions have been met, including a certificate that all the conditions relating to establishment, structure, functions and operations of the SPV are complied with.

4.12 Mission Monitoring

4.12.1 National Level: An apex committee (AC), headed by the Secretary, MoUD and comprising representatives of related Ministries and organisations will approve the proposals for Smart Cities Mission, monitor their progress and release of funds. This Committee will meet periodically, as considered necessary.

AC will provide overall guidance and play an advisory role to the Mission and its key responsibilities are given below.

1. Review the list of the names of cities sent by the State Governments after Stage 1.
2. Review the proposals evaluated by panel of experts after Stage 2.
3. Approve the release of funds based on progress in implementation.
4. Recommend mid-course correction in the implementation tools as and when required.
5. Undertake quarterly review of activities of the scheme including budget, implementation and co-ordination with other missions/schemes and activities of various ministries.

There will be a National Mission Director, not below the rank of Joint Secretary to Government of India, who will be the overall in-charge of all activities related to the Mission. A Mission Directorate will take support from subject matter experts and such staff as considered necessary. The key responsibilities of the Mission Directorate are as under:

1. Develop strategic blueprint and detailed implementation roadmap of the Smart Cities Mission, including the detailed design of the City Challenge.
2. Co-ordinate across Centre, States, ULBs and external stakeholders in order to ensure that external agencies are efficiently used for preparation of SCP, sharing of best practices, developing smart solution etc.
3. Oversee capacity building and assist in handholding of SPVs, State and ULBs. This includes developing and retaining a best practice repository of financial models, land monetization ideas, financial instruments and risk mitigation techniques and mechanism for knowledge sharing across States and ULBs.

4.12.2 State Level: There shall be a State Level High Powered Steering Committee (HPSC) chaired by the Chief Secretary, which would steer the Mission Programme in its entirety. The HPSC will have representatives of State Government departments. The Mayor and Municipal Commissioner of the ULB relating to the smart city would be represented in the HPSC. There would also be a State Mission Director who will be an officer not below the rank of Secretary to the State Government, nominated by the State Government. The State Mission Director will function as the Member-Secretary of the State HPSC.

The key responsibilities of the HPSC are given below:

1. Provide guidance to the Mission and provide State level platform for exchange of ideas pertaining to development of smart cities.
2. Oversee the process of first stage intra-State competition on the basis of Stage 1 criteria.
3. Review the SCPs and send it to the MoUD for participation in the Challenge.

4.12.3 City Level: A Smart City Advisory Forum will be established at the city level for all 100 Smart Cities to advise and enable collaboration among various stakeholders and will include the District Collector, MP, MLA, Mayor, CEO of SPV, local youths, and technical experts.

The CEO of the SPV will be the convener of the Smart City Advisory Forum.

4.13 Convergence with Other Government Schemes

Comprehensive development occurs in areas by integrating the physical, institutional, social and economic infrastructure. Many of the sectoral schemes of the Government converge in this goal, although the path is different. There is a strong complementarity between the Atal Mission for Rejuvenation and Urban Transformation (AMRUT) and Smart Cities Mission in achieving urban transformation. While AMRUT follows a project-based approach, the Smart Cities Mission follows an area-based strategy.

Similarly, great benefit can be derived by seeking convergence of other Central and State Government

Programs/Schemes with the Smart Cities Mission. At the planning stage itself, cities must seek convergence in the SCP with AMRUT, Swachh Bharat Mission (SBM), National Heritage City Development and Augmentation Yojana (HRIDAY), Digital India, Skill Development, Housing for All and other programmes connected to social infrastructure such as health, education and culture.

To sum up, this is the first time, a MoUD programme is using the *challenge* or *competition* method to select cities for funding and using a strategy of area-based development. This captures the spirit of *competitive and cooperative federalism.*

States and ULBs will play a key supportive role in the development of smart cities. Smart leadership and vision at this level and ability to act decisively will be important factors determining the success of the Mission.

Understanding the concepts of retrofitting, redevelopment and greenfield development by the policy makers, implementers and other stakeholders at different levels will require capacity assistance.

Major investments in time and resources will have to be made during the planning phase prior to participation in the Challenge.

The Smart Cities Mission requires smart people who actively participate in governance and reforms. Citizen involvement is much more than a ceremonial participation in governance. Smart people involve themselves in the definition of the smart city, decisions on deploying smart solutions, implementing reforms, doing more with less and oversight during implementing and designing post-project structures in order to make the smart city developments sustainable. The participation of smart people will be enabled by the SPV through increasing use of ICT, especially mobile-based tools.

5

National Mission on Sustainable Habitat (NMSH)

5.1 NMSH: Background

As a part of voluntary actions to address climate change related concerns, India launched National Action Plan on Climate Change (NAPCC) on June 30, 2008. It stresses that maintaining a high growth rate is essential for increasing living standards of the vast majority of people of India and reducing their vulnerability of the impacts of climate change. Accordingly, it identifies measures that promote the objectives of sustainable development of India while also yielding to benefits for addressing climate change.

The NAPCC is co-ordinated by the Ministry of Environment and Forests and implemented through the nodal Ministries and is aimed at advancing relevant actions in specific sectors/areas. NAPCC advocates a strategy that promotes, firstly, the adaptation to climate change and secondly, further enhancement of the ecological sustainability of India's development path.

Eight national missions—in the areas of solar energy, enhanced energy efficiency, sustainable agriculture, sustainable habitat, water, Himalayan ecosystem, increasing the forest cover, and strategic knowledge for climate change—form the core of NAPCC. These National Missions, which form the core of NAPCC, represent multi-pronged, long-term and integrated strategies for achieving key goals in the context of climate change. The focus is on promoting understanding of climate change, adaptation and mitigation, energy efficiency and natural resource conservation.

The eight National Missions of NAPCC are as under:

1. Jawaharlal Nehru National Solar Mission (JNNSM).
2. National Mission for Enhanced Energy Efficiency (NMEEE).
3. National Mission on Strategic Knowledge for Climate Change (NMSKCC).
4. National Mission for Sustaining Himalayan Ecosystem (NMSHE).
5. National Water Mission (NWM).
6. Green India Mission (GIM.)
7. **National Mission on Sustainable Habitat (NMSH).**
8. National Mission for Sustainable Agriculture (NMSA).

In short, NAPCC identifies a number of measures that simultaneously advance the country's development and climate change related objectives of adaptation and mitigation. The implementation of the NAPCC is designed to take place through eight National Missions, which form the core of the National Action Plan and incorporate multi-pronged, long-term and integrated strategies for achieving India's key goals in the context of climate change.

5.2 Coverage of NMSH

NMSH, which is a component of the NAPCC, broadly covers the following aspects:

1. **Extension of the Energy Conservation Building Code:** It addresses the design of new and large commercial buildings to optimize their energy demand. Incentives are provided for re-tooling existing building stock.
2. **Better Urban Planning and Modal Shift to Public Transport:** Making long-term transport plans to facilitate the growth of medium and small cities in such a way that ensures efficient and convenient public transport.
3. **Recycling of Material and Urban Waste Management:** A special area of focus will be development of technology for producing power from waste. The National Mission will include a major R&D programme, focusing on bio-chemical conversion, waste water use, sewage utilization

and recycling options, plasma conversion of waste of biological origin to liquid fuels that can substitute for petroleum based fuels wherever possible.

Apart from the above, the Mission would also facilitate adaptation to vulnerabilities arising out of climate change like adverse impacts on water resources, increased frequencies of extreme weather like droughts, floods, cyclones, storm water surges, rise in sea levels and human health.

5.3 Objectives of NMSH

These are as under:

1. To exploit the potential for mitigating climate change through reduction in demand for energy in the residential and commercial sectors by adopting various energy efficiency and conservation measures. With respect to adaptation, the aim would be to promote greater use of renewable sources and to reduce dependence on a single source. In formulating climate change strategies, mitigation efforts need to be balanced with those aimed at adaptation.
2. To adopt a comprehensive approach in the management of water, municipal solid waste and waste water with a view to realize their full potential for energy generation, recycling and reuse, and composting.
3. To address the issue of mitigating climate change by taking appropriate action with respect to the transport sector such as evolving integrated land use and transportation plans, achieving a modal shift from private to public mode of transportation, encouraging the use of non-motorised transport, improving fuel efficiency, and encouraging use of alternate fuels, etc. To evolve strategies for adaptation in terms of realignment and relocation, design standards and planning for roads, rail and other infrastructure to cope with warming and climate change.
4. To reorient urban planning with a view to address climate change with respect to mitigation as well as adaptation and improve the responsiveness to disasters by strengthening

community based disaster management and to provide better warning systems for extreme weather events.

5. To facilitate adoption of technologies and research and development which lead to energy efficiency and reduction in emissions.
6. To promote patterns of urban growth and sustainable urban development that help secure the fullest possible use of sustainable transport for moving freight, public transport, and encourage cycling and walking; thereby reducing the need to travel, especially by car.
7. To promote measures that improve resilience of infrastructure and human systems to cope with vulnerability consistent with social cohesion and inclusion.
8. To conserve the natural resources that are the key to sustainability of human habitats like water, clean air, flora and fauna, recognising the integrated nature of human and other systems.
9. To reflect the development needs and interests of communities that are especially vulnerable to climate change.
10. To encourage competitiveness and technological innovation in mitigating and adapting to climate change.
11. To develop a transparent, flexible, predictable, efficient and effective planning system that will produce the quality development needed to deliver sustainable development and secure sustainable communities. National policies and regional and local development plans provide the framework for planning for sustainable development and for that development to be managed effectively.
12. To encourage community involvement in ensuring more sustainable patterns of development.
13. To bring together key stakeholders at the central, state, district and local levels for a co-ordinated and comprehensive response to vulnerabilities arising out of climate change.
14. To promote and strengthen efforts aimed at generating awareness related to climate change.

5.4 Strategies and Methodologies for Mitigation

Within the scope of the National Mission for Sustainable Habitat, mitigation measures would encompass promotion of energy efficiency in the residential and commercial sectors, capture of green house gases as part of water, waste water and solid waste management, exploitation of mitigation potential in the area of urban transport and reorienting urban planning. Adaptation measures would include water efficient techniques, reducing leakages in the supply system, water recycling, rain water harvesting, designing of urban storm water management systems and urban planning measures, etc.

5.4.1 Promoting Efficiency in the Residential and Commercial Sectors: Though the current energy saving potential in new and existing buildings along with technology and policy options to implement energy efficiency in the building sector have been identified, it is important to discuss the implementation barriers in order to direct growth in the building sector towards sustainable development. The main barriers include knowledge gaps at several levels, issues related to enforcement and implementation, cost of green technology and lack of technology development. These barriers are discussed further and some of the solutions are identified below.

A. Knowledge Gap: A major barrier to green building development is lack of technical, economic and general knowledge related to green buildings. This knowledge gap exists not only among building designers and architects, but also among politicians, investors, and consumers. Beginning with the design side, there is lack of knowledge among designers regarding how best to incorporate building code requirements into building design. This is due to the novelty of building codes in India as well as the novelty of energy efficiency concepts. Also, since the by-laws vary from state to state and between climatic regions, it has been difficult to implement nationwide education programmes regarding byelaws. Further, the capability of designers and architects to perform energy simulations to quantify the potential savings from energy efficiency is also very limited. There are very few consultancy firms in India that can effectively perform the lighting and thermal analysis of buildings to evaluate their performance. Even where green buildings have been designed effectively, the building and construction industry is not prepared to apply these measures practically on site. The construction industry remains unaware of the environmental impacts of its operations.

B. Enforcement and Implementation: While many strategies to encourage or mandate green buildings or energy efficiency have been introduced by the government as discussed in earlier sections of this report, these programmes still require greater implementation. There is a major gap between the political statements and actual action or changes in building design and construction.

While the government has taken initiatives to encourage integration of the ECBC with the NBC for uniform and larger adoption of the energy code, there is currently no concrete plan for implementation of the code, or monitoring and verification.

Additionally, though the Bureau of Energy Efficiency (BEE) has developed a strategy and implemented energy audits for important government buildings, there is a lack of policy to mandate the energy saving recommendations made during these audits. There is also a lack of such programmes for commercial buildings.

Incentives, both financial and symbolic, are crucial for widespread adoption of these programmes. The following are some suggestions to increase the enforcement and implementation potential of the existing green building strategies.

C. Implementation and Incentives: Building by-laws should be written at the state and city levels to include an energy code incorporating aspects of the ECBC and green design best practices. The by-laws should include a combination of mandatory rules and voluntary guidelines. In particular, meeting minimum energy performance standards should be mandatory for new buildings, but the methods used to achieve these reductions should be voluntary. This would greatly increase energy efficiency but continue to allow for flexibility in design. Significant work has been done in identifying green parameters through initiatives such as GRIHA which need to be factored in.

Since existing policies related to building by-laws are complex and divided between many government departments at the state and federal levels, there is a need to simplify and coordinate building by-laws and building policy. It should be integrated between different government departments at both the union and state levels, to ensure that separate policies do not contradict or hinder the implementation of others.

The government should attract real estate builders' participation and partnership in creating regulation and promoting efficient buildings. Engaging the stakeholders while developing policy will aid in education and implementation. The capacity of the state-level and city-level bodies, which would be responsible for the final implementation of the energy code, should also be strengthened.

D. Building Performance Certification and Rating Systems: In order to encourage the adoption of voluntary energy efficiency measures and the design of buildings that exceed minimum performance standards, certification of energy performance and building rating systems should be put into place to recognize higher performance buildings.

A programme of benchmarking and certification of buildings at the time of rental and sale should be put into place. As in many international examples, certification should be mandatory for buildings beyond a certain size. A simple building certification system could rely on a quantitative assessment of total energy consumption over the year, per square metre. If a building receives a score below a benchmarked level, it should not be possible to sell or rent that structure. This would encourage renovations and efficient new construction. Since the building would be re-evaluated after each rental and sale, each owner and resident would have an incentive to green the building.

Such certification could also be accompanied by mandatory energy audits. The BEE has already made energy audits mandatory for many Government buildings. It has planned to mandate energy audits for all commercial buildings above a certain threshold of connected load. It remains important to develop mechanisms to ensure that the recommendations of the audit are implemented in a stipulated time. Auditing combined with certification of energy performance could work in tandem to ensure implementation of energy efficient systems.

These performance ratings should be harmonized across India, while incorporating regional climatic and cultural differences, as has been successful in Europe.

Building ratings should be voluntary, but the Government should increase recognition and awards for architects who receive high building ratings. Increased marketing of the building rating system is required, so that the rating scheme will become more well-known and more frequently used by consumers to compare performance.

E. Financial Incentives: When energy efficiency measures and codes are put into place, it is important to ensure that developers and architects will be able to fund and finance these efficient projects. A policy directive to public sector banks could mandate that they would only fund buildings that are code compliant or those that reach a set level of energy performance based on building ratings. Government controlled financial institutions could also be encouraged to fund projects that utilize green-labelled products.

F. Technology Development and Lowering Cost: In order for any of the implementation strategies to be successful, green building materials, equipment and systems need to be available and reasonably priced in all parts of India. This will require significant investment in research for suitable technologies, as well as government programmes to push the market development further and faster.

The methods for building more efficient buildings already exist and have proven to be successful. It is up to all stakeholders—from business, government, civil society, and consumer sectors—to join together for the implementation and wider adoption of these methods. To summarize, these measures include the following:

1. Courses with various college curriculums for students along with the quality improvement programme (QIP) at the faculty level should be integrated. These could be offered through the various regional engineering colleges (RECs), National Institutes of Technology (NIT), Councils of Architecture, Associations of Engineers, Institutes of Town Planners, etc. The courses could be developed in association with All India Council for Technical Education (AICTE), Indira Gandhi National Open University (IGNOU), TERI University, etc.
2. Important public buildings in the various climatic zones of the country could be designed as green buildings and serve as demonstration projects for best practices in green buildings. The carbon footprints of such projects could be monitored and information shared for a larger adoption of the green building design principles.
3. The awareness programmes could be launched through radio, television, hoardings and print media with national newspapers (for example, the TEACH India and LEAD India programmes launched by the Times of India).
4. Publishing and projecting the advantages (including life-cycle cost benefits) of using labelled appliances and financial incentives to manufacturers of labelled appliances. Launch awareness campaigns to increase demand for such appliances.
5. Awareness programmes could be introduced as summer projects and classroom discussions.
6. A Sustainable Habitats Mission website could host the

information with regular interaction and blogs from technical experts in the area. Existing information on financial incentives, codes, etc. could be compiled for easy reference by various stakeholders.

7. A legal implementation and monitoring process should be adopted by national, state and city level bodies which could be defined in order to minimise gaps in implementation. The emphasis will be on performance standards and not on particular technologies. Encouragement of solar water heating can also be built into the by-laws.
8. Holding open days for various builders' associations, property developers, material and product manufacturers in addition to technical experts from various regions to present their views that would contribute towards policy creation.
9. Holding training programmes for evaluators, officials of Economic Advisory Councils (EACs) and Student Environmental action coalitions (SEACs) on the ECBC, environmental clearance process, etc.
10. Mandating certification of energy performance for all buildings, rented or sold.
11. Increasing BEE energy auditing and develop monitoring mechanisms to ensure recommendations are implemented.
12. Mandating rating for development of projects of certain size. It could facilitate a single point system for study of carbon footprint, roof top solar programmes and impact land use planning at the zonal level.
13. Increasing recognition and awards for high rated buildings.
14. Offering softer loans for green buildings from public sector banks, encourage private banks to do the same. It should adopt a purchase preference policy for green equipment to increase market demand and guarantee investors a stable market for green products, offer tax incentives to developers, owners, or occupants of efficient buildings, reduce power tariffs or offer rebates on electricity bills for high performance buildings, and

implement time-of-day metering and billing to reduce peak demand. Further, the government should bundle CDM building efficiency programmes and increase awareness of potential for CDM benefits, encourage investment in green technology development through marketing and reduced taxation for green product manufacturers and reduce excise taxes or VAT of green products, systems or materials.

15. The R&D needs should focus on the development of energy-efficient products pertaining to energy efficient buildings and building components/systems, development of energy efficient windows, development of simulation software to predict the energy used in buildings and building integrated renewable energy systems, etc.
16. Incentivizing efficient lighting systems, particularly street lighting.
17. Developing technologies for recycling of construction waste.
18. Developing national standards for energy efficient construction on priority basis in collaboration with Bureau of Indian Standards (BIS). Harmonisation of ECBC with NBC and Environmental Impact Assessment Guidelines (EIAG) of the MoEF also needs to be done.
19. Making national network of building centres to become key institutions for the propagation of energy efficient building materials and technology. Central/state government agencies such as Central Public Works Department and State Public Works Department, Delhi Development Authority, etc. must be mandated to integrate energy efficiency measures in respect of building activity taken up by them.

5.4.2 Water Supply, Wastewater and Solid Waste Management: The potential for mitigation in the water supply sector can be realized through a reduced need for pumping which in turn would reduce the demand for energy, reduction of non-revenue water (NRW), energy audit of all the water utilities, rationalization of water tariff to reduce wasteful use of water, minimization of leakages, metering of all water taps and water audit, etc.

In the wastewater sector, GHG mitigation measures could include full collection, conveyance and treatment of waste water, reuse and recycling of treated effluent and gas recovery from sludge as well as use of treated waste water for artificial recharge of aquifers to improve the ground water potential. At the household level separation of black water and grey water needs to be promoted to enable recycling of the former for fertilizer and the latter for toilets. Designs will have to be developed for this purpose. It should be ensured that systems for the management of human excreta incorporate conservation principles. Low-water use toilets (3-5 litre) and ecological sanitation approaches (including ecological toilets), where nutrients are safely recycled into productive agriculture can be promoted. Replacement of waste water pumping equipment to improve the system efficiency through energy saving should be considered. Decentralized waste water management systems for community, housing complexes, commercial buildings need to be introduced for efficient wastewater management. Institutional capacity of all (ULBs) should be strengthened for effective implementation and O&M of sewerage system.

Lack of local capital is a key constraint for waste management which must be addressed. Inadequate expertise with local bodies on sustainable technologies like a waste recovery project is also an important barrier which needs immediate attention. Uncontrolled and informal disposal should be regulated. Regional solid waste management facilities should be encouraged. In case of existing landfills, bioremediation of waste is recommended with a view to reclaim the land and convert organic waste into useful products which will result in elimination of GHG emission.

All ULBs should comply with the implementation of MSW (Management and Handling) Rules, 2000 notified by the MoEF.

Improved allocation of funds for capital investment and for further operation and maintenance by ULBs may be ensured for efficient SWM systems. Landfill sites, often situated in rural areas adjacent to urban areas, need to be developed scientifically. It should be ensured that areas identified for drainages are not converted to landfill sites since the former plays a crucial role in retaining surface water, maintaining soil moisture, etc.

5.4.3 Urban Transport:

A. Strengthening of Public Transport System through a Combination of Promotional, Regulatory and Fiscal Measures: Promotional measures could include encouraging private participation in the provision of transport services on remunerative as well as non-remunerative routes, greater functional autonomy to state transport undertakings, a quantum jump in the quality of city buses and city bus services by introducing sleek, ergonomically designed buses with wider doors and windows, level boarding and alighting, comfortable seating and suspension, passenger information system, GPS enabled with electronic fare collection, etc; introduction of state of the art ITS-enabled modern buses on PPP mode, reserving of one lane out of three lanes or more for high capacity bus systems/public transport and high occupancy vehicles carrying six people or more. Urban transport demand is characterized by patterned travel and non-patterned travel. Even for patterned travel, patterns are complex. No public authority can acquire complete information about these demand patterns whereas private sources would have a serious pecuniary interest in obtaining such information. A realignment of policy on this basis i.e. public provision for trunk routes and supplementary private provision regulated in terms of safety, omissions and road space can be explored.

B. Reducing the Fuel Consumed per Passenger Travel through Modal Shift: Significant GHG mitigation can be achieved through modal shift by providing all arterial roads more than 25 m right of way to have minimum of 2.5 m pedestrian path (with trees) and proper street furniture and 2.5

m bicycle path preferably in each direction as a mandatory measure. Where it is not possible to provide a dedicated cycle path because of right of way being narrow, traffic calming measures to reduce the speed of traffic to 30 kmph need to be adopted. Without properly engineered pedestrian path and bicycle path, the roads are unsafe for walking and bicycling and safety of walking and bicycling needs to be ensured.

C. Improving Access to Goods and Services through an Integrated Urban Plan: The greatest GHG mitigation can be achieved through linking spatial planning with transportation planning to improve access to goods and services while minimizing the need to travel through charging the cost of externalities such as congestion, pollution, climate change, public infrastructure and reducing subsidies to private vehicles. Urban sprawl is not energy efficient or conducive to the provision of sustainable public transport system. As such, major transport axes need to be identified and the development should take place along pre-defined major transport axes.

D. Integrating Inter-City Road Passenger Transport with Urban Transport Systems: Long-distance passenger travel needs to be closely integrated into the urban environment, facilitating fast traveller-friendly mass-transport access to well located terminals and airports. Carefully planned highway system improvements are required to reduce travel times for goods and passengers while improving road safety, congestion, fuel consumption and emissions.

E. Shifting from Fossil Fuels to Natural Gas, Renewable and Alternate Fuels: With the abundant availability of renewable sources like biomass across the country, India has a vast potential to replace the current usage of fossil fuels in various commercial vehicles. Changing to fuels that have a lower carbon footprint in sufficient quantities would have a major impact on GHG emissions from the road transport.

F. Establishing and Implementing Fuel Efficiency Standards for New as well as Existing Vehicles: Improving the maintenance condition of in-use vehicles (in terms of quality and frequency) is important. Under the Energy Conservation Act, 2001, regulations are to be made for the following three complimentary strategies: (a) fuel economy standards to set benchmarks for efficient engine technology, (b) fuel economy labelling of vehicles to help increase consumers' demand for fuel efficient vehicles and (c) fiscal incentives to be linked to fuel economy of the vehicles.

Energy efficiency standards need be implemented throughout India for all forms of motorized transport for which a time frame for the finalization of the vehicle fuel efficiency standards and its implementation should be set.

G. Facilitating R&D Activities: Automobile industry and R&D organizations should be encouraged to develop and commercialize new products, processes and technologies which have the potential to contribute substantially to energy conservation and protection of the environment.

H. Discouraging Diesel Propelled Personal Vehicles: There has been a considerable increase in diesel vehicles as passenger vehicles and some of them are used as a personal mode of transport, it is important to ensure that these vehicles meet the same performance standards as other vehicles. This has increased pollution levels in some cities. There is a need to restrict the manufacture of these vehicles and to discourage their use as personal transport.

I. Exploring Technological Options: Measures such as reduction in vehicle loads by using light weight materials; improving aerodynamics; reducing roll resistance of the tyres on the road; using mobile air-conditioning systems with new refrigerants such as HFC152a, improving drive train efficiency; adopting advanced direct injecting gasoline engines that can yield about 35 percent greater fuel economy than conventional gasoline engines. Improvements in transmissions and frictional losses in the engines, introducing variable valve timings and hybrid drive trains also need to be undertaken.

J. Creating Public Awareness: The Government should launch intensive awareness especially on health and well-being.

The campaigns should seek people's support for initiatives like greater use of public transport and non motorized vehicles, proper maintenance of their vehicles and adopting "Green Travel Habits". Emphasis should be laid on bringing about such awareness amongst children through inputs in their school curricula, organizing various painting and essay competitions, etc. Use of public transport should be encouraged through instruments such as tax rates, parking policy etc.

K. Multimodal Integration: To provide for seamless connectivity over a widespread network of various public transport modes, the government should insist on setting up Unified Metropolitan Transport Authorities (UMTA) in all one million plus cities. This will facilitate more coordinated planning and implementation of urban transport programmes and projects as well as an integrated management of urban transport systems.

L. Comprehensive Mobility Planning and Management using Intelligent Transport Systems: The advances in information technology and electronics have to be used for setting up of Traffic Information Management Control Centres in all one million plus cities for better traffic management, thereby reducing the problem of congestion and idling of vehicles.

M. Central Financial Support: There is a need for continuous engagement by the Central Government in this sector by providing central financial assistance on a reform based agenda which may be integrated with JNNURM. In addition to JNNURM, there is also a need to create a dedicated central urban transport fund.

N. Service Level Benchmarks: The Ministry of Urban Development brought out service level benchmarking covering public transport facilities, pedestrian infrastructure facilities, non motorized transport (NMT) facilities, level of usage of intelligent transport system (ITS) facilities, travel speed (motorized and mass transit) along major corridors, availability of parking spaces, road safety, pollution levels, integrated land use transport system, financial sustainability of public transport by bus.

5.4.4 Urban Planning:

A. National Level Strategies: At the national level, it is imperative to have a National Urban Policy (NUP) incorporating incentives and disincentives that encourage and support sustainable habitat. Urban Development Plan Formulation and Implementation (UDPFI) guidelines formulated by MoUD would be a useful reference in this regard. It needs to be ensured that plans and policies are based on thorough analysis and a scientific basis. Outcome of the analysis should facilitate policy makers to take appropriate decisions. As envisaged in the National Urban Housing and Habitat Policy (NUHP), 2007, the states should prepare dynamic plans with provision for review every five years. Climate change concerns should be appreciated in the planning process in a manner that optimises development objectives.

B. Regional Level Strategies: Planners should take into account specific effects of climate change while planning for a district/region. Some issues need to be tackled at the regional level such as conservation and sustainable development of natural resources.

The needs and broader interests of the community to secure a better quality of life for the community as a whole need to be ensured through plans that are drawn up for a longer time scale, and need not focus only on short-term gains. Planning authorities should consider both long-term and short-term policies.

The planning process should not impose disproportionate costs in terms of environmental and social impacts, or by unnecessarily constraining otherwise beneficial economic or social development. It should also take into account the resources likely to be available for implementation and the costs likely to be incurred.

C. City Level Strategies: The local role includes enforcing policies and regulations (e.g., restricting urban sprawl). It is the local government which must define the future growth strategies through urban planning. Preparation of master plan and zonal plan should be made mandatory for all urban settlements by considering sustainable development norms.

Land use integrated with transport system in cities should help in reducing the trip length. Greater use of the public transport system and walking and cycling should be encouraged. Building by-laws/building regulations should focus on environmental standards that contribute to sustainability and simultaneously address GHG mitigation. Some of the specific strategies could include the following:

1. Increasing green cover as part of the urban and regional planning exercise.
2. Reduce the heat island effect.
3. Re-development/redensification of existing urban habitat. Mixed land use, integrated and shared social space, and multiple transport options should be considered and implemented. This would minimize infrastructure requirements, energy use in intra-city travel as well as the diversion of agricultural land to urban use. This model would also ensure greater living space per citizen or alternately greater public space.
4. Development of green belts as envisaged in the National Urban Housing and Habitat Policy, 2007.
5. Environmental impact assessment of master plans, and other mega urban infrastructure projects.
6. Promoting mixed use zones as appropriate.
7. Initiating urban renewal programmes.
8. Responsive urban design to climate change and incentivisation.

Poverty reduction is the key for sustainable urban development. As long as there is poverty, environment will not be seen as a priority. People have no choice but to use the cheapest energy options, which may be environmentally harmful (e.g., charcoal). The major concern is poverty itself and its reduction will help in mitigation of climate change. It is therefore imperative for all the state governments to work on poverty reduction mechanisms by partnering with one another to develop new means of tackling the poverty reduction issue.

To sum up, the growth rate of the Indian economy has been increasing over the last few years. Sustaining these growth rates is, however, critically dependent on correcting the infrastructure bottlenecks which exist across various sectors of the economy. One of these bottlenecks is the quality of city infrastructure including roads, water and sanitation. The pressure on city infrastructure has been multiplying on account of the rapid growth in urban population. In the past, municipalities have traditionally relied on state government for funding urban infrastructure projects.

Although some of the larger municipalities have started building capacity, most lack the capacity for sustained long-term planning and preparation of bankable urban infrastructure projects. The size of projects for smaller municipalities has also not been adequate to constitute a marketable size for bond issues. They also lack internal systems for accessing market borrowings. The sharp growth in infrastructure requirement coupled with pressure on state governments' own finances has led to a situation where municipalities may not be able to sustain infrastructure creation solely relying on state government funding. There is, therefore, a need to access alternate sources of funds for bridging municipal infrastructure gaps.

6

Urban Housing and Slum Clearance/Development

Housing is an activity that is typically labour intensive and, therefore, fits in well with the pattern of development envisaged for India. The provision of shelter is a basic need which must be met. Housing construction also creates much-needed employment for the unskilled and, therefore, income for the relatively poor.

The housing problem has become acute in most industrial regions of the world since the Second World War. There is increasing recognition everywhere of the close relation between housing and the health and well-being of the people.

Actually, over a number of years, shortages on a large-scale have developed and conditions worsened a great deal. Private enterprise has proved incapable of meeting the needs and the State has had to assume direct initiative and responsibility in this field to an increasing extent. In some highly industrialised countries, housing accommodation has been provided to a large extent by heavy subsidies from the State in respect of houses of standard design for low-income groups which are not an economic proposition in most countries at present on account of the high cost of construction, building materials and development.

6.1 Constitutional Provisions Regarding Housing

The subject of housing is not specifically mentioned in the Seventh Schedule of the Constitution of India which deals with matters coming within the purview of the Union and State Legislatures. In so far as housing for industrial labour is concerned, Entry 24 of List III (Concurrent List) may be said to cover it because it deals comprehensively with welfare of labour.

Being in the Concurrent List, it is a matter with which both the Union and the State Governments are concerned. The residuary power in relation to subjects not mentioned in List III (Concurrent List) or List II (State List), however, vests in the Union Legislature. As such, the Centre may be said to be directly concerned with the subject of housing in general.

A major situation was created when as a result of the partition of the country about 75 lakh displaced persons came to India from Pakistan and had to be provided with accommodation of some sort. It is in connection with the construction of houses for refugees from Pakistan that the Central Government first undertook a large-scale housing programme for persons other than their employees.

6.2 Importance of Housing

In fulfilling the basic needs of the population, housing, ranks next only to food and clothing in importance. A certain minimum standard of housing is essential for healthy and civilised existence. The development of housing, therefore, must enjoy high priority in a poor country like India where housing amenities are far below the minimum standards that have been internationally accepted. Housing activity serves to fulfil many of the fundamental objectives of national policies:

1. Providing shelter.
2. Raising the quality of life, particularly of the poorer sections of the population.
3. Creating conditions which are conducive to the achievements of crucial objectives in terms of health, sanitation and education.
4. Creating substantial additional employment and dispersed economic activity.
5. Improving urban-rural and inter-personal equity through the narrowing down of difference in standards of living.
6. Generating additional voluntary savings.

6.3 National Housing and Habitat Policy (NHHP), 1998

NHHP provides the basic framework for achieving the

objective of *shelter for all* by 2012. It was evolved in 1998 with the long-term goal of eradicating houselessness, improving the housing conditions of the inadequately housed and providing a minimum level of basic services and amenities to all. It was formulated to address the issues of sustainable development, infrastructure development and for strong public private partnership (PPP) for shelter delivery with the objective of creating surpluses in housing stock and facilitating construction of 2 million dwelling units each year in pursuance of the National Agenda for Governance. However, the housing sector has witnessed several changes since then.

NHHP specifically advocates that Government creates a facilitating environment for growth of housing activity instead of taking on the task of housing itself. Housing is largely a private sector activity in both the rural and urban sectors. This is not to rule out the need for a high degree of involvement of the Government and its agencies in meeting the housing needs of the urban poor.

The National Agenda of Governance also emphasised that housing activity would be an engine for substantial generation of employment, and all legal and administrative impediments that stand in the way of vigorous housing activity should be removed forthwith.

6.4 Role of the Government

In these times, Government cannot afford to confine its role in the field to housing to planning and regulation. Private enterprise is not in a position to do the job so far as low-income groups are concerned. They cannot afford to pay the economic rent for housing accommodation of even the minimum standards. The Government has, therefore, to fill the gap and assist the construction of suitable houses for low and middle income groups, both in urban and rural areas as a part of its own functions. This would involve a large measure of assistance which may take the form of subsidies on a generous scale and the supply of loans on a somewhat low rate of interest. In view of the gravity and vastness of the problem and the financial condition of the States, the Central Government has to accept a large measure of responsibility for financing housing programmes in the industrial centres where congestion and shortage have become very acute in recent years. Provision should also be made to find funds for middle-class housing schemes, preferably through co-operative building societies.

In the field of housing, Government has been giving assistance for the benefit of selected sections of the community and providing accommodation to its employees. Governmental initiatives and facilitating role have a significant impact on the provision of housing and growth of the sector. These initiatives and interventions relate to the following:

1. Legislations concerning ownership.
2. Transfers and development of land.
3. Stamp duty and registration laws.
4. Rent control legislation.
5. Tax policy particularly relating to housing loans.
6. Property and land tax laws.
7. Town planning law and its actual implementation.
8. Zoning regulations.
9. Land use change.
10. Building by-laws.

Government role also covers urban development activities through parastatals and urban development authorities, sites and services schemes, slum policy, provision of urban infrastructure, urban transport policy and facilities, the institutions in the public sector relating to housing development and housing finance, and house construction in the public sector.

6.4.1 National Housing Bank (NHB): Against the milieu of rapid urbanization and a changing socio-economic scenario, the demand for housing in the country has been expanding at a fast pace. In India, investment in housing till recently was mainly financed by own sources or from informal credit market. Since the 1990s, efforts have been directed at the development of housing finance institutions to meet the large resource gap that exists for housing finance in the country. The emergence of organised housing finance has been a relatively late development in India. When the NHB was set up in 1988, nearly 80 percent of the housing stock in the country was financed from informal sources. The organised sources of housing finance included, *inter alia*, the housing finance companies (HFCs) which then numbered about 400 and were essentially non-banking financial companies (NBFCs) that were regulated by the RBI. These included small companies with operations restricted to localised areas and companies engaged in construction/development, which also offered housing credit. Several of the companies relied on public deposits for their resources. A notable exception was the Housing Development Finance Corporation (HDFC).

In recognition of the need for developing a network of specialised housing finance institutions in the country, NHB was set up in July 1988 as a wholly owned subsidiary of the RBI under the National Housing Bank Act, 1987, to function as an apex bank for the housing finance. NHB was established with a mandate 'to operate as a principal agency to promote housing finance institutions both at local and regional levels and to provide financial and other support to such institutions and for matters connected therewith or incidental thereto'.

As a chief refinance institution in the housing sector, NHB regulates housing finance companies (HFCs), refinances their operations and expands the spread of housing finance to different income groups all over the country, while functioning within the overall framework of the housing policy. It has also helped in diverting increasing proportions of annual provident fund accumulations for housing finance through housing linked savings schemes for provident fund subscribers.

Since then the sector has grown with many new HFCs being set up, including several sponsored by banks and financial institutions. The important among these are the following: LIC Housing Finance Ltd., GIC Housing Finance Ltd., BOB Housing Ltd. (since merged with its parent bank, viz. Bank of Baroda), PNB Housing Finance Ltd., IDBI Home Finance Ltd., and ICICI Home Finance Ltd.. Some of these were set up with equity support from the NHB as part of their developmental mandate. These HFCs have provided aspiring home owners with access to housing finance and facilitated home ownership in a big way.

6.4.2 Housing Boards at State Level: The State Governments are responsible for implementing social housing schemes. Almost all the States have set up housing boards in order to facilitate the implementation of the social housing schemes. Community-operative banks have been financing housing schemes. Community-operative banks cater to economically weaker sections, low and middle income groups as well as community-operative or group housing societies.

6.4.3 Housing and Urban Development Corporation (HUDCO): It was set up in April 1970 as an apex techno-finance organization in order to provide loans and technical support to state and city level organizations. Among the HFCs, HUDCO has dominated in terms of profits and total disbursements. Government also recognised the need to strengthen HUDCO through augmenting its resources for meeting the requirements for shelter provisions for lower income groups in a large measure in rural and urban areas including the shelters and the slum dwellers and for expanding infrastructure facilities in the urban areas.

6.5 Private Sector Participation

As in the past, the bulk of housing for the higher income groups continues to be provided by the private sector. In addition, in view of the constraints on public resources, there should be greater encouragement for the private sector to step up its activities in the construction of housing for low and middle income groups. Imaginative schemes of improved facilities for financial intermediation in this sector will have to be investigated in order to achieve this objective.

The public sector has only a marginal, though promotional, role to play in the provision of urban housing. It is clear that the need is great for better and more housing in urban areas. Given the overall resources constraints and more pressing competing claims on public resources, the vast majority of additional housing in urban areas will have to be met from private resources. The role of the public sector will have to be restricted to the improvement of slums, the direct provision of housing to some of the urban poor and encouragement of agencies such as HUDCO which can promote the marshalling of private resource into housing in a constructive manner.

Much of the ills of urban housing and resource mobilisation in larger urban areas can be attributed to the problems inherent in the urban land market. While urban development programmes have to depend largely on a well coordinated land development programme, the existing legal and administrative machinery has impeded supply and development of serviced land. Also, very little efforts have been made to mop up the large appreciation in values of real estate particularly in metropolitan cities.

A corollary to the above process is exploration of avenues through which private initiatives can find a greater role in urban development programme. The role of private sector needs to be expanded. The extent and the manner in which private developers can contribute to urban renewal and squatter settlements and peripheral areas in metropolitan regions (including residential and trunk infrastructure development) needs assessment.

For years to come the bulk of the building activity will still have to be undertaken by private enterprise. In building works on a small-scale, the private builder can often construct at a rate cheaper than public bodies on account of economy in supervision and personal attention to details.

At the same time, while private builders should be

encouraged to the maximum, steps should be taken to eliminate the speculative element in land and to discourage land hoarding in urban areas, for which purpose the taxation structure on vacant lands should be so designed as to make all land hoarding unprofitable.

6.6 Energy Efficiency in Residential and Commercial Buildings

Buildings can be broadly classified under two categories, namely, residential and commercial. Energy end-use in these buildings varies largely across income groups, building construction typology, climate and several other factors.

6.6.1 Residential Energy Consumption: Residential energy consumption can be broadly divided into six categories: lighting, cooking, space conditioning, refrigeration, water heating and others. In summer months, air conditioners and refrigerators dominate electricity consumption. In winter months, consumption is dominated by heaters and geysers. Thus, space conditioning (heating and cooling), refrigerators, geysers and lighting need maximum attention in the residential sector for adoption of efficiency measures.

6.6.2 Commercial Energy Consumption: The commercial sector comprises various institutional and industrial establishments such as banks, hotels, restaurants, shopping complexes, offices and public departments supplying basic utilities. Most commercial energy is used in buildings or structures for the purpose of space heating, water heating, lighting, cooking and cooling.

In India, commercial energy demand estimation and projection are beset with numerous data gaps, particularly with respect to the reporting of the number of commercial establishments/consumers, their energy consumption patterns, degree of usage of energy for different end-use energy consuming activities and penetration of appliances and other end-use devices in the sector. However, the bifurcation of electricity consumption amongst various electricity consuming activities such as lighting, space conditioning, and refrigeration is based on electricity usage norms.

Lighting, space-conditioning, water heating and refrigerators account for maximum electricity consumption in the commercial and residential building sector. Using appropriate architectural design, materials, building components along with renewable energy, it is possible to reduce electrical energy consumption in buildings appreciably. Some Indian architecture traditions are examples of human settlements designed in harmony with the habitat which can be considered to be the first step to conserve energy in buildings.

In order to institutionalize energy conservation efforts in the country, the Government of India passed the Energy Conservation Act in 2001, and established the Bureau of Energy Efficiency (BEE) on March 1, 2002 to promote the efficient use of energy and its conservation.

6.6.3 Energy Conservation Act, 2001: Energy conservation has emerged as a major policy objective in India. Energy Conservation Act (ECA), 2001, was passed by the Indian Parliament in September 2001. This Act requires large energy consumers to adhere to energy consumption norms, new buildings to follow the Energy Conservation Building Codes (ECBCs) and appliances to meet energy performance standards and to display energy consumption labels. In other words, the Act provides a legal framework for energy efficiency initiatives in the country. It has mandatory and promotional initiatives which broadly relate to designated consumers, standards and labelling programme for equipment and appliances and ECBCs for new commercial buildings.

The Act also created the Bureau of Energy Efficiency (BEE) to implement the provisions of the Act.

6.6.4 Bureau of Energy Efficiency (BEE): BEE was set up by the Government of India on March 1, 2002 as a Statutory Body as per Section 3 of Energy Conservation Act (ECA), 2001. Head office of the BEE is located in New Delhi.

BEE is responsible for spearheading the improvement of

energy efficiency through regulatory and promotional instruments. BEE has several programmes to set labels and energy efficient standards for refrigerators, air conditioners, motors and other appliances. Energy labelling on voluntary basis for refrigerators and tubular fluorescent lighting was launched in 2006.

The mission of BEE is to develop policies and strategies with a thrust on self-regulation and market principles within the overall framework of Energy Conservation Act, 2001, with the primary objective of promoting energy saving measures and, in turn, reducing energy intensity (i.e. energy consumed per unit of product/service, practice and procedure) of the Indian economy.

A. Objectives of BEE: BEE strives to achieve the following objectives:

1. Exerting leadership and providing policy framework and direction to national energy conservation and efficiency efforts and programmes.
2. Co-ordinating energy efficiency and conservation policies and programmes and taking it to the stakeholders.
3. Establishing systems and procedures to measure, monitor and verify energy efficiency results in individual sectors as well as at the macro level.
4. Leveraging multilateral and bilateral and private sector support in implementation of ECA, 2001 and efficient use of energy and its conservation programmes.
5. Demonstrating delivery of energy efficiency services as mandated in the ECA, 2001 through private-public partnerships.
6. Interpreting, planning and managing energy conservation programmes as envisaged in the ECA, 2001.

B. Projects and Programmes of BEE: BEE has initiated following projects and programmes to achieve its goals:

1. Indian Industry Programme for Energy Conservation (IIPEC).
2. Professional certification of energy managers and accreditation of energy auditors.

3. Development of manual and energy performance codes for equipment.
4. Standardization and labelling (S&L) programme.
5. Energy efficiency in building and establishments.
6. Energy conservation awareness in schools.
7. National energy conservation awards.

C. Actions Taken by BEE: Actions taken by BEE so far are given below:

1. Conduct of national certificate examinations for selection of energy managers and energy auditors.
2. Accreditation of energy auditing agencies on the basis of their energy auditing capabilities and institutional set up.
3. Framing of draft norms for fixation of specific energy consumption in cement and pulp and paper industries.
4. Setting up of task forces in 7 energy-intensive sectors to frame best practices in energy conservation.
5. Motivation of industries to take up energy efficiency measures through institution of National Energy Conservation Award Scheme of the Ministry of Power, Government of India.
6. Completion of energy audits for a number of Government buildings, including Rashtrapati Bhawan, Prime Minister's Office, South Block (Defence Ministry), Rail Bhawan, Sanchar Bhawan, Shram Shakti Bhawan, Transport Bhawan, Delhi Airport and All India Institute of Medical Sciences (AIIMS).

Ministry of Power, through BEE, has initiated a number of energy efficiency initiatives through a range of measures some of which are as under:

1. Energy Conservation Building Code for large, new commercial buildings.
2. Energy labelling scheme for appliances.
3. Development of energy consumption norms for industrial sub-sectors.
4. Annual examinations to certify energy auditors and energy managers.

However, the effectiveness of these and other measures ultimately depends on their adoption by all energy users and consequently on their awareness of the energy savings opportunities around them.

Keeping this in view, Ministry of Power has initiated National Campaign on Energy Conservation and National Painting Competition on Energy Conservation for school children.

6.6.5 Energy Conservation Building Code (ECBC): Under Section 14(p) of the Energy Conservation Act, 2001, Central Government has powers to prescribe Energy Conservation Building Code (ECBC) for commercial buildings having a connected load of 500 KW or building complex for efficient use of energy and its conservation. The State Governments have the flexibility to modify ECBC to suit local or regional needs. The Central Government is also empowered to include such commercial buildings in the list of designated consumers under Section 14(e). State Governments are empowered, under Section 15(a), to amend and notify ECBC to suit regional/local climatic conditions.

ECBC was launched by the Ministry of Power in May 2007 on a voluntary basis. The major components of the building which are being addressed through ECBC are walls, roofs and windows, lighting systems, air conditioning systems, electrical distribution systems, and water heating and pumping systems. New buildings can save up to 50 percent energy by appropriate design interventions in building envelope, lighting and air conditioning systems.

ECBC is intended for new commercial buildings having a connected load of more than 500 KW and has initially been launched on voluntary basis. ECBC defines norms of energy performance and takes into consideration the climatic regions of the country where the building is located. The major components of the building which are being addressed through the code are the following:

1. Envelope (walls, roofs, windows).
2. Lighting systems.

3. Water heating and pumping system.
4. Electrical distribution system.

ECBC addresses the 5 climatic zones of the country: hot and dry, warm and humid, composite, temperate and cold. In order to ensure administration of ECBC implementation in a uniform and consistent manner all over the country, BEE has set up an ECBC Programme Committee (EPC) by pooling in the expertise of all stakeholders, including state designated agencies, industry etc. This committee: (a) facilitates the development of ECBC compliant building designs, (b) ensures credible implementation of a few demonstration projects in the public sector and (c) makes arrangements for evaluation of the progress and outcomes by creating appropriate institutional mechanism. BEE has come out with the revised edition of ECBC incorporating the comments received from stakeholders and organizations like Central Power and Works Department (CPWD).

With a view to build adequate technical capacity and develop building procedures and tools to effectively implement ECBC, a panel of 44 ECBC expert architects has been shortlisted. The shortlisted architects are resource persons and brand ambassadors for the ECBC. These expert architects support the implementation of ECBC by providing various services to architects who are designing ECBC compliant buildings.

Tip sheets on building envelopes, lighting, and building simulation have been developed and launched by BEE. The capacity building of architects and engineers will be achieved by working closely with architectural/engineering colleges through training of next generation architects and engineers to enable them to design energy efficient and sustainable buildings.

A number of upcoming government buildings in the country are being constructed as per ECBC norms. Government organizations, Centre, State and public sector undertakings, have committed to build their new buildings as ECBC compliant.

In order to promote energy efficiency in existing buildings, a scheme to promote Energy Efficiency in Government Buildings has been developed by BEE. The approved scheme provides for funding of Investment Grade Energy Audits (IGEA) being arranged by the Central Government Agencies/State Designated Agencies. The coverage of government buildings includes large buildings which can have a demonstrative impact like large municipal or local body buildings, hospitals etc.

In order to promote implementation of energy efficiency measures through performance contracting route, BEE has undertaken a process of short-listing of Energy Service Companies (ESCOs) through an open invitation and evaluation process. 35 ESCOs have been accredited. This exercise is expected to aid ESCOs to be able to successfully bid for energy services projects and to arrange financing for the execution of such projects.

President of India launched an initiative *Roshini* which aims at converting the President's Estate into a model township which would be eco-friendly, green and plastic free. BEE has been entrusted the task of taking up energy efficiency measures for the entire President's Estate excluding the Rashtrapati Bhawan.

6.6.6 National Building Code (NBC), 2005: It has been developed by the Bureau of Indian Standards as a guiding code to be followed by municipalities and development authorities in formulation and adoption of building by laws (BBL). NBC deals with various aspects of energy conservation and sustainable development through appropriate design, usage and practices with regard to building materials, construction technologies, and building and plumbing services. It focuses on energy efficiency in the following areas:

1. Use of pozzolanas (such as fly ash, rice husk ash, metakaoline, silica fume, ground granulated blast furnace slag, etc.) in concrete production.
2. Daylight integration (indoor lighting levels to be met via day lighting).

3. Artificial lighting requirements (levels) for indoor spaces.
4. Ventilation standards (natural and mechanical) for optimal human health and well-being.
5. Electrical standards (minimum power factor, allowances for diversity, etc.).
6. Select HVAC design norms.

However, so far the NBC is not integrated with the ECBC.

6.6.7 Energy Efficiency in Small and Medium Enterprises (SMEs): BEE is implementing a programme to improve the energy performance in the identified 25 SME clusters across the country. The objective of the programme is to accelerate the adoption of energy efficient technologies and practices in the chosen SME clusters through knowledge sharing, capacity building and development of innovative financing mechanisms.

Cluster-based approach is adopted in this SME programme because of the similar characteristics like geographical location, markets, products manufactured, technology, development issues and common pool of resources.

The main emphasis of the scheme is to build capacity necessary to enable them to discharge regulatory, facilitative and enforcement functions under the Act, given that the institutional capacity is limited, both in terms of human and infrastructure resources.

State Designated Agencies (SDAs) are statutory bodies set up by states to implement energy conservation measures at state level. SDAs are expected to play three major roles namely: as a development agency, as a facilitator and as a regulator/enforcing body.

6.6.8 Bachat Lamp Yojana (BLY): BLY aims at the large-scale replacement of incandescent bulbs in households by CFLs. It seeks to provide CFLs to households at the price similar to that of incandescent bulbs. BLY is designed as a public-private partnership between the Government of India, private sector CFL suppliers and State level Electricity Distribution Companies (DISCOMs). The CFL suppliers sell high quality CFLs to households at a price of ₹ 15 per CFL within a designated project area in a DISCOM region of operation. A CFL supplier is chosen by the DISCOM through a due diligence process from a list of CFL suppliers empanelled by BEE.

Under the scheme, 40 watt, 60 watt and 100 watt incandescent lamps are replaced with 9-11 watt, 13-15 watt and 20-23 watt CFLs respectively. BEE monitors the electricity saving in each project area in accordance with the monitoring methodology prescribed by the Executive Board of Clean Development Mechanism (CDM). In order to reduce the transaction costs associated with the approval of CDM projects, BEE has developed a programme of activities (PoA) which serves as an umbrella CDM project, registered with the CDM Executive Board. The individual projects, designed in conformance with the umbrella project, are added to the umbrella project as and when they are prepared. The development of the PoA is a voluntary action on the part of BEE, and it does not seek any commercial or CDM revenues from the PoA. On the other hand, BEE, on behalf of the Government of India, takes the responsibility of monitoring of all project areas after the DISCOMs and the CFL suppliers have entered into a tripartite agreement with BEE.

6.6.9 Standards and Labelling Programme: Under Section 14 of the Energy Conservation Act, 2001, BEE has developed a scheme for energy efficiency labelling of equipment. Central Government, under the same Act, has powers to: (a) direct display of labels on specified appliances or equipment (Section 14d) and (b) enforce minimum efficiency standards by prohibiting manufacture, sale, and import of products not meeting the minimum standards (Section 14c).

Standards and labelling programme for end-use appliances and equipments provides for self-certification by the manufacturers based on the standards issued by BEE. The scheme has been developed in collaboration with all the stakeholders, and aims at providing information on energy performance so that consumers can make informed decisions while purchasing appliances. Other than the objective of informed choices to consumers, this programme also leads to energy saving, and thereby the cost saving potential of the marketed household and other equipment. Along with the fact that this would impact the energy saving in the medium and long-run, it will also position domestic industry to compete in such markets where norms for energy efficiency are mandatory.

The scheme was launched by the Minister of Power in May 2006 and energy labels have been put on the following equipments and appliances under programme implementation on voluntary basis:

1. Frost free refrigerators.
2. Tubular florescent lamps.
3. Room air conditioners.
4. Direct cool refrigerators
5. Distribution transformers.
6. Induction motors.
7. Agricultural pump sets.
8. Ceiling fans.
9. Electric geysers.
10. Colour televisions.

The scheme was invoked on voluntary basis for 4 equipments and appliances, viz. air conditioners, distribution transformers, refrigerators and tube lights. The same was made mandatory for all the above 4 equipments/appliances with effect from January 7, 2010 with stakeholders' consultation. The scheme for other equipments/appliances is currently under voluntary phase and depending upon the market transformation will be made into a mandatory scheme. Education and awareness about labels, ensuring credibility of the scheme by check and challenge testing, monitoring and evaluation of the impact of the scheme are the major aims and objectives of the scheme.

6.6.10 National Energy Conservation Awards: These annual awards recognize innovation and achievements in energy conservation by the industry; buildings, railways, state designated agencies and municipalities and raise awareness that energy conservation plays a big part in India's response to reducing global warming through energy saving.

6.7 Integrated Building Solutions

In formulating climate change strategies, mitigation efforts need to be balanced with those aimed at adaptation. There are interactions between vulnerability, adaptation and mitigation in buildings through climate conditions and energy systems. As a result of a warming climate, heating energy consumption will decline, but energy demand for cooling will increase while at the same time passive cooling techniques will becomes less effective. The net impact of these changes on GHG emissions is related to the available choice of primary energy used for heating and the efficiency of technologies that are used for heating and cooling needs.

Fortunately, there are many potential synergies where investments in the building sector may reduce the overall cost of climate change in terms of both mitigation and adaptation. For instance, if new buildings are constructed, the design can address both mitigation and adaptation aspects. Among the most important of these are reduced cooling loads. For instance, using advanced insulation techniques and passive solar design to reduce the expected increase in air conditioning load.

In addition, if high efficiency electric appliances are used, the savings are increased due to reduced electricity demand for air conditioning, especially in commercial buildings. Roof retrofits can incorporate increased insulation and storm security in one investment. In addition, the integrated design of well insulated, air tight buildings, with efficient air management and energy system leads not only to lower GHG emissions, but also reduce thermal stress to occupants, reducing extreme weather related mortality and other health effects.

Policies that actively promote integrated building solutions for both mitigating and adapting to climate change are especially important for the building sector. It has been observed that building users responding to a warmer climate generally choose options that increase energy consumption rather than other means, such as insulation, shading or ventilation, which consume less energy. Good urban planning, including increasing green areas as well as cool roofs in cities, has proven to be an efficient way to limit the heat island effect. Cities like the Municipal Corporations of Rajkot, Nagpur, Pune and Mumbai already offer property tax rebates to implement certain good practices (e.g., use of solar water heaters etc.).

The Ministry of New and Renewable Energy (MNRE) is promoting solar water heating systems for various classes of consumers through its scheme for loans at nominal rates of interest, i.e. 2 percent to 5 percent for domestic, institutional and industrial consumers, capital subsidy for developers and incentives to municipalities/utilities for the amendment of building byelaws/provision of rebate in property tax or electricity tariff. A scheme has also been introduced to incentivize green buildings which includes a rebate in registration fee, to the extent of 90 percent, incentives to architects and design consultants ranging from ₹ 2.5 lakh to ₹ 5 lakh and incentives to urban local bodies that announce rebates in property tax for green buildings as well as awards to the best performing urban local bodies.

MNRE recently announced the Solar City initiative which will provide seed funds to cities for developing and implementing similar strategies at the city level. MNRE has developed climate zone-wise energy efficiency and passive architectural guidelines for residential and commercial buildings which could be followed by CPWD and Municipal Corporations all over the country.

The main barriers in the adoption of various energy efficiency practices are knowledge gaps, issues related to enforcement and implementation and the cost of green technologies and technology development. This also requires a stronger political commitment and more ambitious policy-making, including careful design of policies as well as enforcement and regular monitoring.

6.8 Green Buildings

There needs to be a demand for green buildings from investors, developers, and building occupants. This demand is currently low due to lack of awareness of the financial, social and health benefits of green buildings. Firstly, there is a lack of knowledge about green investment and returns on green buildings in the society. Much analysis has been performed to show that green buildings do not have to cost more initially, and even when initial design or construction costs are higher, the overall returns can be much higher due to efficiency of operations. Very few people have detailed knowledge about the clean development mechanism (CDM) and the possibility to obtain additional funding for their projects through the CDM. Since consumers are also unaware of the comparative costs of future operation and maintenance of buildings, they do not take building efficiency into consideration when making purchasing decisions. Because of this, most builders in India do not consider the future costs of functioning the building during design and construction stage.

Finally, in the actual building operation, there is a lack of awareness of the financial and environmental benefits of operating buildings efficiently. Most consumers are currently unaware about the availability of green products and BEE-labelled products. They are also unaware about the economic, environmental and health benefits of using such green and efficient products or appliances. Since there is a lack of awareness about the life cycle cost benefits of efficient products, the higher upfront cost prevents purchase. Despite the extent of the knowledge gap, there are many ways to address this barrier through effective outreach and education campaigns. Until consumers are more aware of the environmental and financial impacts of buildings, there will remain a limited demand for such designs. Yet designers and architects cannot create green buildings without improved education regarding the ways to incorporate and analyse code requirements and efficiency recommendations. Bridging the knowledge gap will require outreach and education for all sectors simultaneously.

Programmes that educate the engineering and architecture communities—both in universities and for current building professionals—about green design should be undertaken by the government, educational communities and companies. Educational programmes for green buildings should focus on regional solutions, because of the variations in climatic factors and the cultural differences in various parts of India.

Demonstration projects at key geographical locations of the country to test the effectiveness of code recommendations on real time projects would introduce the design and construction industry to best practices. These demonstration projects would also help introduce consumers and investors to the economic, health, environmental and aesthetic benefits of green buildings.

There should also be awareness programmes to motivate consumers and emphasise the importance of energy efficiency in buildings. These should address the economic benefits of green buildings, particularly reductions in operation costs from energy consumption. These could encourage consumers to look for green buildings in all new purchases or retrofit existing buildings. Awareness programmes should also focus on marketing and increasing labelling of life cycle costs and cost saving potential in efficient products. The economic benefits of BEE-labelled products should be disseminated further.

Some outreach programmes should focus on the next generation. One way to do so would be to retrofit energy efficient lighting and appliances into existing schools. Building greener and more efficient school buildings should also be a priority. Monitoring and information collection in schools could demonstrate the benefits to the community. Students could also be educated through a voluntary shutdown of power. In metropolitan areas, social groups or schools could take the responsibility of organizing families to participate. Social events in community centres could be held for families that had shutdown power. Additionally, public offices should participate in such a way as to raise awareness about voluntary shutdowns.

Mandating certification of energy performance for all buildings rented and sold, would allow consumers to compare the energy performance of all buildings. Once the public is made aware of the costs of running a building before purchasing and operating the structure, builders will be held accountable and responsible for creating more efficient buildings.

A general approach to bridge the knowledge gap in all areas would be to create a dedicated website with information and relevant documents related to building efficiency codes, benefits of green buildings and technical recommendations for designing and constructing green buildings.

6.8.1 Financial Incentives for Green Buildings: Furthermore, soft construction loans could be offered for green buildings, with more efficient buildings attracting lower interest rates. Corporate banks could also be encouraged to incorporate these soft green construction loans as part of their corporate social responsibility programmes.

Many stakeholders identified tax incentives as a primary method for encouraging green building adoption and that could be incorporated with a programme of tax penalties for inefficient buildings. These tax incentives and penalties could include tax rebates (either for residents or developers), corporate tax reductions and penalties for inefficiency to phase out old buildings.

Many international cities have had success in implementing tax breaks for green buildings based on efficiency; platinum buildings receive an even bigger tax break than silver buildings. While the developer receives the tax break, this should be passed on to the user because of lower construction costs. Such an incentive can be seen as "priming the system" for green development. As long as the occupants do actually benefit from lower costs, this method would increase their demand.

Another option would be to implement a housing or property tax rebate of between 5 to 10 percent based on energy performance. Again, more efficient buildings would receive larger rebates. There is some concern regarding the split incentives in such a model. While builders and developers will pay the initial cost of green design and construction, only the residents will receive the benefits. However, since building occupants and owners are best suited to push developers to make green buildings, any benefits that they receive will increase their demand for green buildings and force developers to build green.

An additional financial incentive for green buildings would be to adjust power tariffs. Consumers could be offered a lower power tariff based on the efficiency of their buildings. A more efficient building (measured as electricity use per square metre) would pay less per kilowatt-hour than a typical lower performance building. This would provide increased incentives for efficiency, as more efficient homes would already be paying less on their electricity bills just by using less energy. Such schemes already exist in some cities that reward users for installation and use of solar water heating. In Rajasthan, users with solar water heating systems receive a rebate of 5 paise per kwh, while in Karnataka similar rebates are 15 paise per kwh and 40 paise per kwh in West Bengal.

Tariffs could also be adjusted by implementing "Time-of-Day Power Tariffs" which would help utilities to reduce the need for increased energy supply. Time-of-day tariffs have been shown to reduce demand at peak hours, because costs would be higher at those times. This would provide greater incentives for companies to utilize energy storage and to reduce peak demand. To implement this, the partnership of energy companies would be necessary, and meters that would differentiate between times of day would also need to be installed.

While implementing financial incentives such as purchase preferences, policy directives to banks, soft construction loans, tax incentives, property tax, rebates, subsidized power tariffs, etc. it should be ensured that they are economically justified.

While the government has been active in encouraging CDM projects throughout India, greater focus should be placed on encouraging CDM certification for energy efficiency programmes and making developers aware of the financial benefits of CDM certification. One such programme would be a programmatic CDM for BEE-labelled products, where the manufacturers could bundle and sell the products. The Government could also institute utility linked DSM programmes and allow the utilities to bundle efficiency measures for CDM credit as well.

Since energy codes are relatively new in India, green products and services including insulation, compact fluorescent lamps (CFL) and T5 lamps, efficient glass, and efficient HVAC systems, required by buildings to comply with the code requirements are not readily and abundantly available or competitively priced. Market monopoly by a handful of manufacturers of energy efficient products has exacerbated the problem, resulting in a non-competitive market for green products.

Government, research universities and private developers need to identify R&D options for investment to arrive at innovative low-cost technology options for arriving at sustainable development in the building sector.

Large private investors should be encouraged to focus on green growth and to develop local production of efficient materials. This encouragement could occur through government commitments for purchasing green products (thus ensuring a market) or through reduced business taxes for manufacturers of green products.

The Government should have a purchasing preference policy for green equipment. If the Government is a significant product consumer, then the manufacturer will reconfigure the assembly line in order to meet the Government demand for green equipment.

The Government has mandated the use of solar water heating in many applications because such systems have fairly rapid payback periods even at current costs. Such programmes will greatly increase the purchase of such systems, further bringing down the cost and payback time. Similar support should be given to CFLs. If the government mandates the use of CFLs, as Australia has done, the market will expand rapidly, driving down the cost and allowing the CFL to dominate the market for all levels of society in rural as well as urban areas.

Life cycle cost analysis for materials and systems should be used and marketed. Evaluating products based on the full cost of their production and operation makes the benefits of green products and the high cost of inefficiency much more apparent.

Additionally, while developing lower cost technology and encouraging market expansion to drive down costs, the government can also implement financial incentives to overcome the short-term cost barriers of green technology.

An initial boost to promotion of energy efficient products and services is required, and could take the form of reduced excise taxes or reduced VAT for efficient products.

Overcoming these major barriers is a significant task and will require the cooperation and coordination of many Government bodies as well as corporate interests and research groups. However, if green building policies can be implemented and provided with appropriate incentives, major improvements can be made to the existing and new building stock. As mentioned initially, the implementation of existing energy efficiency measures could achieve 30 percent energy savings in new residential buildings and 40 percent energy savings in new commercial buildings. These savings could be even larger as research and development related to energy efficient technologies improve.

6.9 Slum Clearance/Development

Most of the towns in India have grown up haphazardly. They have a large proportion of sub-standard houses and slums containing unsanitary mud-huts of flimsy construction, poorly ventilated, over-congested and often lacking in essential amenities such as water and light. This is particularly so in the large industrial cities. The disgraceful sights presented by the slums of Delhi, Mumbai, Kolkata, Chennai and other big cities are conspicuous examples of this state of affairs. These conditions have developed because of insufficient control over building activity by the State or municipal authorities. Local authorities have been generally indifferent to enforcing such by-laws regarding building and sanitation as have existed. Their own resources have been too meagre to permit any development work worth the name.

The migration of people from villages to towns in search of employment has accelerated the growth of urban population. Adequate facilities and services for the increased urban population are not available. There has been some decline in standards, particularly of housing. The provision of housing through private or co-operative effort is usually directed to the affluent or middle classes and the incoming poor in metropolitan areas give rise to slums.

The experience of public housing so far is that its unit costs are high and that with the constraint of resources it is not possible for public operations to touch even the fringe of the problem. Slum clearance schemes often lead to creation of new slums or deterioration of conditions in some of the older slums. In growing cities of a reasonable size, it should be part of Government policy to encourage, through proper planning and land policy, adequate supply of housing. In cities where the slum population is large, this approach would not be effective and it would be necessary to try to ameliorate the living conditions of dwellers of slums as an immediate measure. Emphasis should be on limiting the rise in the prices of land, providing financial assistance to co-operative and private effort and assuming legal powers for reconditioning of slums.

Some of the difficulties which come in the way of implementation of the slum clearance and improvement programme are: (a) lengthy and time-consuming procedures of acquisition of slum areas, (b) non-availability and high costs of alternative sites near existing places of work, (c) inability of the slum dwellers to pay even the subsidised rent and (d) their reluctance to move from the areas selected for clearance.

The strategy of attempting massive relocation of slums in urban areas has also found critics. Such relocation not only involves substantial hardship to those affected in terms of loss of easy access to employment centres and other amenities, but results in unnecessary destruction of existing housing capital, however sub-standard it may be. It is, therefore, important that substantially increased investments be made in the environmental improvement of slum areas. Low cost sanitation and drainage are key areas of much needed investment in the slums of our cities.

While steps should be taken to clear/improve existing slums, it is equally important that new slums are not allowed to grow up. This is by no means an easy task to accomplish. Besides preparing and strictly implementing master plans for all growing towns and cities, it is essential to enforce municipal bye-laws and building regulations, and at the same time, to expand housing facilities for low-income groups and for economically weaker sections. As transitional measures, night shelters and dormitory accommodation for pavement dwellers and non-family workers have considerable urgency. Similarly, the housing of sweepers and scavengers must receive special attention. In selecting slum areas for clearance and improvement, high priority should be given to areas predominantly inhabited by sweepers and scavengers.

6.9.1 Valmiki Ambedkar Awaas Yojana (VAMBAY): VAMBAY, launched in December 2001, facilitates the construction and upgradation of dwelling units for the slum dwellers, and provides a healthy and enabling urban environment through community toilets under Nirmal Bharat Abhiyan, a component of the Scheme. The Central Government provides a subsidy of 50 percent, with the balance provided by the State Government.

6.9.2 Rajiv Awaas Yojana (RAY): The RAY, which envisages a slum-free India, was launched in 2011 and 54 pilot projects and 228 cities have been included under the preparatory phase of programme with total project cost of ₹ 2468.51 crore of which the central share is ₹ 1361.84 crore.

To sum up, housing provides a large scope for direct and indirect employment of persons with a wide range of skills and also of unskilled persons. Housing is a basic necessity as well as an important economic activity, in that it is a part of the construction industry.

It is clear that housing conditions in the country are rather poor. A large number of people either live without any shelter whatsoever or in units below the lowest possible standards.

With the anticipated entry of FDI into the real estate sector, care has to be taken that the needs of the urban poor and marginalised sections are not ignored. Given the large number of activities impinging on housing directly and indirectly and the multiplicity of agencies involved, designing a framework for orderly and dynamic growth in the housing sector is a challenge to the planners.

There is a need to increase the supply of affordable housing to the economically weaker sections and the low income category through a proper programme of allocation of land, extension of funding assistance and provision of support services. The problem of the urban shelter-less and pavement dwellers has not been given the consideration that is necessary in a welfare or pro-poor State, as seen from the lack of progress in the Night Shelter Scheme. Regulation of building quality and its assurance, especially in areas prone to disasters is an issue whose urgency was reiterated after the earthquake in Gujarat in January 2000. Building designs also need to be gender sensitive and should accommodate the requirements of physically challenged population.

Building cost can be substantially reduced by adopting improved techniques which have already been tried in other countries. For instance, production of bricks can be mechanised, at least in the bigger cities, by use of power and improved types of continuous process kilns. Similarly, building components such as door and window frames and other building equipment can be standardised, thus making mass production possible.

7

Urban Transport Policy and Services

7.1 Need for Efficient Urban Transport

Urban transport is one of the key elements of urban infrastructure. An effective urban transportation system enhances productivity and growth in the economy. Urban transportation covers two broad modes, viz. private transport and public transport. Public transport is energy-efficient and less polluting. Public transport system also helps to maximize urban-rural linkage and improves access of the rural/semi-urban population in the periphery to the city centres for the movement of labour without proliferation of slums within and around cities.

A good network of roads coupled with efficient mass urban transport system makes a substantial contribution to the efficiency of the cities and enables them to become a catalyst of economic and social development.

Little attention has been paid to development of mass rapid transport systems in most major cities. In fact, urban transport is one of the most important components of urban infrastructure which has been neglected due to various reasons. Bus services and urban rail services have been extremely limited.

Till recently, the city of Delhi lacked an efficient mass transport system. The setting up of the Delhi Metro Rail Transit System (DMRTS), which was inaugurated on December 24, 2002, has brought about a great improvement in efficiency and quality of life of the citizens of Delhi. DMRTS is a joint venture between Government of India and Delhi Government. DMRTS is one of the largest infrastructure projects being undertaken, and is being developed on lines of mass rapid transit systems in Hong Kong and Singapore. The project is expected to bring about substantial reduction in pollution, reduction in accident rates and improvement in quality of life.

The objective of urban transport policy should be to ensure safe, affordable, quick, comfortable, reliable and sustainable access for the growing number of city residents to jobs, education, recreation and such other needs within our cities.

7.2 Transport Problems in Urban Areas

For urban areas to be able to support the required level of economic activity, they must provide for the easy and sustainable flow of goods and people. Unfortunately, however, such flow of goods and people has been facing several problems. Most prominent among them are the following:

1. Accessing jobs, education, recreation and similar activities is becoming increasingly time-consuming. Billions of man hours are lost with people stuck in traffic. The primary reason for this has been the explosive growth in the number of motor vehicles, coupled with limitations on the amount of road space that can be provided.
2. Cost of travel, especially for the poor, has increased considerably. This is largely because the use of cheaper non-motorised modes like cycling and walking has become extremely risky, since these modes have to share the same right of way with motorized modes. Further, with population growth, cities have tended to sprawl and increased travel distances have made non-motorized modes impossible to use. This has made access to livelihoods, particularly for the poor, far more difficult.
3. Travel in the city has become more risky with accident rates having gone up. The number of persons killed in road accidents has also gone up. This again has tended to impact the poor more severely as many of those killed or injured tend to be cyclists, pedestrians or pavement dwellers.
4. Increased use of personal vehicles has led to increased air pollution.

Unless the above problems are remedied, poor mobility can become a major dampener to economic growth and cause the quality of life to deteriorate. A policy is, therefore, needed on the approach to dealing with this rapidly growing problem as also offer a clear direction and a framework for future action.

7.3 National Urban Transport Policy (NUTP), 2006

NUTP was formulated with the objective of ensuring easily accessible, safe, affordable, quick, comfortable, reliable and sustainable mobility for all.

It has laid major emphasis on promoting investments in public transport in Indian cities as well as measures that make its use more attractive than in the past. Towards this end, the policy states that the Central Government would encourage all state capitals as well as other cities with a population of more than 1 million to start planning for high capacity public transport systems, and promote shift from personal modes of transportation to public modes of transportation. The composition of vehicle population in India is skewed towards personal transport.

7.3.1 Need for a National Urban Transport Policy: Although the responsibility for management of urban areas (and thus urban transport) rests with the State Governments, a Central policy is considered necessary for the following reasons:

1. Several key agencies that play an important role in urban transport planning work under the Central Government, with no accountability to the State Governments.
2. Several Acts and Rules, which have important implications in dealing with urban transport issues, are administered by the Central Government.
3. A need exists to guide State level action plans within an overall framework.
4. Launching of the Jawaharlal Nehru National Urban Renewal Mission (JNNURM) has provided a timely platform for providing significant financial support from the Central Government for investments in urban transport infrastructure. As such, this offers an opportunity for a meaningful national policy that would guide Central financial assistance towards

improving urban mobility.

5. A need exists to build capacity for urban transport planning and also to develop it as a professional practice.
6. A need exists to take up co-ordinated capacity building, research and information dissemination to raise the overall level of awareness and skills.

7.3.2 Components of Urban Transport Policy:

1. Incorporating urban transportation as an important parameter at the urban planning stage rather than being a consequential requirement.
2. Encouraging integrated land use and transport planning in all cities so that travel distances are minimized and access to livelihoods, education, and other social needs, especially for the marginal segments of the urban population is improved.
3. Improving access of business to markets and the various factors of production.
4. Bringing about a more equitable allocation of road space with people, rather than vehicles, as its main focus.
5. Encouraging greater use of public transport and non-motorized modes by offering state financial assistance for this purpose.
6. Enabling the establishment of quality focused multi-modal public transport systems that are well-integrated, providing seamless travel across modes.
7. Establishing effective regulatory and enforcement mechanisms that allow a level playing field for all operators of transport services and enhanced safety for the transport system users.
8. Establishing institutional mechanisms for enhanced co-ordination in the planning and management of transport systems.
9. Introducing intelligent transport systems for traffic management.
10. Addressing concerns of road safety and trauma response.
11. Reducing pollution levels through changes in travelling

practices, better enforcement, stricter norms, technological improvements etc.

12. Building capacity (institutional and manpower) to plan for sustainable urban transport and establishing knowledge management system that would service the needs of all urban transport professionals, such as planners, researchers, teachers, students etc.
13. Promoting the use of cleaner technologies.
14. Raising finances through innovative mechanisms that tap land as a resource, for investments in urban transport infrastructure.
15. Associating the private sector in activities where their strengths can be beneficially tapped.
16. Taking up pilot projects that demonstrate the potential of possible best practices in sustainable urban transport.

7.4 Integration of Land Use and Transport Planning

Cities in India vary considerably in terms of their population, area, urban form, topography, economic activities, income levels, growth constraints etc. Accordingly, the design of the transport system will have to depend on these city-specific features. Further, transport planning is intrinsically linked to land use planning and both need to be developed together in a manner that serves the entire population and yet minimizes travel needs. In short, an integrated master plan needs to internalize the features of sustainable transport systems. In developing such plans, attention should also be paid to channel the future growth of a city around a pre-planned transport network rather than develop a transport system after uncontrolled sprawl has taken place. Transport plans should, therefore, enable a city to take an urban form that best suits the geographical constraints of its location and also one that best supports the key social and economic activities of its residents. Unfortunately, however, transport planning has not received the extent of attention it should have in drawing up strategic development and land use plans.

7.4.1 Equitable Allocation of Road Space: At present, road space gets allocated to whichever vehicle occupies it first. The focus is the vehicle and not people. The result is that a bus carrying 50 people is allocated only two and a half times the road space that is allocated to a car carrying only 1 or 2 persons. Due to disproportionate space allocated to personal vehicles, the lower income groups have ended up paying in terms of higher travel time and higher travel costs. Users of non-motorized modes have tended to be squeezed out of the roads on account of serious threats to their safety. If the focus of the principles of road space allocation were to be the people, then much more space would need to be allocated to public transport systems than is allocated at present.

Transport policy should encourage measures that allocate road space on a more equitable basis, with people as its focus. This can be achieved by reserving lanes and corridors exclusively for public transport and non-motorized modes of travel. Past experience has been that such reserved lanes are not respected by motorists and therefore lose meaning. In order to facilitate better enforcement of such lane discipline, suitable provisions should be introduced in the Motor Vehicles Act, 1988 and other instrumentalities to enable stringent penalties for violation.

7.4.2 Priority to the Use of Public Transport: It is well-known that public transport occupies less road space and causes less pollution per passenger kilometre than personal vehicles. As such, public transport is a more sustainable form of transport. Therefore, the Government should promote investments in public transport as well as measures that make its use more attractive.

Comprehensive city-wide plans should be drawn up comprising trunk and feeder corridors as well as good integration with personal modes, suburban traffic etc. High cost trunk route systems should, through appropriate hub-spoke arrangements, be integrated with feeder systems that enable higher ridership on such trunk systems.

7.5 Issues in Urban Transport Policy

7.5.1 Quality and Pricing of Public Transport: So far, fares for public transport have been set on the premise that this mode of travel is used by the poor, who have no other means of meeting their travel needs. As such, fares have been kept low as a measure of social equity. This has resulted in most public transport systems being unable to recover their operating costs. It has, in fact, encouraged poorly-operated systems that have been financially sustainable only through serious compromises on the quality of the service they render.

In the present day context, however, public transport serves another social purpose. It helps reduce congestion and air pollution, if users of personal vehicles can be persuaded to shift to public transport. Their needs are, however, for improved quality and not so much for low fares. It is, therefore, necessary to think of different types of public transport services for different segments of commuters. Those who place a premium on cost are the poorest sections of society and need to be given affordable prices. The cost of providing public transport for them needs to be subsidized by other sections of society. However, there is another segment that values time saved and comfort more than price. This segment is comparatively better off and would shift to public transport if high quality systems are available to them. The cost of providing public transport to them need not be subsidized and can be met from the fare revenues. As such, the Government should encourage the provision of different levels of services—a basic service with subsidized fares and a premium service which is of high quality but charges higher fares and involves no subsidy.

7.5.2 Technologies for Public Transport: There is a wide spectrum of public transport technologies. At one end are high capacity, but high cost, technologies like underground metro systems and at the other are low capacity bus systems running on a shared right of way. Within these extremes are a range of intermediate possibilities such as buses on dedicated rights of way, elevated sky bus and monorail systems, electric trolley buses etc. While some of them are most effective over high density trunk corridors others prove useful as feeder systems or sub-systems that serve limited sub-areas within a city. Similarly, there are examples of available waterways being taken advantage of for public transport as also systems like ropeways that suit hilly terrains. While the high capacity rail systems and buses on shared rights of way are the only ones tried out in India, several of the others have proved successful in other parts of the world.

Each of these technologies has its unique characteristics and is best suited to a specific situation. Factors such as the urban form, terrain, availability of waterways, level of demand, direction and extent of sprawl, projections for future growth, extent of population density etc. are major determinants of the technology that should be chosen. While rail-based systems seem to suit dense cities with limited sprawl and only a few spinal corridors, bus systems seem better where urban densities are lower and the city has spread over a large area. Given the wide range of possibilities, it is not possible to prescribe a particular technology in a generic policy and such a choice will have to be made as a part of city-specific land use and transport plans. It would also depend on the kind of city that would need to evolve at the particular location.

It is recognized that there are several proven technologies for public transport around the world that have yet to be adopted in India. In order to build up the necessary capacity to adopt such technologies within the country, the Government should facilitate joint ventures and collaboration agreements between such technology providers and suitable Indian companies. Necessary incentives should be provided to enable such technologies to get commercialized in India. This could be by way of financing customized prototypes, development of designs to suit Indian conditions, trial operations, training of the technical personnel etc. The objective should be to ultimately build a level playing field for all proven technologies.

7.5.3 Integrated Public Transport Systems: All cities have corridors that have varying densities of travel and hence need technologies that best match the level of demand on the corridor. This often requires different operators managing such systems. However, a good public transport system is one that is perceived by the user as a single system and allows seamless travel between one mode and the other as also between systems managed by different operators. Such seamless inter-change is possible if proper inter-change infrastructure is available and users are able to use a single ticket over all such systems. This also requires that a single agency takes responsibility for co-ordination so that there is a common approach to public transport planning and management.

A rapid growth in motorization in most cities is causing the relative share of buses to decline. This is because of the following major factors:

1. Poor quality of public transport service. Although it is low cost, it is often overcrowded, dirty, unreliable and highly polluting and has important personal security and safety issues.
2. Poor access to bus services and service quality.
3. Poor image of bus and public transport.
4. Improper planning and provisioning of infrastructure facilities.
5. Improper route planning, issue of permits without any survey or scientific data.
6. Lack of passenger information systems, institutional and regulatory hurdles.
7. Lack of uniformity regarding institutional arrangements for providing public transport services.

7.5.4 Role of Para-Transit: Para-transit is normally expected to fulfil a need that neither public transport or personal vehicles are able to fulfil. They normally cater to a category of occasional trips such as trips to airports or rail stations with excessive baggage, or emergency trips that have to be undertaken immediately and it is not possible to wait for public transport. Para transit would not normally be used for regular commute trips to work or school. However, when the quality of public transport deteriorates, para-transit tends to substitute for public transport. Unfortunately, this has started happening in many Indian cities.

7.5.5 Priority to Non-motorized Transport: With increasing urban sprawl and rising income levels, non-motorized transport has lost its earlier importance. The longer trip lengths have made cycling more difficult. Further, non-motorized modes are also exposed to greater risk of accidents as they share a common right of way with motorized vehicles. However, non-motorized modes are environmentally friendly and have to be given their due share in the transport system of a city. The problems being faced by them would have to be mitigated.

First of all, the safety concerns of cyclists and pedestrians have to be addressed by encouraging the construction of segregated rights of way for bicycles and pedestrians. Apart from improving safety, the segregation of vehicles moving at different speeds would help improve traffic flow, increase the average speed of traffic and reduce emissions resulting from sub-optimal speeds. Such segregated paths would be useful not only along arterials but also as a means of improving access to major public transport stations. Such access paths, coupled with safe bicycle parking places, would contribute towards increasing the use of public transport. Creative facilities like shade giving landscaping, provision of drinking water and resting stations along bicycle corridors should also be encouraged as they can mitigate, to a large extent, adverse weather conditions.

It has been the experience that many such cycle tracks and pedestrian paths do not get used as initially envisaged. However, a view has been that this is because these facilities are designed badly and without fully recognizing the limitations and problems faced by cyclists or pedestrians. It is, therefore, essential that such facilities are constructed after an open debate on the designs with experts and the community that is expected to use them. Such public appraisal would lead to designs that enable greater use by the potential beneficiaries. Encroachment of footpaths too affects pedestrian safety adversely and requires strict enforcement coupled with public participation. Pedestrian safety is also adversely affected by the lack of safe crossing facilities at busy intersections of even high traffic corridors.

7.5.6 Parking Problems: Land is valuable in all urban areas. Parking places occupy large portions of such land. This fact should be recognized in determining the principles for allocation of parking space.

Levy of a high parking fee, that truly represents the value of the land occupied, should be used as a means to make the use of public transport more attractive. Preference in the allocation of parking space for public transport vehicles and non-motorized modes as well as easier access of work places to and from such spaces would go a long way in encouraging the use of sustainable transport systems. Park and ride facilities for bicycle users, with convenient inter-change, would be another useful measure. Simultaneously, a graded scale of parking fee, that recovers the economic cost of the land used in such parking, should be adopted. The objective should be to persuade people to use public transport to reach city centres.

7.5.7 Freight Traffic: As economic activities in cities expand and city population grows, a substantial amount of freight traffic would be generated. The timely and smooth movement of such freight is crucial to the well-being of the people and the viability of the economic activities they undertake. However, with limited capacity of the transport system, it is essential that freight traffic and passenger traffic are so staggered as to make optimum use of the transport infrastructure. It is a time-honoured and tested practice to use off-peak passenger travel times to move freight. Many cities have earmarked late night hours for the movement of freight and restricted the entry of heavy vehicles into cities during day time. Further, several cities have by-passes that enable through traffic to go around the city and not add to city traffic. These practices are sound and should be encouraged in all cities. For this purpose, cities should be encouraged to build by-passes through innovative and viable public-private partnerships. Similarly, facilities for the parking of freight vehicles outside city limits, such as truck terminals, should also be encouraged through public-private partnerships.

7.5.8 Capacity Building: The responsibility for the planning and implementation of urban transport systems rests with the State Governments and the municipal bodies. However, since the problems associated with urban transport are of relatively recent origin in India, having surfaced only from the early 1990s, the ability to understand and deal with these problems is yet to fully mature. This calls for concerted efforts at strengthening capabilities at the State and city levels to address these issues and undertake the task of developing sustainable urban transport systems.

Capacity building will have to be addressed at two levels—institutional and individual. Institutional capacity would primarily involve creating a pool of knowledge and a knowledge management centre that would sustain and enhance expertise as well as facilitate more informed planning. It should also include regular research to help formulate the right mitigation strategies, without merely adopting what other countries have tried.

At the individual level, a major exercise of training and skill development of the public officials and other public functionaries should be taken up to make such officials aware of the nuances of urban transport planning and the specific issues involved in managing city transport. This should be targeted at personnel belonging to the state transport departments, municipal corporations, metropolitan development authorities, traffic police, environmental authorities, public works departments etc.

7.5.9 Use of Cleaner Technologies: While petroleum based fuels are by far the most commonly used today, other alternatives have been emerging, though slowly. CNG has been adopted in a big way for bus and other modes of public transport in Delhi. Such cleaner technologies need to be encouraged so that the problem of vehicular pollution can be more effectively dealt with. Besides, renewable sources need to be tapped as a measure of sustainable development and in recognition of India's energy security concerns. The Government should, therefore, encourage the research, development and commercialization of cleaner technologies.

New technologies always find it difficult to enter an established market and new auto fuel technologies should also face this problem. However, in view of their many advantages, they should be offered suitable concessions and benefits that would enable them to make an entry and compete with established technologies on more equitable terms. Such competition will also encourage established technologies to improve their performance characteristics and compete with the emerging choices.

7.5.10 Poor Maintenance of Vehicles: Several vehicles on roads tend to be poorly maintained and are overly polluting. This is partly because the requirements of proper maintenance are not stringent and are largely driven only by the owner's motivation to save on fuel cost. Even where such motivation exists, the lack of a widespread network of good quality repair facilities discourages them for the exertion of having their vehicles periodically tested.

In order to overcome these problems, Government should lay down a clear and time-bound schedule of progressively tighter emission norms, with adequate lead-time, to allow the auto and oil industry to make the required investments. Measures should also be introduced to incentivize the use of fuel efficient (zero pollution) and small-sized vehicles that use up little road space and also cause low pollution. Statutory provisions should also be introduced requiring all in-use vehicles in a city, including personal motor vehicles, to undergo a periodic check up and obtain a specified certification.

7.5.11 Private Sector Participation: It is evident that huge capital investments are required in dealing with thc urban transport problems. Whether they are for constructing capital-intensive mass transit systems or segregated rights-of-way for cycles and pedestrians, a substantial financial burden would devolve on the government. Most State Governments and local bodies do not have the required resources and, therefore, alternative methods of financing would have to be explored.

The Central and State Governments should encourage partnerships and greater usc of private capital in areas where the private sector can competitively deliver urban transport services. More specifically, the greater use of private buses in city areas should be encouraged to reduce the dependence on public budgets. The commercial utilization of land resources, available with public transport service providers should be encouraged to raise additional resources.

There are several activities in which the private sector can be beneficially engaged, thereby saving financial resources for activities that only public agencies can best perform. However, these have to be done under conditions that strike a fair balance between the universal obligations of the government and the profit motive of the private operator. Accordingly, Central and State Governments should encourage a more liberal use of the private sector, especially in activities like the operation and maintenance of parking facilities certification facilities, repair facilities, construction and management of terminal facilities etc. Till the mid-1980s most public transport services were largely provided by publicly-owned State Transport Corporations. Since then, however, some States have permitted privately-run services. While public operations have tended to be high cost and most State Transport Corporations have run up heavy losses, the reliability and safety record of inadequately regulated private operators has been poor. Thus, State Governments should involve the private sector in providing public transport services, but under well-structured procurement contracts.

7.5.12 Public Awareness and Co-operation: Urban transport policies cannot succeed without the fullest co-operation of all the city residents. Such co-operation can be best secured if the objective of any initiative is made clearly known to them. It is, therefore, necessary to launch intensive awareness campaigns that educate people on the ill effects of the growing transport problems in urban areas, especially on their health and well being. The campaigns should seek their support for initiatives like greater use of public transport and non-motorized vehicles, proper maintenance of their vehicles, safer driving practices etc. Such campaigns should also encourage individuals, families and communities to adopt *green travel habits* that would make travel less polluting and damaging.

7.6 Strategies for Reducing GHG Emissions

The transport sector GHG emissions are expected to soar if it follows the path of the highly motorised nations without integrated land-use transport policies in place. This will require accelerated urban reform, improved urban structure (for example, to protect mass transit rights-of-way in the early stages of development) and urban road traffic (for example, to implement effective traffic restraint) together with innovative transport demand management and access and mobility planning to support the main social and economic activities that take place in a city.

Broadly speaking, strategies for reducing GHG emissions in the transport sector could include the following.

7.6.1 Greater Use of Non-Motorized Mode: Measures that discourage the use of personal motor vehicles would have to go hand-in-hand with measures that encourage the use of non-motorized modes, as they are *greener* modes of travel. All safety concerns of cyclists and pedestrians have to be addressed by encouraging the construction of segregated right-of-way for bicycles and pedestrians. This can be done by following measures:

1. Investing in a segregated right of way for bicycles and pedestrians.

2. Converting crowded areas like market places into no-vehicle zones.
3. Improving bicycle technology.
4. Providing safer parking facilities for bicycles in workplaces.
5. Launching public cycle programmes on public-private partnership (PPP) basis.
6. Organising cycle rickshaws through PPP.
7. Promoting cycling and walking as healthy activities.

7.6.2 Reducing Travel Demand: The greatest GHG mitigation can be achieved in the medium to long-term through proper integration of land use and transport planning to improve access to goods and services, while minimizing the need to travel through innovative means and without compromising economic growth. Travel demand is a function of population, the per capita trip rate, and the average trip length. With rapid urbanization, there is little possibility of reduction in the per capita trip rate. This is because a larger share of the population would be securing employment (especially women) and more children would be attending schools. Efforts to reduce travel demand have, therefore, to focus on reducing the average trip length.

From a transport perspective in mega cities, small and self-contained clusters are considered desirable as people are expected to move to residences that are closer to their workplace, or seek work closer to home. It is essential that the transport network guides the urban form, rather than the urban form guiding the transport system. Also, it would be equally important to link the peri-urban and rural community with fast mass transit, and promote the use of information and communication technology (ICT) policies to enhance economic development.

7.6.3 Emphasis on Railways for Passenger and Freight Transport: Conventional bus transport in crowded cities is stretched to its limits and cannot meet the rapidly growing transportation demands. Railways have to play an increasing role in the integrated multi-modal transport system to capture the new traffic thrown up by the growing Indian economy. To realize this, the railways need to seriously consider the provision of a complete logistic solution to its customers, in addition to providing superior services, running of suburban trains on SPV mode through partnering with state and city governments.

7.6.4 Tough Fuel Economy Standards: Tougher fuel economy standards would significantly increase new vehicle efficiency across the fleet. The current fuel economy standards should be averaged for each category and should take into account its economic impact. Attempts should be made to increase fuel efficiency. Indeed this may seem to be a tough measure and vehicle manufacturers may protest.

As demonstrated through experience in the USA when tough measures in this regard were taken, the initial protest from vehicle manufacturers turned to compliance. High initial cost is a major obstacle to the widespread production and sale of hybrid and fuel cell vehicles. Tax incentives could be offered in order to stimulate mass production and support initial sales of these innovative vehicles. The amount of the tax incentive (or most of the incentive) should be based on the fuel economy achieved. Also vehicles should have relatively low pollutant emissions as well as high fuel efficiency in order to be eligible for a tax incentive. Taxes and duties on public transport vehicles and taxies should be much lower than that on personal vehicles.

7.6.5 Alternate Fuels: The Ministry of New and Renewable Energy is also promoting programmes for the development of alternative systems of fuel/fuel systems for transportation like battery operated vehicles (BOV), hydrogen and fuel cell based vehicles and bio-fuel operated vehicles. Among the bio-fuels, use of ethanol as a fuel is also one of the prominent alternative fuels.

Battery operated vehicles can have niche applications for replacing fossil fuel vehicles in hospitals, sanctuaries, zoos, bio-sphere reserves etc. However, for general use, more focus should be on development and deployment of hybrid vehicles (HV) which have a better performance in terms of speed and range. The transition to BOVs/HVs can be achieved through the appropriate policy support, fiscal incentives and technology development. Technology development should be supported in the area of BOVs and HVs to achieve increased operational range, mass production and commercial availability at affordable prices. There is a need to develop high energy and power density, light weight and inexpensive batteries and also to improve the overall performance, reliability, and durability of the BOVs. Several companies, research groups/institutions are developing different types of advanced batteries for use in electric vehicles.

7.6.6 Use of Hydrogen: Combustion of hydrogen in engines/turbines does not produce pollutants like carbon monoxide and hydrocarbons as in the case of fossil fuels. However, oxides of nitrogen are present in the exhaust from the engine/vehicle. However, when hydrogen is used as a fuel in fuel cells, there are no pollutants emitted through the tail pipe of the vehicle, and water is the only product of the electro-chemical reaction in fuel cells. A National Hydrogen Energy Road Map has been prepared under the aegis of the Ministry of New and Renewable Energy (MNRE). The road map envisages that about one million hydrogen-fuelled vehicles would ply on Indian roads by 2020. About 75 percent of these vehicles would be two and three wheelers. However implementation of this technology would entail resolution of technological challenges as well as challenges related to creation of distribution infrastructure.

Compressed natural gas (CNG) blended with hydrogen has been used as a fuel in the USA and European countries and it has been observed that emissions (carbon monoxide and unburnt CNG) from the vehicles, which use such blended fuel, are lower as compared to the vehicles using only CNG as fuel. However, emissions of oxides of nitrogen are found to be higher.

7.6.7 Bio-fuels: Bio-fuels can be defined as combustible fuels produced from biomass. These fuels are generally in the form of alcohols, esters, ethers and other chemicals produced from biomass. The two most common types of bio-fuels that can be used in vehicles are ethanol and bio-diesel. Use of bio-fuels as a blend to fossil fuels can provide a solution for reducing the emission problems. Another promising technology is that of cellulosic ethanol as the annual generation of cellulosic biomass from crop residues in India is significant. However, the available technology is not yet competitive with petroleum based fuels.

7.7 Fiscal and Control Measures

Fiscal measures to strengthen public transport system could include charging of fee for using congested parts of a city, levying of high parking fees, increasing vehicle registration charges and increasing fuel tax, pollution-based annual road tax (where low-powered, low-emission, hybrid and newer vehicles pay less road tax than the high-powered, higher-emission and poorly maintained old vehicles), etc. Such fiscal measures can help reduce private vehicle operation leading to reduced congestion and air pollution. Some initiatives in this direction have already been taken by the Ministry of Urban Development at the centre by advising the states to consider levying an additional registration fee on cars and two-wheelers so that the additional cess on vehicles could be set aside in a dedicated transport fund and used for financing public transport at the state as well at the city level.

In addition, the Ministry has suggested that the states levy additional sales tax on vehicles besides imposing cess on renewal of permits of commercial vehicles as also on the renewal fee on driving licences and vehicle registration. If all the States were to agree to the suggestion, the Ministry's calculations estimate an annual mop up of ₹ 25,000 crore through the dedicated taxes that could solve the hardship which the urban commuters face across India. To avail central assistance for transport projects under the JNNURM, the MoUD has requested the state governments to submit action taken reports on NUTP which underlines the need for setting up a dedicated transport fund for revamping the public transport system.

A World Bank estimate shows that the total tax burden per vehicle per km. is 2.3 times higher for public transport buses than cars in Indian cities which needs to be rationalized and harmonised with a view to improve the public transport system. Besides, the existing tax structure for commercial vehicles shows wide variations across states due to different classification of principles for the taxation of vehicles, variations in the application of lifetime and annual tax rates to vehicle categories, use of specific and ad valorem rates and the multiplicity of rates. There is a need to study the economic implications of rationalization and harmonization of the tax structure across the country in terms of its impact on the reduction of transaction costs. In addition, the cost of modern buses has to be brought down through reduction in tax and duties so as to make their introduction financially viable. Presently the cost of various central taxes and duties and also state taxes account for 30 percent to 35 percent of the total cost for the modern buses.

Control measures include physical restrictions on the use of personal vehicles in some corridors, limiting the availability of parking space in city centres, using parking fee as a travel demand management (TDM) measure, banning of parking on arterial roads, having a parking policy for the city, limiting the availability of road space for personal vehicles, restricting ownership of vehicles to mitigate emissions and making owning of parking space compulsory to acquire a new private vehicle. A good parking policy with parking charges reflecting the economic cost of land use of such parking, graded scale of parking fee, differential rate of parking during peak hours and non peak hours and differential rates for street parking (which should be high) etc. can be used as not only as an effective measure of controlling the demand for personal vehicle uses, but also for generating resources for a dedicated urban transport fund which can be used to provide public transport.

A good example of control measures is the congestion-charge operating in Singapore and more recently, in London, as well as the quota-based certificate of entitlement scheme for restricting vehicle ownership in Singapore. Both measures are enforced to change the preferences of people and promote public transport systems.

Besides, with a view to rid the sector of unscrupulous practices and to improve the quality of service, a prerequisite is strict enforcement of rules. For this, specially designated regulatory bodies need to be set up, with the authority to lay down minimum basic service standards for the industry, impose heavy fines, suspend or even cancel licenses and launch and vigorously pursue prosecutions for accidents. Only then will it be possible to attract large players and enhance the attractiveness of investment in this industry.

To sum up, fast growth of urban population, spread of urban areas and spurt in secondary and tertiary activities have led to urban transport problems like severe traffic congestions, slowing down of vehicular movement, high air and noise pollution, longer journey hours, increasing costs of travel etc. Urban transport is an important service sector and plays a crucial role in the development of the urban economy and the time has come to take stock of the urban transport scenario.

India is poised for rapid economic growth. Such future growth will largely come from the secondary and tertiary sectors of the economy, i.e., industrial and service sectors. Since economic activities in these sectors primarily take place in urban areas, the state of towns and cities is crucial to India's future growth. Further, India's urban population is currently around 30 percent of its total population. Experience across the world has been that as economies grow, rapid urbanization takes this proportion to over 60 percent before it begins to stabilize. Hence, cities must not only meet the mobility needs of the current population but also provide for the needs of those yet to join the urban population.

8

Urban Health Security and Services

At the time of Independence in 1947, healthcare services in India were utterly inadequate, urban-based and curative in nature. Majority of the population, especially the poor and those residing in rural areas, did not have access to modern health facilities. Consequently, the morbidity and mortality rates were quite high. Many women died while seeking abortion to get rid of unwanted pregnancy because access to contraceptives for preventing pregnancies was not available. Similarly, antenatal and postnatal care and services were poor and out of reach for majority of women and their families.

Improvement in the health status of the population has been one of the major thrust areas in social development programmes of India since Independence. Over the past six decades, India has built up a vast health infrastructure and manpower at primary, secondary and tertiary care levels in the government, voluntary and private sectors manned by professionals and para-medicals. India has invested massive amounts under the successive Five Year Plans in medical education, training and research which has ensured large manpower from the super-specialists to the auxiliary midwives.

Efforts are continuing to improve the access to and utilization of health, family welfare and nutrition services with special focus on under-served and under-privileged segments of population. Technological improvements and increased access to healthcare have resulted in a steep fall in mortality rate, but the burden of communicable and non-communicable diseases, environmental pollution and nutritional problems continues to be high. In spite of the fact that norms for creation of infrastructure and manpower are similar throughout the country, there remain substantial variations among states and districts within a state in availability and utilization of healthcare services and health indices of the population.

Current policies and programmes are aimed to provide essential supplies, improve efficiency and ensure accountability especially in states where performance is sub-optimal. In view of the massive inter-regional differences in the availability and utilization of health services and health indices of the population, a differential strategy is envisaged so that there is incremental improvement in all states and districts within a state. This in turn is expected to result in substantial improvement in state and national indices and enable the country to achieve the goals set for the future.

Presently, India has a vast network of governmental, voluntary and private health infrastructure manned by large number of medical and paramedical persons.

8.1 Importance of Health

Health is fundamental to national progress in any sphere. In terms of resources for economic development, nothing can be considered of higher importance than the health of the people which is a measure of their energy and capacity as well as of the potential of man-hours for productive work in relation to the total number of persons maintained by the nation. For the efficiency of industry and of agriculture, the health of the worker is an essential consideration.

Health is a positive state of well being in which the harmonious development of physical and mental capacities of the individual lead to the enjoyment of a rich and full life. It is not a negative state of mere absence of disease. Health further implies complete adjustment of the individual to his total environment, physical and social. Health involves primarily the application of medical science for the benefit of the individual and of society. However, many other factors, social, economic and educational have an intimate bearing on the health of the community. Health is thus a vital part of the concurrent and integrated programme of development of all aspects of community life.

The output of an industrial worker in India is low compared with that of the worker in other countries. The productive capacity of an agricultural worker is comparatively low. The loss caused by morbidity in working time is enormous. To this, must be added the expenditure to the individual and to the State in the provision of medical care.

8.2 Healthcare in Indian Constitution

Health security is one of the major components of human development. Good health is not only an end product of development but also a necessary condition for economic development. Improved health contributes to economic growth by reducing production losses due to illness of workers. There is a significant relation between income growth and health.

Healthcare is also an important component of social security. Indeed medical care is widely regarded as the primary branch of social security since health is of concern to all age groups and all categories of employees. All comprehensive social security programmes, therefore, make provision for medical care.

Entry 6 in the State List (List II) in the Seventh Schedule of the Constitution of India reads: "Public health and sanitation, hospitals and dispensaries". Thus public health is a State subject in India. However, population control and family planning are areas of common interest for the Central and State Governments as they find place in the Concurrent List (List III) [Entry 20A] in the Seventh Schedule of the Constitution.

According to the Directive Principles of State Policy laid down in the Constitution, raising the level of nutrition, and the standard of living and the improvement of public health are among the primary duties of the State. Improvement in the health status of the population has been one of the major thrust areas for the social development programmes of the country.

Public spending on health in India at 1 percent of GDP is

amongst the lowest in the world whereas its proportion of private spending on health is one of the highest. Households in India spend about 5-6 percent of their consumption expenditure on health. The cost of services in the private sector makes it unaffordable for the poor and the underprivileged.

8.3 Health Indices of India and Selected Asian Countries

The comparative picture with regard to health indicators such as life expectancy, total fertility rate (TFR), maternal mortality ratio (MMR) and infant mortality rate (IMR) reveals that India is lagging behind other Asian countries such as Indonesia, Sri Lanka and China (Table 8.1).

Table 8.1: Health Indicators of Selected Asian Countries

Country	Life Expectancy (years)		TFR	MMR	IMR
	Male	Female			
Japan	78.9	86.1	1.35	10	3
Sri Lanka	72.2	77.5	1.89	92	15
China	70.6	74.2	1.72	56	32
Indonesia	66.2	69.9	2.25	230	36
India	63.9	66.9	2.90	301	58
Pakistan	64.0	64.3	3.87	500	73

TFR = Total Fertility Rate; MMR = Maternal Mortality Ratio per 1,00,000 live births; IMR = Infant Mortality Rate per 1,000 live births.

Source: Government of India, Planning Commission, *Eleventh Five Year Plan* (2007-12), Vol., II, p. 58, Table 3.1.1 (excerpted).

8.4 Healthcare Trends in India

Improvement in the health status of the population is a major thrust area under the social development programmes being undertaken in the country. This is sought to the achieved through improvement in the access to and utilization of health services in the country with special focus on under-served and under-privileged segments of the population. India has built up a vast health infrastructure and manpower at primary, secondary and tertiary care in government, voluntary and private sectors. Technological advances and improvement in access to healthcare technologies have resulted in a substantial improvement in health indices of the population and a steep decline in mortality (Table 8.2). However, the extent of access to and utilization of healthcare has varied substantially between States, districts and different segments of society.

Table 8.2: Select Indicators of Healthcare Progress of India

Indicator	1950-51	2011-12
Birth-rate (per 1,000)	39.9	21.8
Death-rate (per 1,000)	27.4	7.1
Life expectancy at birth (years)	32.1	66.1
Male	32.5	64.6
Female	31.7	67.7
Registered medical practitioners (per 10,000 population)	1.7	7.6
Hospital beds (per 10,000 population)	3.2	9.5

Source: Government of India, *Economic Survey*, 2012-13, Statistical Appendix, Tables 01, 9.1 and 9.4 (excerpted).

India has entered an era of *dual disease burden.* While communicable diseases have become more difficult to combat due to insecticide resistance among vectors, resistance to antibiotics in many bacteria and emergence of new diseases such as HIV increasing longevity and the changes in life style have resulted in the increasing prevalence of non-communicable diseases.

8.5 Health Indices in Rural and Urban India

Public healthcare system in rural areas in many States and regions is in shambles. Extreme inequalities and disparities persist both in terms of access to healthcare as well as health outcomes (Table 8.3). This large disparity across India places the burden on the poor, especially women, scheduled castes and tribes. Inequity is also reflected in the availability of public resources between the advanced and less developed States.

Urban growth has led to increase in number of urban poor. Though the coverage of health and family welfare services in urban areas is much better than the rural, lack of water and sanitation and the high population density in slums leads to rapid spread of infections. These settlements have high incidence of vector borne diseases, asthma, TB, malaria, coronary heart diseases, diabetes etc. Poor housing conditions, exposure to heat and cold, air and water pollution and occupational hazards add to the environmental risks for the poor. They are further made vulnerable, as they have no back up savings, food stocks or social support systems to tide over the crisis of illness. Despite the presence of so many private and government hospitals in urban areas, large chunk of homeless and those living in slums or temporary settlements are left out of the proper healthcare system. Thus, even though there is a concentration of healthcare facilities in urban areas, the urban poor lack access to them and initiatives in this regard have been limited and fragmented.

Table 8.3: Rural-Urban Health Indicators in India

	CBR	CDR	IMR	Anaemia among Children (6-35 months) (percent)	Anaemia among Pregnant Women (percent)
Urban	19.1	6.0	40	72.7	54.6
Rural	25.6	8.1	64	81.2	59.0
Total	23.8	7.6	58	79.2	57.9

CBR = Crude Birth Rate per 1,000; CDR = Crude Death Rate per 1,000; IMR = Infant Mortality Rate per 1,000 live births.

Source: Government of India, Planning Commission, *Eleventh Five Year Plan* (2007-12), Volume II, p. 61, Table 3.1.3.

8.6 Shortcomings of the Public Health System

The public health system in India has various drawbacks.

The Eleventh Five Year Plan (2007-12) pointed out the following drawbacks:

- "Centralised planning instead of decentralised planning using locally relevant strategies.
- Institutions based on population norms rather than habitations.
- Fragmented disease specific approach rather than comprehensive healthcare.
- Inflexible financing and limited scope for innovations.
- Semi-used or dysfunctional health infrastructure.
- Inadequate provision of human resources.
- No prescribed standards of quality.
- Inability of system to mobilize action in areas of safe water, sanitation, hygiene and nutrition (key determinants of health in the context of our country)—lack of convergence.
- Inability to mobilize AYUSH and RMPs and other locally available human resources". [1]

[AYUSH = Ayurveda, Yoga and Naturopathy, Unani, Siddha and Homeopathy; RMPs = Registered Medical Practitioners].

8.7 National Urban Health Mission (NUHM)

NUHM is designed to meet health needs of the urban poor, particularly the slum dwellers by making available to them essential primary healthcare services. This is done by investing in high calibre health professionals, appropriate technology through public-private partnership and health insurance for urban poor. Recognizing the seriousness of the problem, urban health was taken up as a thrust area during the Eleventh Plan. At the State level, besides the State Health Mission and State Health Society and Directorate, there is a State Urban Health Programme Committee. At the district level, similarly there is a District Urban Health Committee and at the city level, a Health and Sanitation Planning Committee.

At the ward slum level, there is a Slum Cluster Health and Water and Sanitation Committee. For promoting public health and cleanliness in urban slums, Eleventh Plan encompassed experiences of civil society organizations working in urban slum clusters. It sought to build a bridge of NGO-government partnership and develop community level monitoring of resources and their rightful use.

NUHM ensures the following:

1. Resources for addressing the health problems in urban areas, especially among urban poor.
2. Need based city specific urban healthcare system to meet the diverse health needs of the urban poor and other vulnerable sections.
3. Partnership with community for a more proactive involvement in planning, implementation and monitoring of health activities.
4. Institutional mechanism and management systems to meet the health related challenges of a rapidly growing urban population.
5. Framework for partnerships with NGOs, Charitable hospitals and other stakeholders.
6. Two-tier system of risk pooling: (a) women's Mahila Arogya Samiti to fulfil urgent hard cash needs for treatments and (b) a health insurance scheme for enabling urban poor to meet medical treatment needs.

NUHM covers all cities with a population of more than 1,00,000. It covers slum dwellers, other marginalized urban dwellers like rickshaw pullers, street vendors, railway and bus station coolies, homeless people, street children, construction site workers, who may be in slums or on sites.

Urban health posts (UHPs) and urban family welfare centres (UFWCs) function under NUHM. They are marked on a map and classified as urban health centres, on the basis of their current population coverage.

8.8 Sarva Swasthya Abhiyan (SSA)

Tenth Five Year Plan (2002-07) indicated the dismal picture of the health services infrastructure and emphasized the need to invest more on building good primary-level care and referral services. The plan emphasized on restructuring and developing the health infrastructure, especially at the primary level. The plan highlighted the importance of the role of decentralization but did not state how this would be achieved. Programme-driven healthcare was in focus. Verticality and technical solutions were given more importance than the comprehensive primary healthcare. The multi-sectoral approach that is much needed for a vibrant health system had not been well thought out.

Eleventh Five Year Plan (2007-12) envisaged inclusive growth by introducing National Urban Health Mission (NUHM) which along with National Rural Health Mission (NRHM) forms Sarva Swasthya Abhiyan (SSA).

NRHM was launched for meeting health needs of all age groups and reduce disease burden across rural India. NUHM was launched to meet the unmet needs of the urban population. NUHM based on health insurance and public-private partnership provides integrated health service delivery to the urban poor. Initially, the focus was on urban slums. NUHM was aligned with NRHM and existing urban schemes. Besides, SSA aims for inclusive growth by finding solutions for strengthening health services and focusing on neglected areas and groups.

8.9 Ayurveda, Yoga & Naturopathy, Unani, Siddha and Homeopathy (AYUSH)

Health sector trends suggest that no single system of healthcare has the capacity to solve all of society's health needs. The Ministry of AYUSH was formed on November 9, 2014 for enhanced health care to the public. Of late, there is a resurgence of interest in holistic systems of healthcare, especially in the prevention and management of chronic lifestyle-related non-communicable diseases and systemic diseases. India can be a world leader in the area of integrative medicine because it has strong foundations in western biomedical sciences and an immensely rich and mature indigenous medical heritage of its own.

The AYUSH sector across the country supports a network of 3,277 hospitals and 24,289 dispensaries. The health services provided by this network largely focus on primary healthcare. In the private and not-for-profit sector there are several thousand AYUSH clinics and around 250 hospitals and nursing homes for in-patient care and specialized therapies like Panchkarma. In clinics and nursing homes there are anecdotal reports of the role of AYUSH in the successful management of several communicable and non-communicable diseases.

Eleventh Plan envisaged following key interventions and strategies for the AYUSH sector:

1. Training in public health for AYUSH personnel as an essential part of education and continuing medical education.
2. Mainstreaming the system of AYUSH in National Healthcare Delivery System by co-locating AYUSH facilities in primary health network.
3. Restructuring public health management to integrate AYUSH practitioners into the National healthcare system.
4. Promoting scientific validation of AYUSH principles, remedies and therapies.
5. Revitalizing, documenting and validating local health traditions of AYUSH.
6. Improving the status of quality of clinical services by creating specialty AYUSH secondary and tertiary care centres.
7. Ensuring conservation of medicinal plants gene pools as well as promoting cultivation of species in high trade and establishment of medicinal plants processing zones.
8. Strengthening regulatory mechanism for ensuring quality control, R&D and processing technology involving accredited laboratories in the Government and non-government sector.
9. Establishing centres of excellence.
10. Promoting public awareness about the strengths and contemporary relevance of AYUSH.

8.10 Growth of Private Sector in Healthcare

Growth of private health sector in India has been considerable in both provision and financing. There is diversity in the composition of the private sector, which ranges from voluntary, not-for-profit, corporates, trusts, stand-alone specialist services, diagnostic services, pharmacy shops and a range of highly qualified to unqualified providers, each addressing different market segments.

Private sector is flourishing primarily because of the failure of the public sector. The growth of private hospitals and diagnostic centres was also encouraged by the Central and State Governments by offering tax exemptions and land at concessional rates, in return for provision of free treatment for the poor as a certain proportion of outpatients and inpatients. Apart from subsidies, private corporate hospitals receive huge amounts of public funds in the form of reimbursements from the public sector undertakings, the Central and the State governments for treating their employees.

The cost of healthcare in the private sector is much higher than the public sector. Many small providers have poor knowledge base and tend to follow irrational, ineffective and sometimes even harmful practices for treating minor ailments. Bulk of the qualified medical practitioners and nurses are subject to self-regulation by their respective State Medical Councils under central legislation. In practice, however, regulation of these professionals is weak and close to non-existent.

8.11 Health Insurance

Health insurance is a common form of medical protection all over the world and till recently it was available only to Government employees and workers in the organised sector. Private health insurance has been in operation for several years, but its coverage is limited.

Ensuring good health for all, particularly the poor, is a complex issue in India with its huge geographical area, large population and inequity of resources. Health system is a mix of the public and private sectors, with the NGOs and civil society still playing a very small, though important, role.

Coverage of health insurance in India is pathetically limited. Traditionally healthcare insurance in the country has been limited to the Employees State Insurance (ESI) schemes for industrial workers, the Central Government Health Scheme (CGHS) for employees and pensioners of the Central Government and the Ex-servicemen Contributory Health Scheme (ECSH) for the former armed forces personnel.

After general insurance was opened up to the private sector and further to foreign direct investment (FDI), there has been a considerable expansion of health insurance, covering mainly the urban upper-middle class. However, healthcare insurance schemes have experienced problems such as high premium, delay in settling claims and non-transparent procedures in deciding reimbursements. The system of third party administrators (TPAs) has facilitated cash payments and expanded access to providers and as a result delivery of healthcare services to the upper middle class has improved. Other segments of the population, the below poverty line (BPL) categories in particular, have remained deprived of the benefits of health insurance in the country.

Side by side with the development of health insurance on a commercial basis, the country has seen the emergence of community-based health insurance (CBHI). CBHI is a not-for-profit insurance scheme managed by the members themselves on the basis of collective pooling of health risks. CBHI schemes are being operated by organizations such as Karuna Trust, and Self-employed Women's Association (SEWA).

India has a huge working population of about 400 million. Almost 93 percent of this work force is in the unorganized sector. There are numerous occupational groups in economic activities, passed on from generation to generation, scattered all over the country with differing employer-employee relationship. Those in the organized sector of the economy, whether in the public or private sector, have access to some form of health service coverage. The unorganized sector workers have no access. The National Commission for Enterprises in the Unorganized Sector (NCEUS) [Chairman: Arjun Sengupta], 2009 had recommended a specific health scheme in incidences of illness and hospitalization for workers and their families.

8.11.1 Aam Admi Bima Yojana (AABY), 2007: Group insurance schemes do not attract unorganized sector workers or the organizations working for their welfare and development because the schemes do not provide the annuity in the cases of survivor members.

All categories of unorganized workers are not covered under the existing schemes of social security. Further, lack of awareness about schemes amongst rural population and the poor delivery mechanism at the village level contribute to the ineffectiveness of the programmes.

Taking the above factors into account, Government of India launched AABY on October 2, 2007. AABY is a scheme for death and disability cover of rural landless in the country in conjunction with the State Governments. The members of rural landless households, in the age-group of 18-59 years are eligible. The premium of ₹ 200 per member, is borne by the Centre and States equally. The State Government is the Nodal Agency. A sum of ₹ 30,000 in case of natural death and ₹ 75,000 in case of accidental death is payable.

A compensation of ₹ 75,000 is payable in case of total permanent disability and of ₹ 37,500 in case of partial permanent disability. The scheme also has a provision for the payment of a scholarship of ₹ 300 per quarter per child for two children of the beneficiaries studying in 9th to 12th standard for its beneficiaries.

8.11.2 Rashtriya Swasthaya Bima Yojana (RSBY), 2007: In order to provide accessible, affordable and accountable quality health services to households in rural areas, the Government launched the National Rural Health Mission (NRHM). The principle thrust of NRHM is to make public system fully functional at all levels and to place a framework which would reduce the distress of households in seeking healthcare system through health insurance scheme. Many efforts in the past for providing health insurance for the rural poor have not been successful because of inadequacies in design and implementation. The cost of insurance coupled with lack of perception of the benefits in the target group, and the procedure for claiming reimbursements have posed serious challenges in the administration. A transparent scheme which lists the entitlements, administered through a smart card obviating the need for out-of-pocket expenses is needed to streamline the administration, ensuring the benefits.

With these objectives in view, the Government of India launched RSBY for Below Poverty Line (BPL) families in the unorganized sector on October 1, 2007. The scheme covers all BPL unorganized sector workers and their families (of five members), whose identity is verified by the implementing agency and issued a smart card.

RSBY provides for cash-less, smart card based health insurance cover of ₹ 30,000 per annum to each enrolled family, comprising up to five individuals. The beneficiary family pays only ₹ 30 per annum as registration/renewal fee. The scheme covers hospitalization expenses (out-patient expenses are not covered), including maternity benefit, and pre-existing diseases. A transportation cost of ₹ 100 per visit is also paid. The premium payable to insurance agencies is funded by Central and State Governments in a 75:25 ratio, which is relaxed to 90:10 for the North-East region and Jammu and Kashmir. The maximum premium by the Central Government is limited to ₹ 750 per insured family per year.

The package of benefits include: (a) cashless attendance to all covered ailments, (b) hospitalization expenses, taking care of most common illnesses, (c) all pre-existing diseases to be covered, and (d) transportation costs subject to prescribed limits payable to the beneficiary. Flexibility is provided to the States to add to the benefits, by meeting the additional premium requirements from their own resources. State Governments decide the implementing agency and also bear the administrative costs.

RSBY was originally limited to below poverty line (BPL) families but was later extended to building and other construction workers, MGNREGA beneficiaries, street vendors, beedi workers, and domestic workers. The scheme is currently being implemented in 24 States/UTs. About 3.71 crore cards have been issued and 72 lakh persons have availed hospitalisation under the scheme till April 30, 2014.

An important feature of RSBY is that it provides for private health service providers to be included in the system, if they meet certain standards and agree to provide cash-less treatment which is reimbursed by the insurance company. This has the advantage of giving patients a choice between alternative service providers where such alternatives are available. Several State Governments (such as those of Andhra Pradesh and Tamil Nadu) have introduced their own health insurance schemes, which often have a more generous total cover.

8.12 Twelfth Five Year Plan (2012-17) on Health

According to Twelfth Plan, "Health is another critical dimension of human capability, which needs much greater attention in the Twelfth Plan. At present, less than 30 percent of outpatient and less than half of inpatient health care capacity of the country is in the public sector, and the majority of the population relies on private health care provision which often imposes a heavy financial burden. It is, therefore, essential to expand public sector capacity in healthcare especially in the rural areas. The NRHM, launched during the Tenth Plan, made an important start in expanding health care facilities in rural areas. While additional infrastructure has been created, there are large shortages of personnel, especially specialists in rural health facilities, reflecting the fact that trained human resources in health are in short supply and it takes many years to set up new medical colleges to train the required number of doctors.

Ideally, the public health care system must be expanded to address the health needs of the vast majority of citizens, recognising that upper-income groups may opt for private health care. The Twelfth Plan will therefore see the transformation of the NRHM into a National Health Mission, covering both rural and urban areas. Unlike rural residents, those in urban areas have access to private health care providers, but private health care is costly and large numbers of urban residents especially slum dwellers cannot afford it. An important component of the National Health Mission will be the Urban Health Initiative for the Poor, providing public sector primary care facilities in selected low-income urban areas. This will require additional resources in the public sector from the budgets of both the Centre and the States, and cities". [2]

To sum up, health of a nation is an essential component of development, vital to its economic growth and internal stability. Assuring a minimal level of healthcare to the population is a critical constituent of the development process. Considerable achievements have been made since Independence in 1947 to improve health standards such as increase in life expectancy, decrease in infant and maternal mortality, and eradication of small pox and guinea worm. Nevertheless, problems abound. Malnutrition affects a large proportion of the population especially women and children. An unacceptably high proportion of the population continues to suffer and die from new diseases apart from the existing ones. Pregnancy and childbirth related complications also contribute to the suffering and mortality of women.

There is a strong link between poverty and ill-health. Ill health creates immense stress even among those who are financially secure. Onset of a long and expensive illness can drive the economically well-off into poverty. The importance of public provisioning of quality healthcare to enable access to affordable and reliable heath services cannot be underestimated. This is specially so in the context of preventing the non-poor from entering into poverty and reducing the suffering of those who are already below poverty line.

Endnotes

1. Government of India, Planning Commission, *Eleventh Five Year Plan* (2007-12), Volume II, p. 67.
2. Government of India, Planning Commission, *Twelfth Five Year Plan (2012-17)*, Volume I, Chapter 1, paras 1.57 and 1.58.

9

Education, Training and Skill Development

Education has been a thrust sector ever since India attained Independence in 1947. Right from the inception of planning, the crucial role of education in economic and social development has been recognised and emphasised. Efforts to increase people's participation in education and to diversify educational programmes in order to promote knowledge and skills required for nation-building have characterised successive Five Year Plans. Despite a series of problems that the country faced soon after independence, it has been possible to create a vast educational infrastructure in terms of large enrolments and teaching force and massive capabilities for management, research and development.

9.1 Constitutional Provisions Regarding Education

Vide Entry 25 of List III (Concurrent List) in the Seventh Schedule of the Constitution of India, education is a concurrent subject and hence a subject of common interest to both the Central and State Governments.

In a historic move, the Constitution (Eighty-sixth Amendment) Act, 2002, amended the Constitution by inserting Article 21A which reads as follows: "The State shall provide free and compulsory education to all children of the age of six to fourteen years in such manner as the State may, by law, determine". This was a significant measure for achieving the goal of Education for All (EFA) by making free and compulsory elementary education a fundamental right for all children in the age group of 6-14 years.

Again, the year 2010 was a landmark for education in India as the Right of Children to Free and Compulsory Education (RTE), Act, 2009 was enforced with effect from April 1, 2010.

RTE Act, 2009, representing the consequential legislation to the Constitution (Eighty-sixth Amendment) Act, 2002, secures the right of children to free and compulsory education till completion of elementary education in a neighbourhood school. RTE Act, 2009 lays down norms and standards relating to pupil teacher ratios, buildings and infrastructure, school working days and working hours of teachers.

In order to fulfil the constitutional obligation, *Sarva Shiksha Abhiyan* was launched in partnership with the States. The programme is an effort towards recognition of the need for improving the performance of the school system through a community-owned approach and ensuring quality elementary education in a mission mode to all children in the age group of 6-14 years by 2010. It also seeks to bridge gender and social gaps. This programme subsumed all existing programmes (except *Mahila Samakhya* and Mid-day Meal Schemes) including externally-aided programmes with its overall framework with district as the unit of programmes implementation.

9.2 Trends in Literacy Rates

Though the level and quality of education can be measured in a number of ways, literacy figures are essential in any measurement of educational attainment. The level of literacy is an important and the most basic index of the educational achievements of an economy.

Literacy levels in a country are a measure of its degree of commitment to social justice. A literate environment is essential for ensuring universal elementary education, reducing child mortality, curbing population growth, ensuring gender equality and acquiring essential livelihood skills.

Over the decades, literacy rates in India have shown a substantial improvement (Table 9.1).

To enlist the support of all concerned and to mobilize extra budgetary resources for the education sector, *Bharat Shiksha Kosh*, a registered society has been set up for receiving contributions, donations or endowments from individuals,

Central and State governments, and non-resident Indians (NRIs) for various educational purposes. Emphasizing the role of education, Eleventh Five Year Plan (2007-12) observed, "The role of education in facilitating social and economic progress is well recognized. It opens up opportunities leading to both individual and group entitlements. Education in its broadest sense of development of youth is the most crucial input for empowering people with skills and knowledge and giving them access to productive employment in future. Improvements in education are not only expected to enhance efficiency but also augment the overall quality of life". [2]

Table 9.1: Literacy Rates in India (1951-2011)

(percent)

Census Year	Persons	Males	Females	Male-Female Gap in Literacy Rate
1951	18.33	27.16	8.66	18.30
1961	28.30	40.40	15.35	25.05
1971	34.45	45.96	21.97	23.98
1981	43.57	56.38	29.76	26.62
1991	52.21	64.13	39.29	24.84
2001	65.38	75.85	54.16	21.70
2011	74.00	82.2	65.5	16.70

Source: Census Reports.

9.3 Elementary Education

From the stand point of priorities within the field of education, importance should be attached, in terms of coverage, to children in the school going age-groups and those among the socially under-privileged groups. This early childhood stage is the period of maximum learning and intellectual development of the child and hence of great potential educational significance.

In India, within the education sector, elementary education has been given the highest priority in terms of sub-sectoral allocations and the number of schemes launched by the Central Government to meet the needs of the educationally disadvantaged. Elementary education, i.e. classes I-VIII consisting of primary (I-V) and upper primary (VI-VIII) is the foundation of the structure of the education system.

9.3.1 ***Sarva Shiksha Abhiyan*** **(SSA):** Launched in November 2000, SSA is a comprehensive programme and the main vehicle for providing elementary education to all children. The goals of SSA are the following.

1. All children in school, education guarantee centre, alternate school, back-to-school camp by 2005.
2. Bridge all gender and social category gaps at the primary stage by 2007 and at elementary education level by 2010.
3. Universal retention by 2010.
4. Focus on elementary education of satisfactory quality with emphasis on education for life.

SSA, implemented in partnership with the States, addresses the needs of 192 million children in the age group of 6-14 years. It covers 9.72 lakh existing primary and upper primary schools and 36.95 lakh teachers.

SSA is the culmination of all previous endeavours and experiences in implementing various education programmes. SSA has been the single largest holistic programme addressing all aspects of elementary education. SSA has brought primary education to the doorstep of millions of children and enrolled them, including first generation learners, through successive fast track initiatives in hitherto unserved and underserved habitations.

According to Eleventh Plan, "SSA interventions have brought down the number of out of school children from 32 million in 2001-02 to 7.1 million in 2005-06. Forty eight districts in 10 States accounted for over 50,000 out of school children each. The number of such districts declined to 29 in 2005-06". [3]

Strong efforts are needed to address the systemic issues of regular functioning of schools, teacher attendance and competence, accountability of educational administrators, pragmatic teacher transfer and promotion policies, effective decentralization of school management and transfer of powers to panchayati raj institutions (PRIs), to build upon the gains of SSA.

9.4 Secondary and Vocational Education

A sound system of secondary education, which offers openings in a large number of different directions, is an essential foundation for economic development on modern lines. With the expansion of elementary education, an increasing number of students reach the secondary stage. The year 2008-09 was a momentous year for secondary education in India when a new Centrally sponsored scheme to universalise education at secondary stage was launched.

9.4.1 Secondary Education: Secondary education sector prepares students in the age group of 14-18 years for entry into higher education as well as for the world of work. The success of *Sarva Shiksha Abhiyan* (SSA) in achieving large-scale enrolment of children in regular and alternate schools has thrown open the challenge of expanding access to secondary education. Rapid changes in technology and the demand for skills also make it necessary that young people acquire more than eight years of elementary education to acquire the necessary skills to compete successfully in the labour market. Moreover, secondary education serves as a bridge between elementary and higher education.

9.4.2 Vocational Education: Vocational training is broadly defined as training that prepares an individual for a specific vocation or occupation. Vocational education remains within the broader school curriculum and involves provision of specific skills to increase the employability of the students on completion of formal education. Vocational training is especially for a particular trade or economic activity and is conducted outside the schooling system. There are three categories of vocational education prevalent in India today: at the lower school stage, at the class 10+2 stage and at the specialised level.

Secondary education must be closely related to the psychological needs of the adolescents for whom it is being designed. In order to equip the youth adequately for the needs of the existing socio-economic situation, it is necessary to give secondary education a vocational bias. At present, this education is mainly academic and does not provide sufficient scope for adolescents with varying aptitudes especially those with a marked practical bent of mind.

The two flagship schemes of Directorate General for Employment and Training under Ministry of Labour and Employment are the craftsmen training scheme (CTS) and the apprenticeship training scheme (ATS). The CTS provides institutional training whereas ATS is a combination of institutional as well as on-the-job training in which trainees are exposed to real life industrial environment.

The CTS is implemented through over 10,750 industrial training institutes (ITIs) in the country—2,275 in the government sector and 8,475 in the private sector.

9.5 Higher and Technical Education

Higher education is of vital importance for the country in consolidating its comparative advantage in skill- and knowledge-intensive services and in building a knowledge-based society.

9.5.1 Higher Education: At the time of Independence in 1947, the number of universities was no more than 20, of colleges around 500 and the total enrolment was less than 1 lakh.

The investment made in higher education over the years has given the country a strong knowledge base in many fields and contributed significantly to economic development, social progress and political democracy in independent India.

By the end of the Tenth Five Year Plan (2002-07), the Indian higher education system had grown into one of the largest in the world with 378 universities, 18,064 colleges, a faculty strength of 4.92 lakh and an estimated enrolment of 140 lakh students.

According to *All India Survey on Higher Education Survey (AISHE), 2012-2013* released in 2014, in 2012-13, the number of universities stood at 665 and the number of colleges at 35,829 colleges. Of the 665 universities, 44 are central universities, 290 state public universities, 122 state private universities, 130 deemed universities, 61 institutes of national importance plus other institutes, and 5 institutions established under State Legislature Acts.

To quote *Economic Survey 2012-13*, “A number of initiatives have been taken during the Eleventh Plan period with focus on improvement of access along with equity and excellence, adoption of state-specific strategies, enhancing the relevance of higher education through curriculum reforms, vocationalization, networking, and use of IT and distance education along with reforms in governance in higher education.

During the Eleventh Plan, 16 central universities were established which include conversion of three state universities to central universities. Seven new Indian Institutes of Management (IIMs), 8 new Indian Institutes of Technology (IITs), 10 new National Institutes of Technology (NITs), 5 Indian Institutes of Science Education and Research (IISERs), and 2 Schools of Planning and Architecture (SPAs) were also established”.

9.5.2 Technical Education: Educational programmes in the field of engineering and technology and craftsmen training—which are designed to help in building up the trained technical personnel required for schemes of industrial development, teaching and research—are immensely important. In formulating these programmes, it should be recognised that advances in the field of science and technology will call, from time to time, for changes in patterns of training and for improvements in the system of education.

Technical and professional education in the country has played a significant role in economic and technical development by producing quality manpower. Strong linkages have developed between technical institutions and the industry. For strengthening technical education and improving the quality of polytechnic pass outs, various steps have been taken through technical education development programmes.

There is a widespread network of technical education institutions in India. The major among them are the following:

1. 16 Indian Institutes of Technology (IITs) and 13 Indian

Institutes of Management (IIMs), which are institutions of national importance.

2. 6,214 engineering and technology colleges and polytechnics.
3. 1,419 institutions for diploma in pharmacy.
4. 119 schools for hotel management and 165 institutions for architecture.
5. For post-graduate courses, there are 3,764 educational institutions for MBA/PGDM and 1,571 for MCA.
6. Deemed universities, namely:

- Indian Institute of Science (IISc), Bangalore.
- Indian School of Mines (ISM), Dhanbad.
- School of Planning and Architecture (SPA), New Delhi.
- Indian Institute of Information Technology and Management (IIITM), Gwalior.
- Indian Institute of Information Technology (IIIT), Allahabad.
- Indian Institute of Information Technology, Design and Manufacturing Jabalpur.

7. 30 National Institutes of Technology (NITs) which are institutions of national importance.

The number of students in engineering and technology colleges and industrial training institutes has increased sharply. The same picture holds true for other categories like scientists, doctors and agricultural graduates.

Resultantly, India now has the third largest scientific and technical work force in the world. However, the capacity of the system to absorb fully these skills in productive employment has been less than adequate. In pure and applied research, advances have been limited except in a few areas like agricultural research, atomic energy and space. Human skills are a formidable asset since they last not merely during one working life but because they are transmitted for generations. If these assets are used effectively, they may well turn out to be one of the most fruitful results of planning.

9.6 Medical Education

In India, medical education is highly regulated and there is an access barrier for setting up new medical and dental colleges. Eligibility for setting up medical or dental colleges is limited to the following organizations:

1. A State Government/Union Territory.
2. A University.
3. An autonomous body promoted by Central/State Government.
4. A Society registered under the Societies Registration Act, 1860 or corresponding Acts in States.
5. A public religious or charitable trust registered under the Trust Act, 1882 or the Wakf Act, 1954.

Thus, for example, the corporate sector is not eligible and only not-for-profit organizations can apply. The private sector medical and dental colleges that have been established in large numbers have all done so by setting up not-for-profit societies. Besides the problem of the number of healthcare personnel, there is an acute problem of quality as well. Some of the private colleges are producing graduates far below the standards required but the Government colleges have also deteriorated, in part because of shortage of staff, the vacancies remaining unfilled because of unattractive remuneration. In Government medical colleges another reason for deterioration of the quality of medical graduates is that they do not get the opportunity to observe the treatment of patients because of the fall in the number of patients coming to Government hospitals for treatment.

9.7 Adult Education

Literacy is the most essential pre-requisite for individual empowerment. Adult literacy and further education of the literates is as vital an area as universal elementary education.

The National Literacy Mission (NLM) was launched on May 5, 1988 as a Technology Mission to impart functional literacy to non-literates in the country in the age group of 15-35 years in a time-bound manner. This age-group has been the focus of attention because they are in the productive and reproductive period of life. NLM was set up with an initial target to make 80 million persons literate by 1995, which was later enhanced to 100 million by 1997 and the revised target was to achieve a threshold level of 75 percent literacy by 2007.

Total Literacy Campaign (TLC) has been the principal strategy of NLM for eradication of illiteracy in the target group. These campaigns are area-specific, time-bound, volunteer-based, cost-effective and outcome-oriented. They are implemented by *Zila Saksharata Samities* and district level literacy societies.

Keeping pace with its endeavours, campaigns and programmes, NLM has strengthened and revitalized the States Literacy Missions which have been imparted greater autonomy. They now have the authority to plan, implement and monitor literacy programmes and sanction continuing education programmes at the State level. The NLM has also come to recognize the great potential that NGOs have in furthering its programmes and schemes. Given the major role, NGOs are now allowed to receive funds from *Zila Sakshara Samities* and actually run continuing education centres. The *Jan Shikshan Sansthans* have expanded their outreach and are also catering to the rural segment by offering vocational training courses.

9.8 Skill Development

The term *skills* is used in the literature to refer to a wide range of attributes and to that extent there is no clear definition of a skilled worker. In practical terms, the term used is *marketable skill* which commonly refers to any skill/expertise/ability that has a market value, i.e. which has the potential of being utilised for generating income/employment. Skill development is important because of its contribution to enhancing productivity at the individual, industry and also national levels because of the complementarities that exist between physical capital and human capital on the one hand and between technology and human capital on the other.

Fast changing knowledge economies call for new core competencies among all learners in the society.

9.8.1 Coordinated Action on Skill Development: Skill building can be viewed as an instrument to improve the effectiveness and contribution of labour to the overall production. It is as an important ingredient to push the production possibility frontier outward and to take growth rate of the economy to a higher trajectory. Skill building could also be seen as an instrument to empower the individual and improve his/her social acceptance or value.

Co-ordinated action on skill development as proposed by Planning Commission was approved by the Cabinet on May 15, 2008. The coordinated action is the major initiative for achieving Eleventh Plan objective of inclusive growth and development through coordination and harmonization of skill development initiatives of different players. The action aims at creation of a pool of skilled manpower with adequate skills that meet the employment requirements across various sectors of the national economy. The approved Co-ordinated Action on Skill Development envisaged setting up of a three-tier institutional structure involving Prime Minister's National Council on Skill Development (NCSD) for policy direction to be supported by National Skill Development Coordination Board (NSDCB) and National Skill Development Corporation (NSDC). The institutional structure was put in place in 2008 itself.

A. Prime Minister's National Council on Skill Development (NCSD): In pursuance of the decision of the Cabinet at its meeting held on May 15, 2008 on Coordinated Action for Skill Development and setting up of the National Skill Development Corporation, Prime Minister's National Council on Skill Development was constituted. NCSD was set up for giving policy directions and periodic review of efforts to address the issue of skill development by expansion of training capacity in a mission mode. The council will be responsible for vision setting and laying down broad strategies for skill development.

The main functions of NCSD are as under:

1. To lay down overall broad policy objectives, financing and governance models and strategies relating to skill development.
2. To review the progress of schemes, and guide on mid-course corrections, additions and closure of parts or whole of any particular programme/scheme.
3. Coordinate public sector/private sector initiatives in a framework of collaborative action.

NCSD has set a target of creating 500 million skilled persons by 2022 with emphasis on inclusivity so as to deal with divides of gender, rural/urban, organized/unorganized, employment and traditional/contemporary work place. It has laid down the core governing principles and operating strategies for skill development.

Some of the key governance principles for skill development strategy include designing of programmes under which the learner can pay the skill provider directly, skills are fungible and bankable, individuals are enabled to convert their knowledge and skills through adequate testing and certification into higher diplomas and degrees. The emphasis is on promoting multiple models of delivery that can respond to differing situations in various States and to utilize existing available infrastructure of educational institutions for skill development after school hours without affecting the formal education. The State Governments are encouraged to set up the State-level coordination body for skill development.

B. National Skill Development Coordination Board (NSDCB): In pursuance of the decision of the Cabinet at its meeting held on May 15, 2008 on Coordinated Action for Skill Development and setting up of the National Skill Development Corporation, National Skill Development Coordination Board was constituted.

NSDCB is entrusted with the coordination and harmonization of the initiatives of Governments for skill development spread across 17 Central Ministries and State

Governments with the initiatives of the National Skill Development Corporation (NSDC). It has 12 members which include high level government officials and distinguished academicians.

The main functions of NSDCB include the following:

1. Enumerating strategies to implement the decisions of the Prime Minister's National Council on Skill Development (NCSD).
2. Developing suitable operational guidelines and instructions to achieve the objectives of skill development requirement of the economy.
3. Initiating solutions and strategies to address the problems of: (a) regional imbalance in skill development infrastructure, (b) socio-economic, rural-urban and gender divide, (c) quality teachers (d) ensuring effective utilization of investment in terms of money and infrastructure, (e) integrating varying existing regulatory institutions, (f) involving private sector to develop skills for wage/self-employment, and (g) promoting apprenticeship/on-the-job training for creation of skilled personnel to address unemployment problem.
4. Encouraging State Governments to put in place similar institutional structures.
5. Establishing national skill inventory and national database for skill deficiency mapping on national web portal to facilitate exchange of information between prospective employers and job seekers.
6. Coordinating and facilitating the repositioning of employment exchanges as outreach points for storing and providing information on employment and skill development.
7. Coordinating the establishment of a credible accreditation system and a guidance framework for all accrediting agencies of different ministries and private players.
8. Monitoring, evaluating and analyzing the outcomes of the various schemes and programmes and apprising NCSD.

NSDCB has constituted the following 5 sub-committees to

look into various aspects of skill development.

1. Curriculum revision.
2. Remodelling apprenticeship training.
3. Evolving vision on the status of vocational education and training in educational system.
4. Institutional mechanism for skill mapping and skill inventory on real time basis.
5. Improvement in accreditation and certification system.

C. National Skill Development Corporation (NSDC): NSDC, a non-profit company under Section 25 of the Companies Act, 1956 has been set up under the Ministry of Finance. It has a equity base of ₹ 10 crore of which 49 percent is contributed by the Government and 51 percent by the private sector.

NSDC has two tier structure, viz. a 15 member board and a National Skill Development Fund (NSDF) as a 100 percent Government-owned trust to facilitate its mandate of coordinating and stimulating private sector initiative in the area of skill development with enhanced flexibility and effectiveness.

NSDF, operating arm of the NSDC, was created with a corpus of ₹ 995.10 crore as Government-owned trust to receive financial contributions from donors, private entities, governments (both Central and State), statutory bodies, financial institutions etc. NSDC and NSDF would enter into an investment management agreement whereby NSDF would provide funds to NSDC for furtherance of the objective of skill development in accordance with the approved work and financial plan. NSDC would charge a management fee from NSDF for managing its resources. The beneficiaries of the trust are the youth of India who require skill development and vocational training. Its main functions are as follows:

1. Making periodic as well as an annual report of its plans and activities and put them in the public domain.
2. Establishing a trainee placement and tracking system for effective evaluation and future policy planning.

3. Establishing credible independent certification systems for both vocational education (VE) and vocational training (VT) with the scope for permitting vertical and horizontal mobility within and between VE and VT.

9.8.2 National Policy on Skill Development (NPSD), 2009: NPSD was formulated by the Ministry of Labour and Employment and was approved by the Cabinet in its meeting held on February 23, 2009. The objective of NPSD is to create a workforce empowered with improved skills, knowledge and internationally recognized qualifications to gain access to decent employment and ensure India's competitiveness in the dynamic global labour market. It aims at increase in productivity of workforce both in the organized and the unorganized sectors, seeking increased participation of youth, women, disabled and other disadvantaged sections and to synergize efforts of various sectors and reform the present system. The salient features of NPSD are as under:

1. Demand-driven system guided by labour market signals thereby reducing skills mismatch.
2. Expansion of outreach using established as well as innovative approaches.
3. National vocational qualifications framework which will, *inter alia*, include opportunities for horizontal and vertical mobility between general and technical education, recognition and certification of competencies irrespective of mode of learning.
4. System to deliver competencies in line with nationally and internationally recognized standards.
5. Focus on new emerging occupations.
6. Focus on pre-employment training and life-long learning.
7. Adequate participation of women, disabled persons and disadvantaged groups including economically backward and minorities and enhancing their access to training and employment opportunities.
8. Stress on research, planning and monitoring.
9. Involvement of social partners, i.e. responsibility for

management and financing of the system would be shared with all stakeholders and provide greater space for public private partnership (PPP).

10. Promoting excellence.
11. Use of modern training technologies including distance learning, e-learning, web-based learning etc.
12. Skill upgradation of trainers, their quality assurance, and improvement of status.

9.8.3 National Policy for Skill Development and Entrepreneurship (NPSDE), 2015: The Ministry of Labour and Employment, Government of India, had formulated a National Policy on Skill Development in 2009. The objective of this policy was to empower all individuals through improved skills, knowledge, nationally and internationally recognized qualifications to gain access to decent employment and ensure India's competitiveness in the global market. The 2009 policy was superseded by NPSDE, 2015. The new policy tries to bring the world of education and training closer to the world of work so as to enable them together build a strong India.

The Ministry of Skill Development and Entrepreneurship, Government of India, is an integral part of the government policy on *Sabka Saath, Sabka Vikaas* and its commitment to overall human resources development to take advantage of the demographic profile of India in the coming years. The objective of NPSDE, 2015 is to meet the challenge of skilling at scale with speed and standard (quality). It aims to provide an umbrella framework to all skilling activities being carried out within the country, and to align them to common standards and link the skilling with demand centres. In addition to laying down the objectives and expected outcomes, it also identifies the various institutional frameworks which can act as the vehicle to reach the expected outcomes. The national policy also provides clarity and coherence on how skill development efforts across the country can be aligned within the existing institutional arrangements. This policy links skills development to improved employability and productivity.

The salient features and provisions of NPSDE, 2015 are presented below.

A. Vision: To create an ecosystem of empowerment by skilling on a large scale at speed with high standards and to promote a culture of innovation based entrepreneurship which can generate wealth and employment so as to ensure Sustainable livelihoods for all citizens in the country.

B. Mission: The mission is to:

- Create a demand for skilling across the country.
- Correct and align skilling with required competencies.
- Connect the supply of skilled human resources with sectoral demands.
- Certify and assess in alignment with global and national standards.
- Catalyse an ecosystem wherein productive and innovative entrepreneurship germinates, sustains and grows, leading to creation of a more dynamic entrepreneurial economy and more formal wage employment.

C. Objectives of NPSDE, 2015

The core objective of NPSDE, 2015 is to empower the individuals by enabling them to realize their full potential through a process of life-long learning where competencies are accumulated via instruments such as credible certifications, credit accumulation and transfer etc. As individuals grow, the society and nation also benefit from their productivity and growth. This will involve the following:

1. Make quality vocational training aspirational for both youth and employers whereby youth sees it as a matter of choice and employer acknowledges the productivity linked to skilled workforce by paying the requisite premium.
2. Ensure both vertical and horizontal pathways to skilled workforce for further growth by providing seamless integration of skill training with formal education.
3. Focus on an outcome-based approach towards quality skilling that on the one hand results in increased employability and better livelihoods for individuals, and

on the other hand translates into improved productivity across primary, secondary and tertiary sectors.

4. Increase the capacity and quality of training infrastructure and trainers to ensure equitable and easy access to every citizen.
5. Address human resources needs by aligning supply of skilled workers with sectoral requirements of industry and the country's strategic priorities including flagship programmes like 'Make in India'.
6. Establish an IT-based information system for aggregating demand and supply of skilled workforce which can help in matching and connecting supply with demand.
7. Promote national standards in the skilling space through active involvement of employers in setting occupational standards, helping develop curriculum, providing apprenticeship opportunities, participating in assessments, and providing gainful employment to skilled workforce with adequate compensation. Operationalize a well-defined quality assurance framework aligned with global standards to facilitate mobility of labour.
8. Leverage modern technology to ensure scale, access and outreach, in addition to ease of delivering content and monitoring results.
9. Recognise the value of on-the-job training, by making apprenticeships in actual work environments an integral part of all skill development efforts.
10. Ensure that the skilling needs of the socially and geographically disadvantaged and marginalized groups—like the scheduled castes (SCs), scheduled tribes (STs), other backward classes (OBCs), minorities, differently-abled persons—are appropriately taken care of.
11. Promote increased participation of women in the workforce through appropriate skilling and gender mainstreaming of training.
12. Promote commitment and ownership of all stakeholders towards skill development and create an effective

co-ordination mechanism.

Endnotes

1. Government of India, Planning Commission, *Twelfth Five Year Plan* (2012-17), Volume I, paras 1.57 and 1.58.
2. Government of India, Planning Commission, *Eleventh Five Year Plan* (2007-12), Volume II, p. 1.
3. Ibid., p. 2.

10

Urban Water Supply

Provision of clean drinking water, sanitation and a clean environment are vital to improve the health of people, to reduce incidence of diseases and deaths. Women and girls in India spend hours fetching water and that drudgery is undesirable in itself and it also takes away other opportunities for self-development. Lack of covered toilets nearby imposes a severe hardship on women and girls. Also, provision of clean drinking water without at the same time provision of sanitation and clean environment would be less effective in improving health. The two should be treated together as complementary needs.

Water supply and sanitation is a State subject and the State Governments/UTs and urban local bodies are responsible for providing water supply and sanitation services through planning, design, implementation, operation and maintenance. Ministry of Urban Development, Government of India is responsible for formulation of broad policies and programmes and assists State Governments/UTs in providing technical assistance in water supply and sanitation sector.

10.1 Need for Safe Drinking Water

Safe drinking water and improved sanitation play a major role in the overall well-being of the people, with a significant bearing on infant mortality rate, longevity and productivity. The poor, both in rural and urban areas, bear a disproportionately higher burden on the non-availability of water, as well as its poor quality. Seasonal disruption of water supply is common, especially during summer months. Fetching of water for domestic use, sometimes from far-flung sources, is a time-consuming physical burden borne by women, particularly in the rural areas. 70-80 percent of illnesses are related to water contamination and poor sanitation. Women and children are particularly vulnerable to the effects of water contamination. It is also a matter of concern that despite the progress achieved in provision of water supply, the level of water-related sickness continues to be high.

As per 2011 Census of India, approximately 10 percent of urban households do not have access to safe drinking water. According to Census 2001, only 23.55 percent had toilet facilities and 52 percent of the population was left uncovered by sanitation facilities. The coverage in terms of organised sewerage system ranged from 35 percent in class IV to 75 percent in class I cities. The drainage system for rain water disposal covers only 66 percent of the urban population. The city roads are inadequate for traffic requirements, leading to congestion and fast deterioration in quality of roads due to excess loads.

The coverage of urban population with water supply facilities in the past had not been very impressive, due to various reasons, including the fact that the investment made in the urban water supply sector had been inadequate. It is necessary to plan augmentation of water supply in urban areas to reach the prescribed norms, higher degree of reliability, assurance of water quality, a high standard of operation and management, accountability to customers and in particular special arrangements to meet the needs of the urban poor.

The achievement of these tasks depends to a large extent on the willingness of the State Governments and urban local bodies (ULBs) to restructure water supply organisations, levy reasonable water rates, take up reforms in billing, accounting and collection and become credit worthy in order to have access to market funding.

10.1.1 Characteristics of Good Quality Water: These can be listed as follows:

1. It must be pleasant to taste and in appearance.
2. It must be free from pathogenic organisms.
3. It must be free from toxic substances.
4. It should not be corrosive in nature.
5. It should not contain excessive amount of solid substances

which can cause physiological effects on human beings and other consumers.

6. It should have sufficient quantity of dissolved oxygen.
7. It should be available in large quantity.

10.2 Major Issues in Urban Water Supply

10.2.1 Technological Upgradation: Technological upgradation and improved design can hike efficiency and rationalise consumption. Regularity in supply can mean lower project cost and greater willingness to pay on the part of the consumers. Micro-level systems need to be designed to recycle water at the household level. The supply should be metered to plug leakages.

10.2.2 Water Tariff: Pricing should be on cost-recovery basis in the long-term or over the full life of the project. In the short-term, since prices cannot be increased at one go, the government will have to continue to provide subsidies. The water tariff should be increased gradually to reach cost-recovery level. Part of the required increase may be capitalised and charged as connection charges or advance registration charges. Cost recovery may also be made by including water tax, water benefit tax, betterment charges or development charges.

10.2.3 Cross-subsidisation: Cross-subsidisation of domestic use of water by commercial and industrial use may prove self-defeating if the latter diversify their sources of water. Metering of water supply must be promoted. To improve monitoring of leakages, bulk metering should be adopted. A block tariff system may be adopted under which consumption of water is picked at a low initial rate up to a specified volume of use and at a higher rate per block thereafter. Differential pricing may also be related to time of use.

10.2.4 Unaccounted for Water (UFW): UFW—due to leaking water supply systems and illegal tapping—reduces water availability. The average water loss in the leaking water supply systems varies from place to place and it is generally between 20-50 percent. Dedicated efforts to plug the leakages are required in addition to demand management measures for achieving the sustainability and equity.

10.2.5 Long Distance Water Transfer: Sustainability in the urban water supply is addressed mainly through supply side augmentation. Distant perennial sources are identified and long distance piped water transfers to the cities/towns are common. Long distance water transfer has brought in the attendant issues of dependence on other states for urban water supply. For example, Delhi depends on Haryana and Uttar Pradesh for its water supply. There are a few instances when even within the state people object to transfer of water from one district to another. Some times, these issues have a serious implication on the sustainability of supplies to the cities.

10.2.6 Waste Water Management: Most urban centres in India have partial sewerage and sewage treatment facilities. These inadequacies reflect limited capacities of ULBs to invest in capital infrastructure.

Effective management of waste water would result in availability of treated water for reuse, capture of methane gas for power generation and improvement in the quality of the environment. Earning carbon credits is also possible. Methane gas (CH_4) is emitted during waste water transport, sewage treatment process and leakage from anaerobic digestion of waste water sludge. The natural treatment process and septic tanks may result in relatively large emissions of methane. Nitrous oxide (NO_2) is also generated from sewage. In developing countries—due to rapid population growth and urbanization without concurrent development of waste water infrastructure—CH_4 and NO_2 emissions from wastewater are generally higher than the developed countries.

Replacement of waste water pumping equipment to improve the system efficiency through energy saving should be considered. Experiments in utilization of recycled domestic waste water and of bio-gas for power generation in sewage treatment plants (STPs) should be encouraged.

10.2.7 Urban Storm Water Management: Urban areas

always present some risk of flooding when rainfall occurs. Heavy and prolonged rainfall produces very large volumes of surface water in any city, which can easily overwhelm drainage systems. Most of the cities in India do not have proper drainage systems and rely on natural drainage canals. Climate change has the potential to increase flooding risks in two ways: from the sea (higher sea levels and storm surges) and from rainfall. Due to the sea level rise, there may be chances of salt water intrusion in the ground water systems. There is a need for hydrological barriers and alternative sources.

Extreme precipitation is expected to show a substantial increase over a large area over the west coast and in central India. Gujarat, one of India's most prosperous states, has experienced severe flooding for three consecutive years starting in 2004, causing large economic losses in some cities due to extreme precipitation in upstream catchments.

The devastating Mumbai floods of 2005 were caused by an extreme weather event. The bulk of city services were shut down for the first time in recorded history for almost 5 days with no contact via rail, road or air with the rest of the country. Over 1,000 people lost their lives and economic life in the city came to a halt due to a combination of institutional failures, poor preparedness and extremely high vulnerability of the poor.

Since extreme precipitation is expected to show a substantial increase over a large area over the west coast and in Central India, it will require a significant revision of urban planning practices across cities in the flood-affected regions and neighbourhood states to integrate flood and climate change mitigation and adaptation measures into day-to-day urban development and service delivery activities. ULBs have the main responsibility for planning, implementing and managing storm water management systems that can diminish risks of flooding from the direct and indirect impact of climate change through provision of infrastructure and services, disaster preparedness and the planning and regulatory framework. Due to the higher proportion of precipitation in more intense events, there is a need to increase the margin of design safety of buildings, bridges and flyovers to enhance the hydraulic capacity of the sections which will result in additional investments. There is a need for embankment of low lying areas, especially for coastal cities, better disaster warning systems and construction of shelters.

More investment is required to design the urban storm water management system than the current level of funding. An appropriate financing mechanism has to be developed to cope with the costs that will occur from adaptation.

The need for better storm water drainage cannot be overemphasized and needs to be integral component of spatial planning and cities.

10.2.8 Roof Water Harvesting: There is a need to devise systems, drawings and standards for roof water harvesting structures with filters directly connected to households or community sumps or with overflows which are led to recharge structures so that both direct collection of water and recharge of ground water can be taken up simultaneously as a part of the design of buildings. Such standards besides being adopted in the National Building Code (NBC) should give a range of options which may be suitable for all types of houses and buildings. A specific design should be encouraged for all newly developed townships/peripheral urban areas which are in the process of designing systems. There is a need to observe caution in preventing surface water or other pollutants from polluting ground water aquifers through recharge mechanisms. A separate manual suggesting different recharge mechanisms for different soil types can be prepared. Due precautions such as in-built filtering may be considered to prevent contamination of ground water. In addition water harvesting through check dams needs to be given importance.

10.3 Twelfth Five Year Plan (2012-17) on Water Management

Outlining its strategy for efficient management of water resources, the Twelfth Plan observed, "Management of water resources poses increasingly difficult challenges that will require attention in the Twelfth Plan. The total quantity of usable fresh water annually available in India is fixed, but its demand from expanding agriculture and other sectors is increasing. Water resources in many parts of the country are under severe stress leading to excessive exploitation of ground water. There is some scope for increasing water availability. While these opportunities must be fully exploited, the real solution has to come from greater efficiency in water use.

Agriculture accounts for 80 percent of water needs at present, and there is considerable scope for increasing efficiency of water use in this area. This requires better management of water in areas of large and medium irrigation projects. It also requires putting in place more holistic aquifer management strategies. Separation of electricity feeders for agriculture and domestic use can help limit the availability of electricity for pumping ground water thus breaking the vicious cycle between free energy and excess use of groundwater. Wherever this has been done in combination with large-scale watershed programmes, there is evidence that groundwater levels have recovered.

Normally, efficient use of scarce resources requires appropriate pricing, but pricing of water is a sensitive issue. This problem can be solved by providing *lifeline* water supplies for drinking and cooking at very low prices, while charging appropriately for additional water use by domestic consumers. There is a stronger case for rational pricing reflecting the scarcity of water for commercial and industrial use. There is also a strong case for rational pricing of water for agricultural purposes. The proportion of water recycled in urban areas, and by Indian industry needs to be significantly increased. This will happens if supply for commercial purposes is appropriately priced.

Even if we succeed in bringing about a major rationalisation of water prices, by itself, it will not lead to optimal use. For this, a rational pricing must be accompanied by regulatory measures to ration water to different agricultural users, and stronger measures to discourage pollution. Contamination of drinking water is the principal cause of health disorders, particularly amongst children. It is estimated that up to 13.0 percent of drinking water in rural areas contains chemical contaminants including fertilizer run-offs (particularly urea and its decomposition products)". [1]

To sum up, water supply in urban areas is also far from satisfactory. Water is supplied only for few hours of the day which leads to a lot of waste as taps are kept open and water that is stored, not all of it is used productively.

It may be necessary to define priority water uses and to find appropriate ways to implement prioritization. Choices may have to be made concerning the allocation of water resources, and criteria need to be developed on the basis of which such choices can be made. Water management and the implementation of water policy needs to be capable of responding to unexpected developments caused by climate change. Strategies for adaptation need to be developed and implemented in a flexible way in order to take into account further progress of scientific knowledge. Local and regional authorities will need more practical guidance on how to cope with the local and regional impacts of climate change on water.

Investments that appear to be cost-effective under current conditions may become economically and ecologically unviable when considering climatic predictions and their impacts on water resources. Appropriate financing mechanisms have to be developed to cope with the costs that will occur from adaptation. For this, information on the share of costs and benefits of proposed measures and on the scale, time frame and the cost effectiveness of investments needed for a given region is required.

In water supply projects, it is possible to privatise sourcing, treatment and bulk supply. The retail distribution and pricing may remain with the public sector. Low-cost sanitation may be privatised fully on the model of Sulabh Shauchalaya. Maintenance of roads can be entrusted to the private sector subject to quality control.

Endnote

1. Government of India, Planning Commission, *An Approach to the Twelfth Five Year Plan*, October 2011, pp. 10-11.

11

Urban Sanitation, Sewerage and Solid Waste Management

11.1 Sanitation and Sewerage

Census data 2011 indicated that the total urban population of the country stands at 37.7 crore and is projected to touch 60.0 crore by the year 2030. The number of cities and towns too has increased from about 5,161 towns in 2001 to 7,935 in 2011 while the share of urban population has increased from about 28 percent to 31.15 percent of the total population. By the year 2050, it is expected that 50 percent of the country's population will be urban. The Census 2011 also reflected that in 4,041 statutory towns, close to 80 lakh households do not have access to toilets and defecate in the open. It is an accepted fact that weak sanitation has significant health costs and untreated sewage from cities is the single biggest source of water pollution in India. This indicates both the scale of the challenge ahead of the Indian cities and the huge costs incurred from not addressing them.

The status of urban sanitation, as per Census 2011 is as under:

1. 81.4 percent of urban households are having toilets within the premises.
   - 32.7 percent of urban households are connected to a piped sewer system.
   - 38.2 percent dispose of their wastes into septic tanks.
   - 16.50 percent of urban households use other types of latrines.
2. 18.6 percent do not have toilets within the premises.
   - 6 percent use community latrines.
   - 12.6 percent are forced the indignity of open defecation.

The poor, particularly those living in slums and squatter settlements, are generally deprived of basic sanitation facilities. The imperative is to provide sanitation to all and to ensure that the facility is hygienic and does not add to pollution. Currently, people living in cities greatly vary as to their sanitation status. At the bottom are those with no access to sanitation facilities and at the top are those connected to a flush toilet, which in turn is connected to the official underground sewage network. The challenge is enormous and needs urgent intervention, which provides both sanitation facility and disposal.

Table 11.1 gives details of sanitation facilities in urban India.

Table 11.1: Sanitation Facilities in Urban India

No.	Facility	Percent
1.	**Flush/pour toilet latrine of which connected to:**	**72.6**
A	Piped sewer system	32.7
B	Septic system	38.2
C	Other system	1.7
2.	**Pit latrine of which:**	**8.3**
A	With slab/ventilated improved pit	6.4
B	Without slab/open pit	0.7
C	Night soil disposed into open drain	1.2
3.	**Service latrine of which:**	**0.5**
A	Night soil removed by human	0.3
B	Night soil serviced by animals	0.2
4.	**No latrine within premises of which:**	**18.6**
A	Public latrine	6.0
B	Open	12.6
	Total	100.00

Source: Census of India 2011, Houses, Household Amenities and Assets: Latrine Facility, Office of the Registrar General and Census Commissioner, India.

The pollution effect of sanitation is enormous. Poor sanitation conditions, particularly in slums, are often linked to outbreaks of cholera and gastro-enteritis. Water borne diseases are major cause of mortality throughout India and impose a huge burden in terms of loss of life and productivity. Water and sanitation diseases are responsible for most of the environmental health burden. The single major cause of this burden of disease is diarrhoea, which disproportionately affects the children under the age of five.

The major issues in urban sanitation are the following:

1. How to expand sewerage and sanitation facilities to cover all the people in all cities and towns?
2. How to find resources to do that?
3. How to create awareness about the importance of sanitation and solid waste management?
4. How to prepare and execute plans that keep up with growing population?
5. How to finance the operational and maintenance costs of the facilities created?

Landfill sites have not yet been identified by many municipalities and in several municipalities, the landfill sites have been exhausted and the respective local bodies do not have resources to acquire new land. Due to lack of disposal sites, even the collection efficiency gets affected.

Use of low cost technologies like that of *Sulabh Shauchalayas* must be promoted. Cost of drainage and sewerage can be piggybacked on to the water tariff since these projects can be taken up as one package. The cost of storm-water drainage projects can be recovered by commercial use of adjacent lands. Taking up of integrated area development schemes rather than isolated water supply or sanitation schemes should be given priority. Even in older areas, augmentation of water supply schemes and other facilities can be financed out of impact fees or valorisation charges or by a temporary surcharge on property tax.

11.1.1 National Urban Sanitation Policy: It was launched in 2008 with the vision of all Indian cities and towns becoming totally sanitised, healthy and liveable and ensuring good public health and environmental outcomes for all citizens. It has a special focus on hygienic and affordable sanitation facilities for the urban poor and the women. Various activities are being taken including rating of towns and cities on sanitation.

Service level benchmarks have been laid down for municipal services. Ministry of Urban Development (MoUD) is supporting capacity building at various levels, including the urban local bodies and the State personnel in areas related to governance, financial management, and service delivery. (MoUD) has set up 14 centres of excellence, nine for urban development, four for urban transport and one in the field of e-governance in reputed institutions across the country.

11.1.2 Swachh Bharat Mission (SBM): SBM emanates from the vision of the Government articulated in the address of the President of India to the Joint Session of Parliament on June 9, 2014, "We must not tolerate the indignity of homes without toilets and public spaces littered with garbage. For ensuring hygiene, waste management and sanitation across the nation, a *Swachh Bharat Mission* will be launched. This will be our tribute to Mahatma Gandhi on his 150th birth anniversary to be celebrated in the year 2019".

The Government of India launched SBM on October 2, 2014 with a target to make the country clean by October 2, 2019. This is a sub-Mission of the Ministry of Urban Development with a view to achieve the objective of providing sanitation facilities to all 4,041 statutory towns in the country over a period of 5 years commencing from October 2, 2014. The specific objectives of the scheme are to eliminate open defecation, conversion of unsanitary toilets to pour flush toilets, eradication of manual scavenging etc.

The objectives of the Mission are as under:

1. Elimination of open defecation.
2. Conversion of unsanitary toilets to pour flush toilets.
3. Eradication of manual scavenging.
4. 100 percent collection and scientific processing, disposal,

reuse, recycle of municipal solid waste.

5. Bringing about a behavioural change in people regarding healthy sanitation practices.
6. Generating awareness among the citizens about sanitation and its linkages with public health.
7. Strengthening of urban local bodies to design, execute and operate systems.
8. Creating enabling environment for private sector participation in capital expenditure and operation and maintenance expenditure (O&M).

11.1.3 Sanitation-Water Supply Integration: Sanitation and clean drinking water are critical determinants of health and are complementary to each other. Without proper sanitation, the incidence of diarrhoeal diseases due to contaminated drinking water will not come down, and without adequate water supply, improved sanitation is generally not possible. It is, therefore, necessary to adopt a habitation approach to sanitation and to institutionalize the integration of water supply with sanitation in each habitation.

The problem of sanitation in urban areas is also very serious since almost all cities, including even the State capitals and major metros, have a large percentage of the population not connected to the sewer system. Urban development must give top priority to planning for water, toilets and sewerage as an integrated whole taking into account the likely expansion of the urban population.

In short, large parts of the modern cities remain unconnected to the sewage system as they live in unauthorized or illegal areas or slums, where the state services do not reach. In this situation, it is critical to invest in sewage systems. It is equally and even more critical to invest in building affordable and scalable sewage networks, which require a fresh look at the current technology for sewage and its treatment. If sewage systems are not comprehensively spread across the city to collect, convey and intercept waste of all, then pollution will not be under control.

11.2 Solid Waste Management (SWM)

SWM is a part of public health and sanitation, and falls under Entry 6 of List II (State List) in the Seventh Schedule of the Constitution of India.

Since this activity is non-exclusive, non-rivalled and essential, the responsibility for providing the service lies within the public domain.

As this activity is of local nature, it is entrusted to the urban local bodies (ULBs). ULBs undertake the task of solid waste service delivery, with its own staff, equipment and funds. In a few cases, part of the said work is contracted out to private enterprises. The management of municipal solid waste is one of the most important obligatory functions of ULBs which is closely associated with urban environmental conditions.

The cost of collection, treatment and disposal of the solid waste should be reduced through various mechanisms. Technological innovation to improve the reusability of the recycled waste will increase returns and make projects viable. Privatisation of as many operations as is feasible in an urban area will improve efficiency and reduce costs.

The following measures need to be adopted for solid waste management.

1. Greater attention should be paid to segregation of different kinds of waste at the collection point itself to reduce cost of disposal.
2. Toxic waste should be collected and disposed of separately.
3. Biodegradable waste should be tackled locally to avoid storage and transportation over longer distances. This waste can also be coupled with the local sewers and horticulture waste from streets in bio-digesters. This will produce three important by-products—biogas, compost and recyclable water, which will improve the viability of disposal.
4. Building debris (*malba*) should be kept separately and

used for filling building sites and low-lying areas.

5. Remaining waste gets recycled by rag pickers. The small components left over can be disposed of through incineration or sanitary landfills.
6. Wherever environmentally acceptable, disposal can be decentralised to save on transportation cost.
7. Appropriate technologies should be used to improve the quality of processed waste. An improved quality of compost may fetch a higher price and reduce process time and mechanisation. Similarly, refuse-derived fuel (RDF) seems to have good scope for providing cooking fuel, process steam and power generation. Converting waste management into biogas with fertiliser as the by product is a commercially viable method. Landfills can be scientifically organised to minimise pollution from leaching. The biogas produced in a properly-designed landfill can be harnessed and utilised.
8. The *polluter pays* principle should be applied. Operations which create waste may be charged a levy and the returns from the same may be used for financing waste disposal programmes.
9. Solid waste delivery (SWD) services can be unbundled and most functions entrusted to the private sector. This is one area where privatisation has shown consistent productivity gains and cost reductions.

11.2.1 Municipal Solid Waste (Management and Handling) Rules, 2000: These Rules stipulate that all local bodies should undertake segregation of waste and its collection, storage, transportation, processing and disposal.

Biomedical waste is generally disposed of by incinerators or conventional methods. Some of the healthcare facilities have installed their own biomedical waste treatment facilities and others are availing services of common bio-medical waste treatment facilities (CBWTF).

An institutional mechanism is required to be put in place to ensure that issues related to handling of industrial, hazardous and biomedical waste are dealt with properly. Funding should be made conditional upon appropriate measures being taken in respect of these issues. An effective mechanism should be put into place to ensure strict monitoring and compliance by the concerned local authorities. A framework for management of e-waste also needs to be put into place.

Collection, treatment and disposal of solid waste are the responsibility of the ULBs. These bodies must be made specifically accountable in this respect.

There has been no major effort in the past to create community awareness, either about the likely perils due to poor waste management or the simple steps that every citizen can take, which will help in reducing waste generation and promote effective management of solid waste generated. The degree of community sensitization and public awareness is low.

Since in most of cities of India there are many unauthorised housing colonies which are not provided sewerage facilities, their waste go untreated polluting the water bodies in which it is drained.

Most urban centres lack systems for scientific management of municipal solid waste system. MSW is rarely segregated at source in accordance with the Municipal Solid Waste (Management and Handling) Rules, 2000. Mixed waste is dumped into the depression or earmarked low lying areas in and around the towns. The organic fraction of municipal solid waste can be profitably converted into useful products like compost (organic manure), methane gas (used for cooking, heating, lighting, production of energy) etc.

11.3 Energy from Urban Waste

In the solid waste management sector, it should be recognized that urban waste, with a significant proportion of organic constituents, has emerged as a resource for the generation of energy in an environmentally sustainable manner. In developed countries, environmental concerns rather than energy recovery is the prime motivator for waste-to-energy facilities, which help in treating and disposing of wastes. Energy in the form of biogas, heat or power is seen as a bonus which improves the viability of such projects. While biomethanation, refuse-derived-fuel (RDF) and incineration are the most common technologies, pyrolysis and gasification are also emerging as preferred options.

A common feature in most developed countries is that the entire waste management system is being handled as a profitable venture by private industry or NGOs with tipping fee for treatment of waste being one of the major revenue streams. The major benefits of recovery of energy from urban wastes are the following:

1. Reduction in the quantity of waste by 60 percent to 90 percent.
2. Reduction in demand for landfill sites.
3. Reduction in the cost of transportation of wastes to faraway landfill sites.
4. Net reduction in environmental pollution.
5. Generation of substantial quantity of energy.

The treatment and processing of waste being generated in Indian cities requires a mix of technologies as composting alone cannot be the favoured option. With a view to facilitate use of compost as manure, composting either through biomethanation or aerobic processes should be considered only in case of source segregated biodegradable organic fraction and not for the mixed waste.

Besides, requirement of land can also be an issue in the selection of technological options for waste processing and treatment. Some of the key areas for R&D in waste-to-energy are: (a) development of processes/equipments for separation of different components of MSW for energy recovery, (b) bio-methanation of mix of bio-degradable solid wastes from various streams, (c) gasification of MSW for energy recovery, (d) low cost emission control equipment for waste-to-energy conversion technologies.

SWD services can be unbundled and most functions entrusted to the private sector. This is one area where privatisation has shown consistent productivity gains and cost reductions.

To sum up, very few urban local bodies (ULBs) in the country have prepared long-term action plans for effective SWM in their respective cities. For obtaining a long-term economic solution, planning of the system on long-term sustainable basis is very essential. The Ministry of Environment and Forests, Government of India has notified Municipal Solid Waste (Management and Handling) Rules, 2000 to tackle this problem. Increase in quantity of municipal solid waste generation with increase in the urban population is quite obvious. Efforts towards waste recycle, reuse and resource recovery for reduction in waste and adoption of more advanced technological measures for effective and economical disposal of municipal solid waste are urgently needed.

To address the issue of mitigation of GHG emission from municipal waste, appropriate actions are required through adoption of scientific solid waste management systems with options for recovery of wealth from waste, i.e. compost and energy recovery from solid waste. Improved waste management will not only provide for significant GHG mitigation, but will also improve public health and environment quality.

12

Climate Change and Urbanization

One of the challenges of sustainable urban form is to strike a balance between economic performance objectives and environmental sustainability. The land use and transport policies will have to match the demand of different activities. The idea is to create a city that performs well economically and conforms to the objectives of environmental sustainability. In order to be economically efficient a city needs to reduce production costs, e.g. costs of receiving inputs and distributing outputs. It also needs to reduce travel time by proper organisation of land use and activities in a city.

The urban *heat island* effect compounds and exacerbates climate change. Pavement, buildings and other structures typical of urban areas replace natural vegetation and minimise cooling provided by vegetation through both shade and evapo-transpiration. This contributes to the formation of ground-level ozone, which is detrimental to human health. In urban areas rise in temperature due to this process can be between two and ten degrees Fahrenheit. Further, the compounding effects of the urban heat island and increased temperatures from climate change result in increased demand for air conditioning. Increased air conditioning means increased generation of electricity which again contributes to the emission of greenhouse gases. These issues need to be examined in the context of new paradigms for evolving solutions through settlement planning.

12.1 Evidence on Climate Change

The Intergovernmental Panel on Climate Change (IPCC), established in 1988 by the World Meteorological Organization (WMO) and the United Nations Environment Programme

(UNEP), has worked extensively on evaluating past trends and the future prospects of climate change. IPCC reviews and assesses the most recent scientific, technical, and socio-economic information produced worldwide relevant to climate change.

According to IPCC, the global temperature may rise by 2-4.5 degree centigrade by the end of this century, including a 2.7-4.3°C increase over India by 2080s if adequate actions are not taken to reduce emissions globally. At the national level, the observed increase in surface air temperatures over the past century is 0.4 degree centigrade.

12.1.1 The Fourth Assessment Report (AR4) of IPCC, 2007: AR4 of IPCC, released in November 2007, concluded that the fact of global warming is unequivocal and there is enough evidence to indicate that this is due to anthropogenic reasons. Recent years have been the warmest since 1860, the year from when regular instrumental records are available. It is important to note that global warming will affect mankind seriously.

AR4 of IPCC brought climate change issue to the fore and led the parties to make serious efforts to address the problem through long-term cooperative actions as agreed under the Bali Action Plan. [1] IPCC made serious projections of the future scenario in terms of global warming and predicted that there may be adverse impact of climate change on agriculture, water resources, eco-systems, sea levels, human health and result in rise in extreme weather events.

12.1.2 Fifth Assessment Report (AR5) of IPCC, 2014: IPCC in its AR5 observed that there has been an increasing trend in the anthropogenic emissions of greenhouse gases (GHGs) since the advent of the industrial revolution, with about half of the anthropogenic CO_2 emissions during this period occurring in the last 40 years. The period 1983-2012 is likely to have been the warmest 30 year period of the last 1,400 years. CO_2 emissions from fossil fuel combustion and industrial processes have contributed a major portion of total GHG emissions during the period 1970-2010.

The change in the climate system is likely to have adverse impact on the economy, livelihoods, cropping pattern, and food security. According to the various projections by the IPCC, extreme heat events are likely to be longer and more intense in addition to changes in precipitation patterns. The change in climate could: (a) affect the production of wheat, rice, and maize in the tropical and temperate zones, (b) have negative impact on health by exacerbating health problems that already exist especially in developing countries and (c) adversely impact productive activities like growing food and working outdoors.

12.2 United Nations Framework Convention on Climate Change (UNFCCC)

Recognizing the problem and the need for international co-operation, the international community in 1992 established the UNFCCC which accepted the principle of *common but differentiated responsibility* between the industrialized countries and the developing countries.

The objective of UNFCCC is to achieve stabilization of greenhouse gas concentrations in the atmosphere at a level that would prevent dangerous anthropogenic interference with the climate system. The Convention enjoins Parties to communicate information about the implementation of the Convention, taking into account the common but differentiated responsibilities and respective capabilities and their specific regional and national development priorities, objectives and circumstances. Article 12 of the Convention relates to the communication of information pertaining to implementation in accordance with Article 4(1) of the Convention, whereby each Party is required to communicate to the Conference of the Parties. The elements of information in the communication are provided in the context of national circumstances and include:

1. A national inventory of anthropogenic emissions by sources and removals by sinks of all greenhouse gases not controlled by the Montreal Protocol, to the extent its

capacities permit, using comparable methodologies to be promoted and agreed upon by the Conference of Parties;

2. A general description of steps taken to implement the Convention including an assessment of impacts, vulnerability due to climate change and associated adaptation needs; and
3. Any other information that the Party considers relevant to the achievement of the objective of the Convention and suitable for inclusion in its communication, including, if feasible, material relevant for calculations of global emission trends.

12.2.1 Kyoto Protocol: In 1997, parties signatory to UNFCCC adopted the Kyoto Protocol which set legally binding targets for GHG reductions by individual industrialized countries during *first commitment period, 2008-12*, totalling 5.2 percent below their aggregate 1990 emissions. The protocol did not involve any binding commitments by developing countries in recognition of the fact that historically it was the industrialized countries that were responsible for the overwhelming bulk of the stock of GHGs.

Kyoto Protocol made provisions for use of any of the three mechanisms including the Clean Development Mechanism (CDM) to help developed countries meet their quantified emission limitation and reduction commitments domestically and through acquisition of greenhouse gas reduction credits from activities outside their own boundaries at relatively lesser costs. India is a major participant in the projects aimed at using Clean Development Mechanism.

Kyoto Protocol took a more *top-down* but highly differentiated approach, establishing negotiated, binding emissions targets for developed countries, and no new commitments for developing countries.

175 countries including India ratified the Protocol. The US and some other countries did not ratify the Protocol. As it happens, most of those that did ratify the protocol have failed to live up to the commitments they had undertaken.

Under the provisions of the Kyoto Protocol, India as a non-Annex I party, is not obliged to reduce emission of GHGs. Under the Asia-Pacific Partnership on Clean Development and Climate, India has also been working with the US, Australia, China, Japan and Republic of Korea on possible development and promotion of clean technologies for dealing with climate change.

Kyoto Protocol came to an end in 2012.

12.2.2 Copenhagen Accord, 2009 and Cancún Agreements, 2010: With the Copenhagen Accord and Cancún Agreements, parties established a parallel *bottom-up* framework, with countries undertaking national pledges for 2020 that represented political rather than legal commitments. This approach attracted much wider participation, including, for the first time, specific mitigation pledges by developing countries. However, countries' pledges fell far short of the reductions needed to meet the goal set in Copenhagen and Cancún of keeping average warming below 2 degrees Celsius above pre-industrial levels.

12.2.3 Paris Agreement, 2015: The negotiations toward a Paris agreement were launched with the Durban Platform for Enhanced Action adopted at Seventeenth Conference of Parties (COP 17) in 2011. The Durban Platform called for *a protocol, another legal instrument or an agreed outcome with legal force under the Convention applicable to all Parties*, to apply from 2020, but provided no further substantive guidance.

COP 19 in Warsaw called on parties to submit *intended nationally determined contributions* (INDCs) well before the Paris conference, signalling an important bottom-up feature of the emerging agreement. Heading into Paris, more than 180 countries producing more than 90 percent of global emissions had submitted INDCs, a much broader response than many had anticipated.

The Paris Agreement marks the latest step in the evolution of the UN climate change regime, which originated in 1992 with the adoption of the Framework Convention. The

UNFCCC established a long-term objective, general principles, common and differentiated commitments, and a basic governance structure, including an annual Conference of Parties (COP).

The U.N. Climate Change Conference in Paris (November 30 to December 12, 2015) presented a critical opportunity for parties to the U.N. Framework Convention on Climate Change (UNFCCC) to strengthen the global response to climate change. The negotiating mandate for the Paris talks called for a post-2020 climate agreement under the UNFCCC *with legal force* and *applicable to all Parties*. In fulfilling this mandate, the Paris conference was asked to produce a package: a core legal agreement and related instruments and decisions.

Parties to the UNFCCC reached a landmark agreement on December 12, 2015 in Paris, charting a fundamentally new course in the two-decade-old global climate effort.

Culminating a four-year negotiating round, the new treaty ended the strict differentiation between developed and developing countries that characterized earlier efforts, replacing it with a common framework that commits all countries to put forward their best efforts and to strengthen them in the years ahead. This included, for the first time, requirements that all parties report regularly on their emissions and implementation efforts, and undergo international review.

A. Highlights of Paris Agreement: The agreement and a companion decision by parties were the key outcomes of the conference, known as the 21st session of the UNFCCC Conference of the Parties (or COP 21). The Paris Agreement:

1. Reaffirmed the goal of limiting global temperature increase well below 2 degrees Celsius, while urging efforts to limit the increase to 1.5 degrees.
2. Established binding commitments by all parties to make *nationally determined contributions* (NDCs), and to pursue domestic measures aimed at achieving them.
3. Committed all countries to report regularly on their emissions and *progress made in implementing and achieving* their

NDCs, and to undergo international review.

4. Committed all countries to submit new NDCs every five years, with the clear expectation that they will *represent a progression* beyond previous ones.
5. Reaffirmed the binding obligations of developed countries under the UNFCCC to support the efforts of developing countries, while for the first time encouraging voluntary contributions by developing countries too.
6. Extended the current goal of mobilizing US$ 100 billion a year in support by 2020 through 2025, with a new, higher goal to be set for the period after 2025.
7. Extended a mechanism to address *loss and damage* resulting from climate change, which explicitly will not *involve or provide a basis for any liability or compensation.*
8. Required parties engaging in international emissions trading to avoid *double counting.*
9. Called for a new mechanism, similar to the Clean Development Mechanism under the Kyoto Protocol, enabling emission reductions in one country to be counted toward another country's NDC.

The strong momentum toward an agreement that built over the preceding months was dramatically underscored on the opening day of the summit by the presence of 150 presidents and prime ministers, the largest ever single-day gathering of heads of state. Impetus came also from a vast array of *non-state actors*, including governors, mayors and CEOs, and the launch in Paris of major initiatives like the Breakthrough Energy Coalition announced by Bill Gates and other billionaires.

Negotiations on many issues were hard fought and, in typical COP fashion, progress through most of the conference was painstakingly slow. But thanks to deft diplomacy by the French presidency, the Summit was remarkably free of the kind of procedural showdowns that marred previous COPs.

Many operational details of the new framework were left to be decided by future COPs. The agreement will take effect only once enough countries have formally ratified it.

12.3 Impact of Climate Change on India

India has always been subject to a large degree of climate variability. This is likely to be accentuated by climate change. Warming trends along the west coast, in central India, the interior peninsula, and north-eastern India and cooling trends in north-west India and parts of south India have been observed. Coasts are projected to be exposed to increase in risk including coastal erosion due to climate change and sea level rise. Geological Survey of India (GSI) projects that the glaciers of Himalaya are receding at varying rates in different regions. India is conscious of these challenges and has implemented several major programmes addressing the climate variability concerns. These include: (a) cyclone warning and protection, (b) coastal protection, (c) floods and drought control and relief, (d) major and minor irrigation projects, (e) control of malaria, (f) food security measures and (g) research on drought resistant crops.

12.3.1 Climate Change and Human Settlements: Climate change causes vulnerability of human settlements which is related to extreme weather events and such gradual changes in the climate exceed the adaptive capacity of human systems. Climate change adds to the existing stress on the sustainability of human settlements and society. Non-climate sources of change like rapid urbanisation are often the main source of stress.

Human settlements are accustomed to variability in environmental conditions and are resilient to normal variations. Vulnerabilities arise out of experiences that are beyond the normal experience and due to limited adaptive capacity. Climate change is likely to affect infrastructure related to water, sanitation, energy, transportation, healthcare, fire services and other forms of emergency measures.

The urban-heat island effects could get exacerbated due to increase in baseline temperatures, affecting climatic comfort of the urban populations and may consequently lead to additional costs in climate control.

Sustainable development concerns in the sense of enhancement of human well-being, broadly conceived, are a recurring theme in India's development philosophy. The present day consensus reflects three foundational aspirations. *First that human beings should be able to enjoy a decent quality of life; second, that humanity should become capable of respecting the finiteness of the biosphere; and third, that neither the aspiration for the good life, nor the recognition of biophysical limits should preclude the search for greater justice in the world.* Sustainable habitat would mean achieving a balance between the economic and social development of human habitats together with the protection of the environment, equity in employment, shelter, basic services, social infrastructure and transportation. In the context of rapid urbanisation, there is wide awareness about the need to minimize the environmental costs of urbanisation. Environmental damage and depletion of non-renewable resources need to be addressed to meet present and future challenges such as climate change and associated vulnerabilities.

12.3.2 Climate Change and Water Supply: Climate change could affect water supply systems in any number of ways. It can affect the water demand for drinking and cooling systems. Where climate change leads to failure of small local water sources such as wells, it could lead to greater demand for regional water supplies. Changes in precipitation patterns could lead to reduction in water availability and fall in water tables. In coastal areas, it could lead to saline intrusions in rivers and ground water. Loss of melt water could reduce river flows during critical times.

A change in water availability and supply also affects sewered sanitation and drainage systems. When water supplies reduce, sewerage systems also become vulnerable. Further, sewage treatment plants are vulnerable to floods or sea level rise, as these are often located near rivers or seas. Where the sewer outfalls are in the sea, sea level rise will affect the functioning of such systems. Storm water drainage systems could become frequently overloaded and cause flooding if heavy storms become more frequent due to climate change. The impact of inadequate drainage systems in cities like Mumbai are already being felt leading to flooding and huge economic losses. More frequent floods could also present a significant threat if these lead to contamination of flood waters with faecal material.

12.3.3 Occurrence of Droughts: One of the climate change risks to the Indian economy and its people, and therefore to sustainability of habitats, is the increased intensity, frequency and geographical coverage of drought. Its primary impact is on rural areas where agriculture, animal husbandry, and to a lesser extent forestry and fishing, are significantly impacted leading to cycles of seasonal and distress migration. Droughts lead to drinking water shortages and increase in food and biomass fuel prices that hurt the urban poor and middle classes and hence the city economy. It also leads to a number of other impacts like depressed demand for secondary goods and services because of depressed agricultural demand. Climate change related impacts may render subsistence agriculture uneconomical in parts of semi-arid central, western and southern India, fuelling migration of rural population to urban areas.

Climate change may increase droughts in semi-arid peninsular and western India, leading to further misery for the landless and small and marginal farmers, who are typically forced to migrate to cities. They form the most vulnerable groups in cities—having limited skills, education, capital and access to social networks that underpin much economic and social mobility in urban India. They are also more likely to live in illegal and unserviced settlements that are exposed to a wide range of environmental risks varying from flooding to fire and continual cycles of demolition and eviction by civil authorities. They are therefore, dual victims of existing natural hazards and emerging climate change—displaced from their original places of residence and occupations and challenged by urban risks at their new places of residence.

12.3.4 River Hydrology and Inland Flooding: The most serious regional impact of climate change could be changes in the river hydrology in the Indo-Gangetic plain and the Brahmaputra valley due to glacial melt and regression of the Himalayan glaciers. The sustainability of habitats in these regions would be at risk. Inter-basin transfers could be amongst the options that might need to be considered.

Climate change is also expected to increase the severity of flooding in many Indian river basins, especially of the Godavari and Mahanadi along the eastern coast. Floods are expected to increase in north-western India adjoining Pakistan, and in most coastal plains in spite of existing upstream dams and multi-purpose projects. Extreme precipitation is expected to show a substantial increase in some parts of the country. Sanitation infrastructure is the main determinant of the contamination of urban flood-water with faecal material presenting a substantial threat of enteric diseases. In addition to flood hazards, more extreme rainfall events associated with climate change will also cause hazards from landslides in many urban centres in hilly regions.

Dealing with likely increase in risks associated with storm water will require a significant revision of urban planning practices across cities in the flood affected regions. Flood and climate change mitigation and adaptation measures will have to be integrated into day-to-day urban development and service delivery systems. Due to higher precipitation in more intense events, there is a need to increase the margin of design safety to enhance the hydraulic capacity of the sections. This will require additional investments.

12.3.5 Cyclonic Storms, Storm Surges and Coastal Flooding: Yet another important climate change induced risk is that of cyclonic storms, storm surges and accompanying coastal inundation. The high concentration of population, especially on the eastern coast, has led to extremely high vulnerability in this region, leading to devastating loss of life and property. The 1999 Orissa super cyclone killed over 10,000 people, devastated buildings, lifeline infrastructure and economic assets across 10 coastal and six inland districts, which included a number of towns and cities due to a mixture of devastating storm surges, cyclonic winds and coastal flooding.

Cyclones and storm surges could have a devastating impact on large urban centres including the mega cities of Mumbai and Chennai, the million plus cities of Vishakapatnam and Surat as well as other cities like Bharuch, Bhavnagar and Jamnagar apart from causing critical bottlenecks in important ports such as Kandla. Increased migration to the coast, powered by huge investments in coastal infrastructure, settlements and enterprises could lead to a substantial rise in losses.

12.3.6 Sea Level Rise: Rising sea levels in coastal areas would increase the risk of flooding and increase the vulnerability of communities residing in these areas, especially the poor.

It is estimated that sea level could rise by 3.5 to 34.6 inches between 1990 and 2100, making coastal groundwater saltier, endangering wetlands, and inundating valuable land and coastal communities. The most vulnerable stretches along the Western Indian coast are Khambhat and Kachchh in Gujarat, Mumbai and parts of the Konkan coast and south Kerala. The deltas of the Ganga, Krishna, Godavari, Cauvery and Mahanadi on the east coast may be threatened, along with irrigated land and a number of urban and other settlements that are situated in them. The loss of these important economic and cultural regions could have a considerable impact in some states.

There is also a need for better empirical data regarding storm surge and tidal gauge data for better appreciation of the impact of climate change in coastal areas. Tools like micro-modelling could help in developing better understanding.

According to Inter-Governmental Panel on Climate Change (IPCC), Indian coasts will be exposed to increasing risks such as coastal erosion due to climate change and sea level rise. Sea water intrusion is likely to increase the habitat of brackish water fisheries but coastal inundation is likely to damage the aquaculture industry significantly. Changes in currents, water temperature, salinity, strength of upwelling and mixing layer thickness in the West Pacific and North Indian Oceans are expected due to climate change. Sea level rise will exacerbate the already declining fish productivity in Asia. Flooding caused by sea level rise is expected to affect millions of additional people, with small islands and the crowded delta regions around large Asian rivers (such as the Ganges and Brahmaputra) facing the highest risk. The IPCC has identified four deltas along the coast of India that are particularly vulnerable: Ganges-Brahmaputra (extremely vulnerable), Godavari (highly vulnerable), Krishna and Mahanadi (medium vulnerability). Stability of wetlands including mangroves and coral reefs around Asia is likely to be increasingly threatened.

12.4 India's Approach to Climate Change

The climate of India may be broadly described as tropical monsoonal type. India's climate is affected by two seasonal winds: the North-East monsoon and the South-West monsoon. The North-East monsoon, commonly known as the winter monsoon blows from land to sea, whereas the South-West monsoon, known as the summer monsoon blows from sea to land after crossing the Indian Ocean, the Arabian Sea, and the Bay of Bengal. The South-West monsoon brings most of the rainfall during a year in the country.

India is a large developing country with nearly 700 million rural population directly dependent on climate-sensitive sectors (agriculture, forests and fisheries) and natural resources (water, biodiversity, mangroves, coastal zones, grasslands) for subsistence and livelihoods. Further, the adaptive capacity of dry land farmers, forest dwellers, fisher folk and nomadic shepherds is very low.

Climate change may alter the distribution and quality of India's natural resources and adversely affect the livelihoods of its people. With an economy closely linked to its natural resource base and climatically-sensitive sectors, India may face a major threat because of the projected change in climate. With climate change, there would be increasing scarcity of water, reduction in yields of forest biomass, and increased risk to human health. The contribution of India to the cumulative global emissions is only 5 percent. Thus, historically and at present, India's share in the carbon stock in the atmosphere is relatively miniscule when compared to its distribution over the nation's population.

Climate change, resulting from anthropogenic emissions and increasing concentrations of a suite of gases called *greenhouse gases* (GHGs)—mainly due to fossil fuel use, certain agricultural and industrial activities, and deforestation—has the potential, over the next few generations, to significantly alter global climatic conditions. This would result in large changes in ecosystems, leading to possibly catastrophic disruptions of livelihoods, economic activity, living conditions, and human health. On the other hand, the abatement of GHGs involves significant economic costs.

While climate change is a global environmental issue, different countries bear different levels of responsibility for increases in atmospheric GHG concentrations. Further, the adverse impacts of climate change will fall disproportionately on those who have the least responsibility for causing the problem, in particular, developing countries including India.

Though India is a signatory to UNFCCC, it is not required to contain its GHG emissions. India's policies for sustainable development—by way of promoting energy efficiency and the use of renewable energy, changing the fuel mix to cleaner sources, energy pricing, pollution abatement, afforestation, mass transport—themselves result in a relatively GHG benign growth path.

12.5 National Action Plan on Climate Change (NAPCC)

As a part of voluntary actions to address climate change related concerns, India launched NAPCC on June 30, 2008. It stresses that maintaining a high growth rate is essential for increasing living standards of the vast majority of people of India and reducing their vulnerability of the impacts of climate change. Accordingly, it identifies measures that promote the objectives of sustainable development of India while also yielding to benefits for addressing climate change.

NAPCC estimated the per capita emissions of carbon dioxide in India at 1.02 metric ton per capita which is well below the world average of 4.25 and that for China at 3.60. The energy intensity of the economy is also demonstrated as having declined very considerably since the 1980s, to the present level comparing favourably with that of the least energy-intensive developed countries.

The NAPCC is co-ordinated by the Ministry of Environment and Forests and implemented through the nodal Ministries and is aimed at advancing relevant actions in specific sectors/areas.

NAPCC advocates a strategy that promotes, firstly, the adaptation to climate change and secondly, further enhancement of the ecological sustainability of India's development path.

Eight national missions—in the areas of solar energy, enhanced energy efficiency, sustainable agriculture, sustainable habitat, water, Himalayan ecosystem, increasing the forest cover, and strategic knowledge for climate change—form the core of NAPCC. These National Missions, which form the core of NAPCC, represent multi-pronged, long-term and integrated strategies for achieving key goals in the context of climate change. The focus is on promoting understanding of climate change, adaptation and mitigation, energy efficiency and natural resource conservation.

State Governments are also preparing, under the advice of the Central Government, State Action Plans aimed at creating institutional and programme-oriented capacities to address climate change. These, together with the National Missions, will enhance climate change-related actions in the public and private domains.

The eight National Missions of NAPCC are as under:

1. Jawaharlal Nehru National Solar Mission (JNNSM).
2. National Mission for Enhanced Energy Efficiency (NMEEE).
3. National Mission on Strategic Knowledge for Climate Change (NMSKCC).
4. National Mission for Sustaining Himalayan Ecosystem (NMSHE).
5. National Water Mission (NWM).
6. Green India Mission (GIM).
7. National Mission on Sustainable Habitat (NMSH).
8. National Mission for Sustainable Agriculture (NMSA).

12.6 Other National and Sub-National Initiatives

In addition to the National Action Plan on Climate Change, the Government of India has taken several other measures to promote sustainable development and address the threat of climate change. These initiatives operate at the national and sub-national level and span domains that include climate change research, clean technology research and development, finance, and energy efficiency and renewable energy policy and deployment.

12.6.1 National Clean Energy Fund (NCEF): The Government of India created NCEF in 2010 for the purpose of financing and promoting clean energy initiatives and funding research in the area of clean energy in the country. The corpus of the fund is built by levying a cess of ₹ 50 (subsequently increased to ₹ 100 in 2014) per tonne of coal produced domestically or imported.

12.6.2 State Action Plan on Climate Change: In 2008, the Government of India launched the National Action Plan on Climate Change (NAPCC) establishing eight priority missions. For the realisation of these proposed actions at the sub-national level, in August 2009 the Prime Minister called upon State Governments to prepare their own State Action Plan on Climate Change (SAPCC) consistent with strategies in the NAPCC.

A common framework for the preparation of SAPCC was

developed to harmonise national and state level actions. The common framework drew largely on the principles of territorial approach to climate change which focused on sub-national planning, building capacities for vulnerability assessment and identifying investment opportunities based on the priorities of a state. The framework provided broad, systematic and step-wise process for the preparation of SAPCC and advocated a participatory approach so that states have enough ownership for the process and the final plan. The recommended approach retained a level of flexibility in order to integrate state level variations in ecosystems, geographic conditions, socio-economic scenario, and other factors.

Almost all states have prepared their State Action Plan. The SAPCCs have both adaptation and mitigation component to address climate change impacts, though adaptation has been identified as a more important element of the plan. These plans have been reviewed and endorsed by the Expert Committee on Climate Change under the Ministry of Environment, Forests and Climate Change, Government of India.

12.6.3 Prime Minister's Council on Climate Change: Government of India set up an elaborate institutional mechanism to consider and address issues relating to climate change. A Council chaired by Prime Minister called Prime Minister's Council on Climate Change was constituted in June 2007 to coordinate national action for assessment, adaptation and mitigation of climate change. The Council provides the overall guidance to climate change related actions taken by various Ministries of the Government and other agencies. The Council was reconstituted in November 2014 with the following objectives:

1. Co-ordinate national action plans for assessment, adaptation and mitigation of climate change.
2. Advise government on pro-active measures that can be taken by India to deal with the challenge of climate change.
3. Facilitate inter-ministerial coordination and guide policy in relevant areas.

12.6.4 Indian Network for Climate Change Assessment (INCCA): To enhance knowledge about the impacts of climate change at the national and sub-national level, INCCA was launched on October 14, 2009.

INCCA has been conceptualised as a network-based scientific programme designed to:

- Assess the drivers and implications of climate change through scientific research.
- Prepare climate change assessments once every two years (greenhouse gas estimations and impact of climate change, associated vulnerabilities and adaptation).
- Develop decision support systems.
- Build capacity towards management of climate change related risks and opportunities.

The programmes envisaged under the aegis of INCCA include those on Black Carbon, Ecosystem Monitoring, Centre for Advance Studies, Impact Assessments, Greenhouse Gas Inventory Programme, Integrated Vulnerability & Adaptation (V&A) Assessments and Developing Scenarios.

Under the Greenhouse Gas Inventory Programme, a report on 'India's Greenhouse Gas Emission, 2007' was published in May 2010. This report contains updated information on India's greenhouse gas emissions for the year 2007. The assessment was prepared by 83 experts belonging to 19 institutions from across the country.

Under the Impact Assessments Programme, a "Climate Change in India: 4x4 Assessment" has been undertaken to ascertain impacts in 2030s. This assessment brings together four major regions in India, namely Himalayan region, the North-Eastern region, the Western Ghats and the Coastal Region in regard to observed climate and climate change projections in the year 2030 on 4 key sectors of agriculture, water, natural ecosystem, biodiversity, and health.

The National Carbonaceous Aerosols Programme (NCAP) aims to enhance the understanding of the role of carbonaceous aerosols on climate change, to prepare an inventory of black carbon emissions in the country and to assess its impacts on glacier melting. The science plan for the "Black Carbon Research Initiative—National Carbonaceous Aerosols Programme (NCAP)" was launched in March 2011.

12.6.5 National Institute for Climate Change Studies and Actions (NICCSA): NICCSA is being set up by the Government of India under the Climate Change Action Programme (CCAP) of the Ministry of Environment, Forests and Climate Change. The Institute will conduct analytical studies on scientific, environmental, economic development and technological issues related to climate change.

12.6.6 Expert Group on Low Carbon Strategies for Inclusive Growth: This Expert Group was set up by the Planning Commission, Government of India, in 2010 to suggest low carbon pathways consistent with inclusive growth in India. The high-level Expert Group was composed of representatives from relevant government ministries, industry, think tanks and research institutions.

The Expert Group was required to report on the following:

- Its evaluation of some key alternative low carbon options with an analysis of their cost-benefit, and relative merits and demerits.
- An Action Plan comprising of critical low carbon initiatives to be undertaken, including sector-specific initiatives, along with a suggested timeline and targets starting 2011, that can feed into the Twelfth Five Year Plan (2012-17).
- List of enabling legislations, rules or policies required to operationalise the lowcarbon roadmap.

The Expert Group submitted its Interim Report in May 2011. This report provided a menu of options and showed that it is possible for India to reduce its emission intensity by 20-25 percent over 2005 levels by the year 2020. The Final Report, submitted in April 2014, provides a more detailed and longer term assessment of these options, and the macroeconomic and welfare implications of the low carbon strategy.

The Expert Group gave high priority to inclusive growth and noted that pursuit of low carbon development is consistent with growth and inclusion. In the low carbon strategy assessed, energy efficiencies in households, buildings, industry and transport play important roles. At the same time, low carbon supply technologies, such as solar and wind in the power sector, and greater use of public transport and non-motorized transport are critical. Increased sequestration through enlarged green cover through Green India Mission also helps. Reduced local environmental pollution and dependence on imported energy were also identified as benefits of a low carbon strategy.

However, the Expert Group recognised that the additional investment required for a low carbon strategy would leave less investment available for other sectors.

To sum up, India is extremely vulnerable to the impacts of climate change and significant measures are needed to build climate resilience and assist communities with adaptation. Several programmes are already underway in many parts of India, often in partnership with local financial institutions and grassroots non-governmental organisations that are working with local communities on project implementation. Through its corporate social responsibility programmes and other initiatives, Indian industry is also promoting sustainable livelihoods and infrastructure development across the country. Additionally, there are measures that India can take to promote sustainable and inclusive growth in a less carbon-intensive manner. Many of these actions will have to be designed and implemented by industry and civil society organisations.

India, as a party to UNFCCC, 1992 has been committed to address the global problem on the basis of the principle of *common but differentiated responsibilities and respective capabilities* of the member Parties. Since India is highly vulnerable to climate change, it is in its interest to have a global agreement. This, however, has to be consistent with its National Environmental Policy, 2006 which requires *equal per capita entitlements of global environmental resources to all countries.*

Endnote

1. Bali Action Plan on Technological Options, agreed in December 2007, launched a comprehensive process to enable the full, effective and sustained implementation of the United Nations Framework Convention on Climate Change (UNFCCC, 2007) through long-term cooperative action, now, up to and beyond 2012, in order to reach an agreed outcome and adopt a decision in Copenhagen in December 2009. The Bali Action Plan attaches equal weight to mitigation and adaptation, and identifies technology and finance as the key mechanisms to enable developing countries to respond to climate change. Recent years have seen a surge in research and policy analysis on ways in which technology and finance can support mitigation. Similar studies for adaptation are much more recent, and their results therefore less mature.

   The traditional view of adaptation tends to assume that a national government is responsible for implementing technological adaptation measures (e.g., new seed varieties, dams, early-warning systems and irrigation schemes) based on specific knowledge of future climate conditions.

   Even though climate science has made great advances over the past years, it often remains difficult to project future impacts of climate change in sufficient detail to justify investment in technological adaptation measures, in particular on a local scale. An important uncertainty relates to the effect of a changing climate on the frequency, magnitude and spatial occurrence of extreme weather events, such as floods, cyclones and droughts. Planning specific measures based on projections of future climate conditions therefore presents a great challenge to developing countries.

13

India's Five Year Plans on Urban Development and Services (First Plan to Twelfth Plan)

13.1 First Five Year Plan: 1951-52 to 1955-56

First Plan witnessed the first steps in a national housing programme which assumed growing importance in future plans. This included a subsidised industrial housing scheme and a low income group housing scheme. Housing schemes for plantation labour and for labour in coal and mica mines were also implemented as part of the programme. These programmes were substantially expanded during the Second Plan, in the course of which three new programmes, namely rural housing, slum clearance and sweepers' housing and middle income group housing were taken up.

Early in 1952 a new policy was announced whereby the Central Government was prepared to pay a subsidy up to 20 percent of the cost of construction, including the cost of land, provided the balance was met by the employers who would also let out the houses to genuine workers. The houses thus constructed remained the property of the employers.

The provision for housing in the State Plans was of the order of ₹ 10.19 crore.

Housing programmes were also undertaken by the Ministries of Rehabilitation, Defence, Railways, Iron and Steel, and Communications. State Governments and a certain number of local authorities also had their own housing programmes.

13.2 Second Five Year Plan: 1956-57 to 1960-61

During the Second Plan, the Life Insurance Corporation began to provide funds for house building to middle income groups and to State Governments for undertaking rental housing for their low paid employees. Housing on a considerable scale was also undertaken by the Central Government Departments and public enterprises for their employees.

A scheme for giving financial assistance to State Governments and local bodies to enable them to clear some of the worst slums in big cities was initiated during the Second Plan. By the end of the Second Plan, 208 projects costing about ₹ 19 crore and involving re-housing of 58,200 families living in slum conditions were taken up in different towns and cities. About 18,000 units were completed. For such of the families as could not afford to pay even the subsidised rent of a pucca tenement, the scheme provided for skeletal housing and open developed plots with a separate washing platform and latrine for each family, leaving it to the slum dwellers to build huts of a prescribed pattern themselves on a self-help basis in accordance with the technical directions of the State Government.

The housing programme which had its beginning in the First Plan was directed mainly towards housing for industrial workers and low income groups. The programme was considerably expanded during the Second Five Year Plan with the introduction of schemes of slum clearance and slum improvement, plantation labour housing, village housing and land acquisition and development.

A few other specific schemes designed to benefit sections of the community like scheduled castes, scheduled tribes and backward classes in rural areas, handloom weavers, displaced persons etc. were undertaken. The housing programme for workers in the coal and mica industries was implemented with resources provided by the labour welfare funds for these industries.

13.3 Third Five Year Plan: 1961-62 to 1965-66

Third Plan provided ₹ 142 crore as against the revised outlay of ₹ 84 crore in the Second Plan for housing and urban development programmes. In addition, funds for housing were also provided by the Life Insurance Corporation, whose contribution was at about ₹ 60 crore.

Third Plan provided for a programme of about ₹ 29 crore for slum clearance and improvement.

Some States like Mysore, Madras, Madhya Pradesh, Assam, Punjab, West Bengal and Delhi Administration enacted legislations for speedier acquisition of slum areas and for scaling down the rate of compensation.

In the Third Plan, 529 new urban water supply and sanitation schemes were taken up at a cost of ₹ 13 crore in addition to 53 schemes continuing from the Second Plan period. Most of them were completed.

Rural water supply schemes were taken up under the programmes for community development, local development works and welfare of backward classes. These were supplemented by the National Water Supply and Sanitation Programmes of the Ministry of Health. The latter was confined to those groups of villages, where the tapping of water resources required a measure of technical skill. In executing this programme, emphasis was laid on providing water to areas which suffered from water scarcity and salinity and where water-borne diseases were endemic. At an estimated cost of ₹ 27 crore, 1,764 schemes were completed during the Third Plan.

13.4 Fourth Five Year Plan: 1969-70 to 1973-74 [1]

The Plan laid emphasis on cheaper houses to be provided by organising the supply of material and by pursuing research into practicable schemes of cheaper ways of building. States, local authorities and statutory bodies were asked to play a more active role in organising this effort. The private sector was required to standardise building components and manufacture them on a large scale.

Introduced in 1957, the village housing projects scheme provided for assistance to villagers for construction or improvement of houses, for house sites to landless agricultural workers and for streets and drains in selected villages. The scheme did not make much progress.

13.5 Fifth Five Year Plan: 1974-75 to 1978-79 [2]

Provision made in the State Plans for integrated urban development was supplemented by funds provided for the scheme of integrated urban development in the Central Sector. This scheme provided loan assistance to State Governments for developing the necessary infrastructure. It was expected that over a period of time the State Governments would be able to build up a corpus of seed money for expansion programmes.

Urban development programmes were taken up in the three metropolitan cities of Calcutta, Bombay and Madras and nine other cities in 1974-75. Additional six cities were taken up in 1975-76.

The main thrust of the programmes in the Fifth Plan was directed towards ameliorating the conditions of the backward sections of the society. This was sought to be achieved by augmenting the programmes for the construction of housing colonies by State Housing Boards and by taking up on a large scale a programme for the provision of house-sites for landless labourers in rural areas. While the bulk of this programme was undertaken in the State Plans, the activities of the Housing and Urban Development Corporation in the Central sector were geared up to meet the expanding demand. A provision was made to increase the Equity participation in HUDCO to enable it to generate resources of the order of ₹ 150 crore in the Fifth Plan period. Separate provisions were made for the scheme of subsidised housing for plantation labourers and dock labourers. Adequate emphasis was placed on research and development activities for generating better and cheaper designs.

13.6 Sixth Five Year Plan: 1980-81 to 1984-85 [3]

The Sixth Plan addressed the problems of the spatial distribution of population, housing, water supply and sanitation in an integrated manner. Given the resource constraints, public intervention in these fields had to be highly selective and centred on the areas of greatest need. The thrust of planning measures was inevitably towards the assistance of the poor—in rural as well as in urban areas. Priority was given to providing sites to the rural landless along with construction assistance wherever possible. Similarly, priority was attached to providing at least one source of safe water supply in every problem village.

The Sixth Plan viewed the problems of shelter and urban development as being inexorably connected with the provision of safe water supply and adequate sanitation.

The objectives of the Plan were to reduce substantially the number of absolutely shelterless people and to provide conditions for others to improve their housing environment. Specifically, the objectives of the Sixth Plan were as follows:

1. Provision of house-sites and assistance for the construction of dwellings for rural landless labourers. This included an element of housing extension services to assist in proper planning of layouts, sanitation etc.
2. In view of the severe constraints of public resources, public sector social housing schemes were designed to benefit the maximum number of people. They were directed towards the economically weaker sections of the community and designed so that they were within their paying capacity. For the rest, investment policies were framed so as to promote and encourage self-help housing. In addition, resources of institutional agencies like HUDCO and State Housing Boards were augmented to enable them to provide infrastructural facilities as a means of encouraging housing in the private sector.
3. Specific efforts were made to secure a reduction in costs in public housing schemes by reviewing standards and by using cheap and alternative building materials. This necessitated the promotion of research in building technology and the development of cheap and local building materials. Attention was paid to the possibilities of energy conservation in construction technology by

utilising existing materials in local use in the construction of shelter.

4. Specific attention was given to housing activity in small, medium and intermediate towns which had been neglected hitherto.
5. Low cost housing techniques including existing local methods so as to bring down unit costs.
6. Modification of existing building by-laws, land use controls, minimum plot requirements and land requirements for roads which often made it difficult to reduce the costs of shelter.
7. Avoidance of direct subsidies in urban housing. In the case of higher and middle income housing, subsidies were totally avoided. For low income housing, where some direct subsidies were inevitable, they were in the form of infrastructural and sanitation facilities which improved the environment for people to invest in their own shelter.
8. Greater stimulus and support was given to private housing in the middle and lower income groups so that there were incentives to channelise savings into housing construction.
9. In order to ensure a balanced distribution of urban population and to slow down the growth of metropolises, a centrally sponsored scheme of Integrated Development of Small and Medium Towns (IDSMT) was introduced during the Sixth Plan to provide infrastructure and other facilities in these towns. The Sixth Plan made a provision of ₹ 96 crore in the Central sector with a matching provision in the States' sector for the development of about 200 towns. During the Sixth Plan the scheme was applicable to small and medium towns having a population of less than 1 lakh.

13.7 Seventh Five Year Plan: 1985-86 to 1989-90

The Seventh Plan had the following objectives as regards housing:

1. Promotion and encouragement of self-help housing.

2. Provision of house sites to the balance of rural families identified so far and assistance for construction of dwellings for those rural families already provided house-sites.
3. Reducing the cost of housing units so that they were within the paying capacity of the targeted groups, like economically weaker sections, low income group and middle income group.
4. Providing stimulus and support for private housing especially for the middle and lower income groups so as to channel increased savings into housing.
5. Securing reduction in construction costs not only by adopting low-cost housing techniques and standards but also modifications in building by-laws, land use control, minimum plot requirements etc.
6. Harnessing science and technology efforts for improving building technology and development of cheap and local building materials.

In the Seventh Plan, emphasis was placed on the following major programmes:

1. Environmental Improvement of Slums (EIS) programme was continued with greater vigour and steps were taken to provide security of tenure to the slum dwellers so that they could develop a stake in maintaining and improving their habitat.
2. The Plan included a provision of ₹ 930 crore in the States' share for provision of infrastructure facilities like roads, pavements, minor civic works as well as such amenities as bus sheds, market and shopping complexes and theatres. This provision also included the States' contribution against the centrally sponsored scheme of Integrated Development of Small and Medium Towns (IDSMT). A provision of ₹ 317.58 crore was included for the development projects being undertaken in the Calcutta Metropolitan Development Area (CMDA) as part of the externally aided programmes and for the development of

State Capital Projects of Gandhi Nagar, Bhopal and Chandigarh.

3. An outlay of ₹ 35 crore was included in the Plan of the Ministry of Works and Housing for the development of the National Capital Region (NCR) around Delhi. This was in addition to the provisions included in the plans of other Central Ministries like Railways, Shipping and Transport etc. The NCR Plan envisaged deconcentration of economic activity from the core of Delhi into regional towns located in Haryana, Rajasthan and Uttar Pradesh. A statutory Planning Board for NCR was constituted under the Chairmanship of the Minister for Works and Housing and a detailed Plan for Development of NCR was prepared.
4. It was proposed to set up an Urban Infrastructure Development Finance Corporation to deal with the emerging urban problems that the country was facing. The Plan provided ₹ 35 crore in the urban development sector and ₹ 20 crore in the water supply and sanitation sector, as initial capital for the Corporation which augmented its resources by raising funds from institutional sources.

13.8 Eighth Five Year Plan: 1992-93 to 1996-97

The Eighth Plan emphasized the role of Government in the following areas:

1. Creating an enabling environment to remove constraints of housing activity for various sections of the population.
2. Promoting a substantial increase in the supply of housing and basic services.
3. Supporting standardisation and upgradation of the housing stock and to stimulate rental housing.

The long-term objective of the Plan was provision of *Shelter for All.*

The distinctive features of the Eighth Plan on urban development were as follows:

1. Consolidation and operationalisation of spatial and economic dimension of planning for the urban sector.

2. Convergence of all related programmes to create the desired impact in small and medium towns beyond the threshold level.
3. Taking measures—legal, financial and organisational—for enhanced and equitable supply of urban land.
4. Exploring innovations in funding pattern and role of private developers in specific areas.
5. Modification of conventional city plans to incorporate the measures needed for restoration of healthy environment.
6. Emphasising both employment generation and access to basic services involving community level organisations.

13.9 Ninth Five Year Plan: 1997-98 to 2001-02

The Ninth Plan took cognisance of three critical components of development of human settlements, namely drinking water, sanitation and housing. In this perspective, the major sectoral objectives of the Ninth Plan were the following:

1. Development of urban areas as economically efficient, socially equitable and environmentally sustainable entities.
2. Accelerated development of housing, particularly for the low income groups and other disadvantaged groups.
3. Development and upgradation of urban infrastructure services to meet the needs of a growing population.
4. Alleviation of urban poverty and unemployment.
5. Promoting accessibility and affordability of the poor to housing and basic services.
6. Promoting efficient and affordable mass urban transportation systems in metropolitan cities.
7. Improvement of urban environment.
8. Promoting private sector participation in the provision of public infrastructure and of the community and NGOs in urban planning and management of specific components of urban services.
9. Democratic decentralisation and strengthening of municipal governance.

13.10 Tenth Five Year Plan: 2002-03 to 2006-07

The Tenth Plan highlighted the role of the urban local bodies as follows:

1. To be responsive and accountable to the community.
2. To develop cities with standards of service comparable to the best in that particular category.
3. To constantly improve their capabilities so as to equip themselves to undertake their tasks in resource-raising, service provision, and poverty alleviation.

The Tenth Plan envisaged augmentation of water supply in urban areas to reach the prescribed norms, higher degree of reliability, assurance of water quality, a high standard of operation and management, accountability to customers and in particular special arrangements to meet the needs of the urban poor and levy and recovery of user charges to finance the maintenance functions as well as facilitate further investment in the sector. The achievement of these tasks depended to a large extent on the willingness of the State Governments and urban local bodies to restructure water supply organisations, levy reasonable water rates, take up reforms in billing, accounting and collection and become credit worthy in order to have access to market funding. Measures were suggested for water conservation, re-use and recycling of waste water.

While there were progress in some of the suggestions of Tenth Plan like adoption of the rain water harvesting, tariff revision for sustaining O&M, augmenting the water supply and reducing the leakages etc., this progress was confined to some pockets of the country. However the Tenth Plan triggered the realisation that institutions have to be self-sustaining and efficient service was the key to realise that.

13.11 Eleventh Five Year Plan: 2007-08 to 2011-12

The Jawaharlal Nehru National Urban Renewal Mission (JNNURM), which commenced in the Tenth Plan, continued in the Eleventh Plan to be the main vehicle for raising the level of infrastructure and utilities in the existing cities. The aim of the Mission is to create economically productive, efficient, equitable and responsive cities and the focus is on the following:

1. Improving and augmenting the economic and social infrastructure of cities.
2. Ensuring basic services to the urban poor including security of tenure at affordable prices.
3. Initiating wide ranging urban sector reforms whose primary aim is to eliminate legal, institutional and financial constraints that have impeded investment in urban infrastructure and services.
4. Strengthening municipal governments and their functioning in accordance with the provisions of the Constitutional (Seventy-fourth) Amendment Act, 1992.

Urban poverty alleviation and slum development was an important component of the Eleventh Plan. Tenth Plan schemes under the JNNURM for providing affordable shelter and decent living and working conditions to the poor and for helping them to develop self-employment enterprises were continued. The Swaran Jayanti Shahri Rozgar Yojana (SJSRY), a Centrally Sponsored Scheme to provide gainful employment to the urban unemployed (below the poverty line) was implemented in a revamped form during the Eleventh Plan period.

13.12 Twelfth Five Year Plan: 2012-13 to 2016-17

Urbanization is a key indicator of economic development and should be seen as a positive factor for overall development. As an economy grows, its towns and cities expand in size and volume. Urbanization is a natural consequence of economic changes that take place as a country develops. At the same time, urbanization helps to contribute to the growth process at large. This is manifest in the increasing contribution of urban sector to national income.

The process of urbanization has gathered considerable momentum in recent times and this has put urban infrastructure and services under severe strain. For example, several cities in India have only two to four hours of water supply during the entire day. Smaller cities, because of inadequate financial resources, have found it particularly difficult to cope with the increasing demands on services.

The positive role of urbanization is often over-shadowed by the evident deterioration in the physical environment and quality of life in the urban areas caused by widening gap between demand and supply of essential services and infrastructure. This results from increasing population, pressure on urban centres, most of which are financially and organisationally ill-equipped to respond to infrastructural needs. Public investment in urban infrastructure has also been less than adequate. The challenge of reorienting the urbanization process, thus, lies in overcoming the infrastructural deficiencies and taking the best advantage of economic momentum inherent in urbanization.

Unfolding its strategy for improved and effective urbanization, the Twelfth Plan has focused on the following five enablers:

1. Strengthening urban governance.
2. Urban planning.
3. Financing urban infrastructure.
4. Building capacity for managing urbanization.
5. Leveraging innovation to solve the challenges of urbanization.

Endnotes

1. Regular planning process in India was disrupted when the country came under severe shocks such as hostilities with Pakistan (1965), droughts for two successive years (1965-66 and 1966-67), devaluation of the rupee (1966) and inflationary pressure. On account of these adverse circumstances, the draft outline of the Fourth Plan prepared in 1966 had to be abandoned. Instead, three Annual Plans (1966-67, 1967-68 and 1968-69) were prepared and implemented. Proper planning process was resumed when the Fourth Five Year Plan (1969-70 to 1973-74) became operational on April 1, 1969.
2. The Fifth Five Year Plan (1974-75 to 1978-79) was introduced when the country was reeling under severe economic strains such as run-away inflation caused by unprecedented increase in

international oil prices in the wake of 1973 Gulf Crisis and the failure of the Government to takeover the wholesale trade in wheat. When the Janata Government assumed power at the Centre in 1977, it did not allow the Fifth Plan to run its full course of five years (1974-75 to 1978-79) and truncated it at the end of the fourth year (i.e. on March 31, 1978). The Plan was disrupted and replaced by the so-called rolling plan which proved to be a non-starter.

3. The political turmoil of the late 1970s witnessed two Sixth Plans. (a) The Sixth Five Year Plan (1978-79 to 1982-83) of the Janata Party Government which was abandoned when Mrs. Indira Gandhi returned to power at the Centre in early 1980; (b) The Sixth Five Year Plan (1980-81 to 1984-85) introduced by the new Government led by Mrs. Indira Gandhi. The latter ran its full course successfully. It focused on direct attack on poverty.

14

Recent Finance Commissions on Local Bodies

14.1 Tenth Finance Commission (FC-X) on Local Bodies

FC-X did not have any mandate, in its terms of reference, to make recommendations for the local bodies. However, the Seventy-third and Seventy-fourth Constitutional amendments had become effective before the Commission had finalised its report and, therefore, it took the view that in terms of the sub-clauses (bb) and (c) of Article 280(3), it was obliged to make recommendations regarding measures needed to augment the Consolidated Fund of the States for supplementation of the resources of the panchayats and the municipalities. FC-X analysed the scope of such duty cast on it and made the following observations:

1. The need for augmentation of the Consolidated Fund of the States should first be ascertained and only thereafter the measures for such augmentation be recommended.
2. Such measures need not necessarily involve transfer of resources from the Centre.
3. Once the SFCs complete their task, the Finance Commission becomes duly bound to assess and build into the expenditure stream of the States the funding requirements for supplementing the resources of the panchayats and the municipalities. Measures needed for augmentation of the Consolidated Funds of the States may be determined accordingly.
4. The responsibility for sharing and assigning taxes and providing grants to the local bodies rests with the States and does not stand transferred to the Centre.
5. The transfer of duties and functions listed in the Eleventh and Twelfth Schedules of the Constitution would also involve concomitant transfer of staff and resources.

Transfers of duties and functions to the local bodies should, therefore, not entail any extra financial burden.

Since the recommendations of the State Finance Commissions were not available to the FC-X, the latter was in doubt whether it could recommend measures for augmenting State resources for the purpose of supplementing the resources of panchayats and municipalities. To resolve the dilemma, it decided to make *ad hoc* provision of specific grants to States in the following manner.

1. An *ad hoc* provision of ₹ 100 per capita of rural population in each State to be distributed amongst panchayats over and above their due by way of their share of the assigned taxes, duties, tolls, fees etc.
2. A provision of ₹ 1,000 crore for the 5 year period (1995-2000) covered by its recommendations for urban local bodies.

While making these provisions for grants to panchayats/municipalities, the FC-X made it clear that this need not necessarily be a precedent for future Commissions.

14.2 Eleventh Finance Commission (FC-XI) on Local Bodies

FC-XI was the first to be required by the President, in terms of the Seventy-third and Seventy-fourth Amendments to the Constitution, to recommend the measures needed to augment the Consolidated Fund of a State to supplement the resources of the panchayats and municipalities in the State on the basis of the recommendations of the State Finance Commissions.

The FC-XI recommended grants totalling ₹ 10,000 crore for local bodies during 2000-2005, to be utilised mainly for maintenance of civic services. Of this, ₹ 1,600 crore per annum was for rural local bodies and ₹ 400 crore per annum was for urban local bodies. FC-XI recommended that the amounts of ₹ 1,600 crore and ₹ 400 crore provided for the panchayats and municipalities respectively, for each of the five years (2000-05) be distributed among the States on the following criteria and weights.

1. Population—40 percent.
2. Index of decentralisation—20 percent.
3. Distance from highest per capita income—20 percent.
4. Revenue effort—10 percent.
5. Geographical area—10 percent.

The grants given to local bodies were primarily meant for maintenance of civil services including primary health and family welfare, education as well as other public utility services.

14.3 Twelfth Finance Commission (FC-XII) on Local Bodies

FC-XII made the following recommendations regarding local bodies.

1. A total grant of ₹ 20,000 crore for the panchayati raj institutions and ₹ 5,000 crore for the urban local bodies may be given to the states for the period 2005-10.
2. PRIs should be encouraged to take over the assets relating to water supply and sanitation and utilize the grants for repairs/rejuvenation as also the O&M costs. The PRIs should, however, recover at least 50 percent of the recurring costs in the form of user charges.
3. Out of the grants allocated for the panchayats, priority should be given to expenditure on the O&M costs of water supply and sanitation. This will facilitate panchayats to take over the schemes and operate them.
4. At least 50 percent of the grants provided to each state for the urban local bodies should be earmarked for the scheme of solid waste management through public-private partnership. The municipalities should concentrate on collection, segregation and transportation of solid waste. The cost of these activities, whether carried out in house or out sourced, could be met from the grants.
5. Besides expenditure on the O&M costs of water supply and sanitation in rural areas and on the schemes of solid waste management in urban areas, PRIs and ULBs should, out of the grants allocated, give high priority to expenditure on

creation of data base and maintenance of accounts through the use of modern technology and management systems, wherever possible. Some of the modern methods like GIS (geographical information systems) for mapping of properties in urban areas and computerization for switching over to a modern system of financial management would go a long way in creating strong local governments, fulfilling the spirit of the Seventy-third and Seventy-fourth Constitutional amendments.

6. States may assess the requirement of each local body on the basis of the principles stated by us and earmark funds accordingly out of the total allocation recommended by us.
7. Grants have not been recommended separately for the normal and the excluded areas under the Fifth and Sixth Schedule of the Constitution. The states having such areas may distribute the grants recommended by us to all local bodies, including those in the excluded areas, in a fair and just manner.
8. Central Government should not impose any condition other than those prescribed by us, for release or utilization of these grants, which are largely in the nature of a correction of vertical imbalance between the centre and the states.
9. Normal practice of insisting on the utilization of amounts already released before further releases are considered, may continue and the grants may be released to a state only after it certifies that the previous releases have been passed on to the local bodies. The amounts due to the states in the first year of our award period i.e. 2005-06 may be released without such an insistence.
10. State Governments should not take more than 15 days in transferring the grants to local bodies after these are released by the central government. The entre should take a serious view of any undue delay on the part of the state.
11. Central Government should take note of our views on the issues, while formulating or revising various policy

measures. In particular, action may be taken to raise the ceiling on profession tax.

12. States should adopt the best practices to improve the resources of the panchayats.
13. Suggestions made by us in respect of state finance commissions should be acted upon with a view to strengthening the institution of SFCs, so that it may play an effective role in the system of fiscal transfers to the third tier of government.

14.4 Thirteenth Finance Commission (FC-XIII) on Local Bodies

Regarding the functioning of local bodies, the FC-XIII observed, "There has been considerable progress in the empowerment of panchayati raj institutions (PRIs) and municipalities since the Tenth Finance Commission (FC-X) first made a provision for explicitly supporting local bodies through grants, subsequent to the passage of the 73rd and 74th amendments to the Constitution in 1993. Approximately 30 lakh representatives are regularly elected to about 2.5 lakh local institutions all over the country. Providing basic services at the grassroots level makes them the primary interface of the citizens' interaction with the government. The principle of subsidiarity implies that matters are best handled by the least centralised competent authority. Following this, these institutions need to be adequately empowered—both functionally and financially—to enable them to fulfil the role envisaged for them in the Constitution. The State Finance Commissions (SFCs), which buttress the functioning of local bodies, also need to be strengthened so as to make their functioning more predictable and the process of implementing their recommendations more transparent. A number of recommendations were made by FC-XI and FC-XII towards this end. Some of these recommendations, though important, have not been implemented so far. More needs to be done to promote effective decentralisation". [1]

14.5 Fourteenth Finance Commission (FC-XIV) on Local Bodies

After studying the structure and functioning of local bodies, the Fourteen Finance Commission made the following main recommendations:

1. Local bodies should be required to spend the grants only on the basic services within the functions assigned to them under relevant legislations.
2. Grants should go to gram panchayats, which are directly responsible for the delivery of basic services, without any share for other levels. We expect that the State Governments will take care of the needs of the other levels. The earmarked basic grants for gram panchayats will be distributed among them, using the formula prescribed by the respective SFCs for the distribution of resources. Similarly, the basic grant for urban local bodies will be divided into tier-wise shares and distributed across each tier, namely the municipal corporations, municipalities (the tier-II urban local bodies) and the nagar panchayats (the tier-III local bodies) using the formula given by the respective SFCs. The State Governments should apply the distribution formula of the most recent SFC, whose recommendations have been accepted.
3. Stern action should be ensured if irregularities in the application of funds are noticed or pointed out.
4. State Governments should strengthen SFCs. This would involve timely constitution, proper administrative support and adequate resources for smooth functioning and timely placement of the SFC report before State legislature, with action taken notes.
5. Vacant land tax by peri-urban panchayats be considered. In addition, a part of land conversion charges can be shared by State Governments with municipalities and panchayats.
6. States should review the position and prepare a clear framework of rules for the levy of betterment tax.

7. States may like to consider steps to empower local bodies to impose advertisement tax and improve own revenues from this source.
8. States review the structure of entertainment tax and take action to increase its scope to cover more and newer forms of entertainment.
9. State Governments take action to assign productive local assets to the panchayats, put in place enabling rules for collection and institute systems so that they can obtain the best returns while leasing or renting common resources.
10. Urban local bodies rationalise their service charges in a way that they are able to at least recover the operation and maintenance costs from the beneficiaries.

Endnote

1. *Report of the Thirteenth Finance Commission*, December 2009, p. 149.

Appendix

Appendix

Jawaharlal Nehru National Urban Renewal Mission (JNNURM)

Jawaharlal Nehru National Urban Renewal Mission (JNNURM) was launched on December 3, 2005 to give focused attention to integrated development of urban infrastructure and services in select 65 Mission cities with emphasis on provision of basic services to the urban poor including housing, water supply, sanitation, slum improvement, community toilets etc. There were also sub-components under JNNURM to cater to similar needs of the small towns and cities. Priority had been accorded in sanctioning of projects for water supply, sewerage and drainage sectors. Also, projects had been sanctioned for urban transport sector which include construction of roads, flyovers, bus rapid transport system (BRTS). To support and develop public transport system, procurement of buses was also funded under this programme. Initially the duration of the Mission was 7 years from 2005-06 to 2011-12. The Mission period ended on March 31, 2014 after its extension for completion of projects sanctioned under first phase of JNNURM.

A.1 JNNURM-I (2005-12)

JNNURM-I, which was launched in December 2005, was co-terminus with the Eleventh Five Year Plan (2007-12).

JNNURM-I was launched by the Prime Minister on December 3, 2005 to encourage cities to initiate steps to bring about improvement in the existing service levels in a financially sustainable manner. The objectives of the mission, *inter alia*, included planned development of identified cities including semi-urban areas, outgrowths and urban corridors and improved provision of, basic services to the urban poor. Duration of the mission was 7 years beginning from 2005-06.

The JNNURM-I was implemented in cities with focus on upgradation of urban infrastructure, creation of housing stock, and provision of basic services to the poor through community participation and accountability of urban local bodies. The mission was implemented through: (a) the Basic Services to the Urban Poor (BSUP) programme and (b) the Integrated Housing and Slum Development Programme (IHSDP). The BSUP was applicable to 65 select cities in the country and the remaining cities were covered under the IHSDP.

JNNURM-I subsumed the following ongoing schemes:

1. Infrastructure Development in Mega Cities.
2. Integrated Development of Small and Medium Towns.
3. Accelerated Urban Water Supply Programme.

Cities/urban agglomerations/parastatals were required to prepare detailed project reports for undertaking projects under identified areas. Funds for the identified cities were released to the designated State Nodal Agency, which in turn leveraged, to the extent feasible, additional resources from the financial institutions, private sector and capital market. Private sector participation in development, management and financing of urban infrastructure was clearly delineated.

The admissible components under the mission included urban renewal, water supply (including de-salination plants) and sanitation, sewerage and solid waste management, urban transport, development of heritage areas, preservation of water bodies etc. A provision of ₹ 50,000 crore was agreed to as Central assistance for JNNURM-I for a period of 7 years beginning from 2005-06.

JNNURM-I was a Mission mode approach that integrated the two pressing needs—massive investments/resource required for infrastructure development and at the same time urban reforms those were required to sustain big investments. JNNURM-I was a reform-oriented Government of India assisted fund which was provided as a grant to a set of 63 identified large cities in the country and covered all other census towns under Urban Infrastructure Development Scheme for Small and Medium Towns (UIDSSMT) a component of JNNURM. The Mission aimed to encourage reforms and fast track infrastructure development. The focus was on efficiency in urban infrastructure and services delivery mechanism, community participation, accountability of ULBs/Parastatal agency towards citizens.

A.1.1 Mission Statement: The aim was to encourage reforms and fast track planned development of identified cities. Focus was on efficiency in urban infrastructure and service delivery mechanisms, community participation, and accountability of ULBs parastatal agencies towards citizens.

A.1.2 Objectives of the Mission: The objectives of JNNURM-I were to ensure that the following were achieved in the urban sector:

1. Focussed attention to integrated development of infrastructure services in cities covered under the Mission.
2. Establishment of linkages between asset-creation and asset-management through a slew of reforms for long-term project sustainability.
3. Ensuring adequate funds to meet the deficiencies in urban infrastructural services.
4. Planned development of identified cities including peri-urban areas, outgrowths and urban corridors leading to dispersed urbanization.
5. Scale-up delivery of civic amenities and provision of utilities with emphasis on universal access to the urban poor.
6. Special focus on urban renewal programme for the old city areas to reduce congestion.
7. Provision of basic services to the urban poor including security of tenure at affordable prices, improved housing, water supply and sanitation, and ensuring delivery of other existing universal services of the government for education, health and social security.

A.1.3 Scope of the Mission: The Mission comprised two Sub-Missions, namely:

A. Sub-Mission for Urban Infrastructure and Governance: This was administered by the Ministry of Urban Development through the Sub-Mission Directorate for Urban Infrastructure and Governance. The main thrust of the Sub-Mission was on infrastructure projects relating to water supply and sanitation, sewerage, solid waste management, road network, urban transport and redevelopment of old city areas with a view to upgrading infrastructure therein, shifting industrial and commercial establishments to conforming areas etc.

B. Sub-Mission for Basic Services to the Urban Poor: This was administered by the Ministry of Urban Employment and Poverty Alleviation through the Sub-Mission Directorate for Basic Services to the Urban Poor. The main thrust of the Sub-Mission was on integrated development of slums through projects for providing shelter, basic services and other related civic amenities with a view to providing utilities to the urban poor.

A.1.4 Strategy of the Mission: The objectives of the Mission were met through the adoption of the following strategy:

A. Preparing City Development Plan: Every city was expected to formulate a city development plan (CDP) indicating policies, programmes and strategies, and financing plans.

B. Preparing Projects: The CDP was required to facilitate identification of projects. The Urban Local Bodies (ULBs)/parastatal agencies were required to prepare detailed project reports (DPRs) for undertaking projects in the identified spheres. It was essential that projects were planned in a manner that optimised the life-cycle cost of projects. The life-cycle cost of a project covered the capital outlays and the attendant O&M costs to ensure that assets were in good working condition. A revolving fund was created to meet the O&M requirements of assets created, over the planning horizon. In order to seek JNNURM-I assistance, projects were needed to be developed in a manner that ensured and demonstrated optimisation of the life-cycle costs over the planning horizon of the project.

C. Release and Leveraging of Funds: It was expected

that the JNNURM-I assistance would serve to catalyse the flow of investment into the urban infrastructure sector across the country. Funds from the Central and State Government flowed directly to the nodal agency designated by the State, as grants-in-aid. The funds for identified projects across cities were disbursed to the ULB/parastatal agency through the designated State Level Nodal Agency (SLNA) as soft loan or grant-cum-loan or grant. The SLNA/ULBs in turn leveraged additional resources from other sources.

D. Incorporating Private Sector Efficiencies: In order to optimise the life-cycle costs over the planning horizon, private sector efficiencies could be inducted in development, management, implementation and financing of projects, through public private partnership (PPP) arrangements.

A.1.5 Duration of the Mission: The duration of the Mission was 7 years beginning from the year 2005-06. Evaluation of the experience of implementation of the Mission was undertaken before the commencement of Eleventh Five Year Plan (2007-12) and the programme was suitably calibrated.

A.1.6 Expected Outcomes of the JNNURM-I: On completion of the Mission period, it was expected that ULBs and parastatal agencies would have achieved the following:

1. Modern and transparent budgeting, accounting, financial management systems, designed and adopted for all urban service and governance functions.
2. City-wide framework for planning and governance would be established and become operational.
3. All urban residents would be able to obtain access to a basic level of urban services.
4. Financially self-sustaining agencies for urban governance and service delivery would be established, through reforms to major revenue instruments.
5. Local services and governance would be conducted in a manner that is transparent and accountable to citizens.
6. E-governance applications would be introduced in core

functions of ULBs/parastatal resulting in reduced cost and time of service delivery processes.

A.1.7 Financial Assistance under JNNURM-I: The Government of India proposed substantial assistance through the JNNURM-I over the seven-year period. During this period, funds were provided for proposals that met the Mission's requirements.

Under JNNURM-I, financial assistance was available to the ULBs and parastatal agencies which could deploy these funds for implementing the projects themselves or through the special purpose vehicles (SPVs).

Assistance under JNNURM-I was additional central assistance, which was provided as grant (100 percent central grant) to the implementing agencies.

Further, assistance from JNNURM-I was expected to facilitate further investment in the urban sector. To this end, the implementing agencies were expected to leverage the sanctioned funds under JNNURM to attract greater private sector investments through PPP that enabled sharing of risks between the private and public sector.

A.1.8 Areas of Assistance under JNNURM-I:

A. Assistance for Capacity Building, City Development Plan (CDP), Detailed Project Reports (DPRs), Community Participation, Information, Education and Communication (IEC): The JNNURM-I provided assistance for the above-stated components with a provision of 5 percent of the total central assistance or the actual requirement, whichever was less. In addition, not more than 5 percent of the Central grant or the actual requirement, whichever was less could be used for administrative and other expenses (A&OE) by the States.

For capacity building, ULBs and parastatal agencies could engage consultants, in consultation with the SLNA, and seek reimbursement from the Ministry of Urban Development (MoUD) of the Ministry of Urban Employment and Poverty Alleviation (MoUEPA).

B. Investment Support Component: Investment support

was provided to implementing agencies on a project-specific basis for eligible sectors and projects proposed to be undertaken in eligible cities subject to approval of the Central Sanctioning and Monitoring Committee (CSMC) of MoUD/ MoUEPA.

As part of the process for seeking investment support, each ULB seeking assistance from the JNNURM were required to prepare a CDP that shall *inter alia* include strategy to implement reforms, city-level improvements and an investment plan to address the infrastructure needs in a sustainable manner.

Assistance under investment support could be deployed in the following forms:

(a) Enhancing Resource Availability: The JNNURM-I assistance could be used to leverage additional resources available with the ULBs in addition to their existing resources and transfers from the State. These resources could be utilised for capital investment and O&M investments in a project.

(b) Enhancing Commercial Viability of Projects: In respect of projects, which were not commercially viable on a stand-alone basis, assistance under the JNNURM-I could be sought for enhancing project viability. This assistance could be in the nature of viability gap support to projects.

(c) Ensuring Bankability of Projects: Cash flows of infrastructure projects having long gestation periods are susceptible to variations in cash flows, rendering a project non-bankable. To enhance predictability of underlying cash-flows, credit enhancement mechanisms such as establishing liquidity support mechanisms, up-front debt-service reserve facility, deep discount bonds, contingent liability support and equity support are required in order to make the projects bankable. The JNNURM-I assistance could, therefore, be used for funding such support mechanisms.

A.1.9 Eligible Cities, Sectors and Projects:

A. Eligible Cities: JNNURM-I gave assistance for infrastructure development in the eligible cities/urban agglomerations (UAs) across States in the country. These cities/UAs were selected based as per the following criteria:

Category A: Mega cities/UAs, i.e. cities/UAs with 4 million plus population as per 2001 Census. These were the following: Delhi, Greater Mumbai, Ahmedabad, Bangalore, Chennai, Kolkata and Hyderabad (07).

Category B: Million plus cities/UAs, i.e. cities/UAs with 1 million plus but less than 4 million population as per 2001 Census. These were the following: Patna, Faridabad, Bhopal, Ludhiana, Jaipur, Lucknow, Madurai, Nashik, Pune, Cochin, Varanasi, Agra, Amritsar, Vishakhapatnam, Vadodara, Surat, Kanpur, Nagpur, Coimbatore, Meerut, Jabalpur, Jamshedpur, Asansol, Allahabad, Vijayawada, Rajkot, Dhanbad and Indore (28).

Category C: Cities/UAs with less than 1 million population, i.e. selected cities/UAs (state capitals and other cities/UA of religious/historic and tourist importance): These were the following: Guwahati, Itanagar, Jammu, Raipur, Panaji, Shimla, Ranchi, Thiruvananthapuram, Imphal, Shillong, Aizawl, Kohima, Bhubaneshwar, Gangtok, Agartala, Dehradun, Bodhgaya, Ujjain, Puri, Ajmer-Pushkar, Nainital, Mysore, Pondicherry, Chandigarh, Srinagar, Mathura, Haridwar and Nanded (28).

The cities were required to have elected bodies in position.

B. Sectors and Projects Eligible for Assistance under the Sub-Mission Directorate for Urban Infrastructure and Governance. These were as under:

1. Urban renewal, that is, redevelopment of inner (old) city areas [including widening of narrow streets, shifting of industrial and commercial establishments from non-conforming (inner city) areas to conforming (outer city) areas to reduce congestion, replacement of old and worn out pipes by new and higher capacity ones, renewal of the sewerage, drainage, and solid waste disposal system etc.
2. Water supply (including desalination plants) and sanitation.
3. Sewerage and solid waste management.
4. Construction and improvement of drains and storm water drains.

5. Urban transportation including roads, highways, expressways, MRTS, and metro projects.
6. Parking lots and spaces on PPP basis.
7. Development of heritage areas.
8. Prevention and rehabilitation of soil erosion and landslides only in cases of special category States where such problems are common.
9. Preservation of water bodies.

Note: Land cost was not financed except for acquisition of private land for schemes and projects in the North-Eastern States and hilly States, namely Himachal Pradesh, Uttaranchal and Jammu and Kashmir.

C. Sectors and Projects Eligible for Assistance under the Sub-Mission Directorate for Basic Services to the Urban Poor: These were as follows:

1. Integrated development of slums, housing and development of infrastructure projects in slums in the identified cities.
2. Projects involving development, improvement, and maintenance of basic services to the urban poor.
3. Slum improvement and rehabilitation of projects.
4. Projects on water supply, sewerage, drainage, community toilets, and baths etc.
5. Projects for providing houses at affordable cost for slum dwellers, urban poor, economically weaker sections (EWS) and lower income group (LIG) categories.
6. Construction and improvement of drains and storm water drains.
7. Environmental improvement of slums and solid waste management.
8. Street lighting.
9. Civic amenities like community halls, child care centres etc.
10. Operation and Maintenance of assets created under this component.
11. Convergence of health, education and social security schemes for the urban poor.

Note: Land cost was not financed except for acquisition of

private land for schemes and projects in the North-Eastern States and hilly States, namely Himachal Pradesh, Uttaranchal and Jammu and Kashmir.

D. Inadmissible Components for JNNURM-I Assistance: Projects pertaining to the following were not eligible for JNNURM-I assistance: (a) power, (b) telecom, (c) health, (d) education, (e) wage employment programme and staff components and (f) creation of fresh employment opportunities.

A.1.10 Agenda of Reforms: The thrust of the JNNURM-I was to ensure improvement in urban governance and service delivery so that ULBs became financially sound and sustainable for undertaking new programmes. It was also envisaged that, with the charter of reforms that were followed by the State governments and ULBs, a stage would be set for PPPs.

All mandatory and optional reforms were expected to be completed within the Mission period.

A. Mandatory Reforms:

(a) Mandatory Reforms at the Level of ULBs, and Parastatal Agencies:

1. Adoption of modern accrual-based double entry system of accounting in ULBs and parastatal agencies.
2. Introduction of a system of e-governance using IT applications, such GIS and MIS for various services provided by ULBs and parastatal agencies.
3. Reform of property tax with GIS. It became a major source of revenue for ULBs and arrangements for its effective implementation so that collection efficiency reached at least 85 percent within next seven years.
4. Levy of reasonable user charges by ULBs and Parastatals with the objective that the full cost of O&M or recurring cost was collected within the next seven years. However, cities and towns in the North-East and other special category States could recover only 50 percent of O&M charges initially. These cities and towns were expected to graduate to full O&M cost recovery in a phased manner.
5. Internal earmarking, within local bodies, budgets for basic

services to the urban poor.

6. Provision of basic services to the urban poor including security of tenure at affordable prices, improved housing, water supply and sanitation. Delivery of other existing universal services of the government for education, health and social security is ensured.

(b) Mandatory Reforms at the Level of States:

1. Implementation of decentralisation measures as envisaged in 74th Constitutional Amendment Act. The State should ensure meaningful association and engagement of ULBs in planning the function of parastatal agencies as well as the delivery of services to the citizens.
2. Repeal of ULCRA.
3. Reform of Rent Control laws balancing the interests of landlords and tenants.
4. Rationalisation of stamp duty to bring it down to no more than 5 percent within next seven years.
5. Enactment of the public disclosure law to ensure preparation of medium-term fiscal plan of ULBs and parastatal agencies and release of quarterly performance information to all stakeholders.
6. Enactment of the community participation law to institutionalise citizen's participation and introduce the concept of the area sabha in urban areas.
7. Assigning or associating elected ULBs with "city planning function". Over a period of seven years, transferring all special agencies that deliver civic services in urban areas to ULBs and creating accountability platforms for all urban civic service providers in transition.

B. Optional Reforms (Common to States, ULBs and Parastatal Agencies): The following optional reforms were expected to be undertaken by ULBs, parastatal agencies and State governments:

1. Revision of by-laws to streamline the approval process for construction of buildings, development of site etc.
2. Simplification of legal and procedural frameworks for

conversion of land from agricultural to non-agricultural purposes.

3. Introduction of property title certification system in ULBs.
4. Earmarking at least 20-25 percent of developed land in all housing projects (both public and private agencies) for EWS and LIG category with a system of cross subsidisation.
5. Introduction of computerised process of registration of land and property.
6. Revision of by-laws to make rain water harvesting mandatory in all buildings and adoption of water conservation measures.
7. Byelaws for reuse of recycled water.
8. Administrative reforms i.e. reduction in establishment costs by adopting the voluntary retirement scheme (VRS), not filling posts falling vacant due to retirement etc., and achieving specified milestones in this regard.
9. Structural reforms.
10. Encouraging PPP.

JNNURM-I was an ambitious programme to bring about urban renewal in the country.

A.2 JNNURM-II (2012-17)

A new JNNURM-II incorporating the learning from JNNURM-I is a major feature of the Twelfth Five Year Plan (2012-17). It gives priority to the strengthening of human and institutional capabilities, local planning and improvements in governance, which are the foundations for a more financially and environmentally sustainable and a more inclusive process of governance.

JNNURM-II is a landmark initiative because it has put India's urban agenda at the centre stage. It has set about providing resources to the States linked to incentives for reforms which would trigger to focus on improvements to cities and towns. The seven years (2005-12) experience with JNNURM-I has been a substantial learning experience which has also revealed weaknesses in the governance systems and the capabilities of cities, States and even the Centre to manage the process of urbanization.

The salient features of JNNURM-II are as follows:

A.2.1 Objectives: The objectives of JNNURM-II are as under:

1. Alleviating urban poverty.
2. Improving service delivery standards in urban areas including basic services for urban poor.
3. Empowering urban local bodies.
4. Facilitating participatory governance.
5. Effectively managing land resources.
6. Fostering sustainable, inclusive and faster growth.

A.2.2 Strategies of JNNURM-II: To realise these objectives, the key strategies of the programme are as follows:

1. Build adequate capacity including dedicated municipal cadre.
2. Planned urbanization by preparing a development plan through a participatory process.
3. Remove distortions in land market.
4. Establish efficient governance structures.
5. Promote financial sustainability and accountability of ULBs.
6. Attract more private investment, in particular, through PPP.
7. Adoption of service level benchmarks and social and gender audit of the outcomes of programme.
8. Slum rehabilitation and creation of affordable housing.
9. Planned development of smaller towns and periurban areas.
10. Incentivising innovation and rapid learnings across urban systems.

A.2.3 Components of JNNURM-II: The programme has the following components:

1. Urban Infrastructure and Governance (UIG).
2. Rajiv Awas Yojana (RAY).
3. Slum rehabilitation in cities not covered under RAY.
4. Capacity-building.

The scheme for Urban Infrastructure Development in Satellite Towns was merged with the sub-mission on UIG under JNNURM-II. Further, while BSUP and IHSDP were discontinued, RAY is a sub-mission under JNNURM-II for the purposes of achieving convergence.

A.2.4 Coverage of JNNURM-II: Under JNNURM-I, a *Mission city* approach was followed. About 70 percent of the central assistance was provided to 65 Mission cities. In the Twelfth Plan, adequate attention will also be paid to encourage the medium and small town to realise their full economic potential. Hence under JNNURM-II, the limiting concept of *Mission Cities* has been dispensed with and while all cities are eligible to participate, a fair system of selection of cities to be covered under the programme is in place.

A.2.5 Division of Outlay for JNNURM-II: The five year budgetary outlay for JNNURM-II is divided as follows:

- Base Fund (80 percent of the total outlay of JNNURM-II).
- Capacity Building Fund (10 percent of the total outlay of JNNURM-II).
- Incentive Fund (10 percent of the total outlay of JNNURM-II).

A.2.6 Capacity-building under JNNURM-II: Capacity-building at different levels of government is a key focus area under the programme. The main thrust of capacity-building activities is as under:

1. Creation and professionalisation of the municipal cadre.
2. Identifying the gap in capacity at different levels to establish the demand.
3. Opening of suitable institutions in case the existing ones are unable to meet current requirements.
4. Creation of a dedicated PPP cell for developing model bid documents.
5. Creation of cell on municipal finance and framework for land monetisation and other innovative method of generating finances and so on.
6. Dissemination of national and international best practices in urban governance.
7. Conducting annual reform audits to monitor the progress of reforms across participating States and cities.

Bibliography

Bibliography

Agarwal, Anil and Sunita Narain (1992), "Towards a Green World: Should Global Environmental Management be Built on Legal Conventions or Human Rights?", Centre for Science and Environment, New Delhi.

Bose, Ranjan K. and V. Srinivasachary (1997), "Policies to Reduce Energy Use and Environmental Emissions in the Transport Sector: A Case of Delhi City", *Energy Policy,* Vol. 25, pp. 1137-1150.

Briceno-Garmendia, C., A. Estache and N. Shafik (2004), "Infrastructure Services in Developing Countries: Access, Quality, Costs and Policy Reform", World Bank Policy Research Working Paper 3468.

Central Institute of Road Transport, Pune (1988), "Pre-feasibility Studies of Expressways in India".

Centre for Science and Environment (CSE) (1990), "Proceedings of the Seminar on Traditional Water Harvesting System in India", October 9-11, New Delhi.

Chandavarkar, A. (1995), "Infrastructure Finance; Issues, Institution and Policies", World Bank Policy Research Working Paper No. 1374.

Consulting Engineering Services Ltd. (1990), "Long-term Development of Expressways in India", Ministry of Surface Transport, Government of India.

Dalvi, M.Q. (1997), "Transport Planning and Policy in India", Himalaya Publishing House, Mumbai.

Dasgupta, Biplab (1978), "The Environment Debate: Some Issues and Trends", *Economic and Political Weekly*, Annual.

Dreze, Jean and A. Sen (2002), "India: Development and Participation", Oxford University Press, New Delhi.

ESCAP (1994), "Infrastructure Development as Key to Economic Growth and Regional Economic Cooperation", United Nations.

ESCAP (1997), "Mobilising Private Sector Resources for Infrastructure", United Nations.

Gadgil, Madhav and Ramchandra Guha (1992), "This Fissured Land: An Ecological History of India", Oxford University Press, New Delhi.

Gautham Naviakha (2000), "Urban Pollution: Driving Workers to

Desperation", *Economic and Political Weekly*, 35 (51), December 16-22.

Government of India, Ministry of Finance, *Economic Survey* (various issues).

—Ministry of Finance, *Budget Papers* (various years).

—Ministry of Finance, *Reports of Finance Commissions*.

—Ministry of Urban Development, *Annual Report* (various years).

—Ministry of Housing and Urban Poverty Alleviation, *Annual Report* (various years).

—Ministry of Law, Justice, and Company Affairs, *Constitution of India.*

—Planning Commission, *Five Year Plan Documents*.

—Ministry of Environment and Forests, *Annual Report* (various years).

—Ministry of Water Resources, *Annual Report* (various years).

—*National Action Plan on Climate Change,* 2008.

International Finance Corporation (1996), "Financing Private Infrastructure: Lessons and Experience".

Kapur, A. (1995), "Airport Infrastructure: Emerging Role of the Private Sector", World Bank Technical Paper No. 313.

Kothari, Rajni (1988), "Rethinking Development in Search of Humane Alternatives", Ajanta Publications.

Luthra, A. (1999), "Vehicular Emissions in India: Retrospect and Prospects", *Environment and People,* Vol. 16 (4).

Nagdeve, D. (2004), "Air Pollution in Mega Cities of India", International Institute for Population Sciences.

Ravindranath, N.H. and J. Sathaye (2002), "Climate Change and Developing Countries", Kluwer Academic Publishers, Netherlands.

Rupa, Kumar K. et al. (2005), "High-resolution Climate Change: Scenarios for India for the 21st Century", *Current Science*, Vol. 90, pp. 334-345.

Rupesh, Kumar (2003), "Water Pricing in India", *Journal of Hydrology,* Vol. 26, Number1-2.

Sagar, A., M. Bhattacharya and Vinod Joon (2007), "A Comparative Study of Air Pollution-Related Morbidity among Exposed Population of Delhi", *Indian Journal of Community Medicine*, Vol. 32 (4).

Sapru, R.K. (ed) (1987), "Environmental Management in India", Ashish Publishing House, New Delhi.

Sathaye, J., P.R. Shukla and N.H. Ravindranath (2006), "Climate Change, Sustainable Development and India: Global and National Concerns", *Current Science,* Vol. 90 (3).

Singh, Shekhar (1985), "Some Aspects of Ecological Crisis in India", *Social Scientist.*

Sriraman, S. (1998), "Road Transport Development in India", *Current Science*, Vol. 75.

UNIDO (1998), "BOT Guidelines", United Nations, New York.

Vanish, Kathuria and G.S. Haripriya (2000), "Industrial Pollution Control: Choosing the Right Option", *Economic and Political Weekly*, October 28.

World Bank (1989), "Vehicle Fleet Modernisation, Road User Cost Study".

——*World Development Report* (various years).

——*Private Sector in Infrastructure: Strategy, Regulation and Risk,* 1997.

Yamazawa, Ippei (2000), "Developing Economies in the Twenty-First Century: The Challenge of Globalisation", Institute of Developing Economies, Japan.

Websites

Ministry of Urban Development

Ministry of Housing and Urban Poverty Alleviation

Planning Commission of India

Ministry of Environment and Forests

Ministry of Water Resources

Ministry of Health and Family Welfare

Ministry of Road Transport and Highways

Index

Index